266.6 B934j
Burnet, David Staats
The Jerusalem mission under
the direction of the

THE JERUSALEM MISSION

This is a volume in the Arno Press collection

AMERICA AND THE HOLY LAND

Advisory Editor
Professor Moshe Davis

Editorial Board
Professor Robert Theodore Handy
Professor Jules Davids
Dr. Nathan M. Kaganoff

America-Holy Land Studies
A Joint Project of the
American Jewish Historical Society
David R. Pokross, President

Dr. Maurice Jacobs, Chairman
of the American Jewish Historical Society-Institute
of Contemporary Jewry Liaison Committee
and the
Institute of Contemporary Jewry
The Hebrew University of Jerusalem
Dr. Daniel G. Ross, Chairman
of the Institute's International Planning Committee

See last pages of this volume for a complete list of titles.

THE

JERUSALEM MISSION

UNDER THE DIRECTION OF THE

AMERICAN CHRISTIAN MISSIONARY SOCIETY

COMPILED BY

D[avid] S[taats] Burnet

ARNO PRESS

A New York Times Company

New York / 1977

Editorial Supervision: JOSEPH CELLINI

Reprint Edition 1977 by Arno Press Inc.

Reprinted from a copy in the
 Yale Divinity School Library

AMERICA AND THE HOLY LAND
ISBN for complete set: 0-405-10220-8
See last pages of this volume for titles.

Manufactured in the United States of America

Library of Congress Cataloging in Publication Data

Burnet, David Staats, 1808-1867, comp.
   The Jerusalem mission under the direction of the
American Christian Missionary Society.

   (America and the Holy Land)
   Reprint of the 1853 ed. published by the American
Christian Publication Society, Cincinnati.
   1. Missions--Jerusalem. 2. Missions to Jews--
Jerusalem. 3. Disciples of Christ--Missions. I. Ti-
tle. II. Series.
BV3200.B8 1977   266'.6'656944   77-70687
ISBN 0-405-10233-X

In tribute to
DANIEL G. ROSS
for his leadership, friendship and counsel

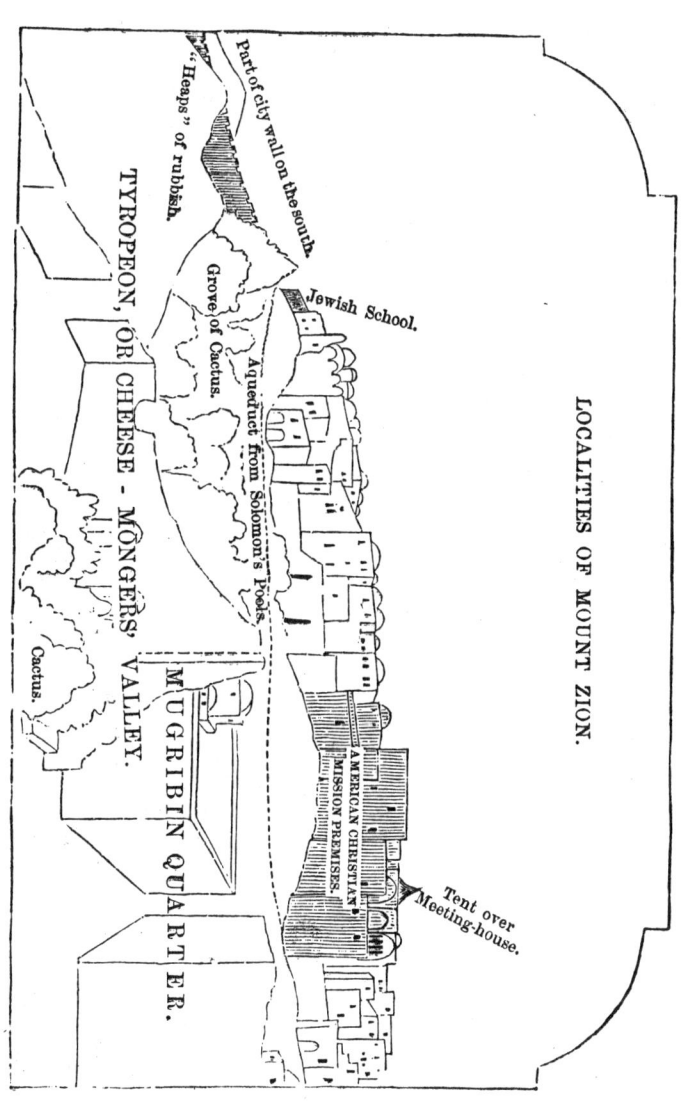

THE AMERICAN CHRISTIAN MISSION, ON MOUNT ZION.

THE

JERUSALEM MISSION:

UNDER THE DIRECTION OF THE

AMERICAN CHRISTIAN MISSIONARY SOCIETY.

COMPILED BY

D. S. BURNET,
CORRESPONDING SECRETARY.

CINCINNATI:
AMERICAN CHRISTIAN PUBLICATION SOCIETY.
1853.

Entered, according to Act of Congress, in the year 1853, by
D. S. BURNET,
In the Clerk's Office of the District Court for the District of Ohio.

CINCINNATI:
C. A. MORGAN & CO., STEREOTYPERS,
HAMMOND STREET.

MORGAN & OVEREND,
PRINTERS.

REV. JAMES T. BARCLAY.

MRS. JULIA A. BARCLAY.

PREFACE.

THE commencement of the nineteenth century was remarkable for the benevolent institutions which distinguished it. Bible and Missionary Societies, before that time, were only the tenants of enthusiastic dreams. Now, there are thirty or forty millions of Bibles; and missionaries can almost shake hands around the globe. These are the grandest enterprises of the age. In politics almost no advances have been made; while the Bible and Mission enterprises have laid the foundation, not only of a great, moral and evangelical reform in the more benighted regions of the earth, but also of enlightened political government in the countries of feudal and nomadic institutions.

The first Foreign Mission of the churches denominationally called Christian, in the United States, was commenced in Jerusalem, in February, 1851. From its conception to its inception, and from the latter time to the present, it has been a subject of great interest to the brotherhood. It has been the occasion of more prayer, more deep-felt solicitude, and more hearty rejoicings and gratitude, than any similar undertaking. Every letter from the Mission is read with eagerness, and the next arrival anxiously expected. The reprint of the following Journal and Letters, therefore, will doubtless be hailed by thousands with great pleasure.

The work will be continued while incidents of interest are reported; the whole making, after awhile, a valuable addition to our Evangelical, and more especially, to our Sunday School, literature.

D. S. BURNET.

CONTENTS.

View of Mount Zion and Localities of Mount Zion (Frontispiece), drawn by Sarah Barclay.
Portrait of Dr. J. T. Barclay.

	PAGE.
Dr. Barclay's offer of himself and Family,	5
" " first letter to Missionary Board,	6
Where should we first establish a Foreign Mission,	10
First Missionary impulse in the minds of the Barclay family,	27
Dr. Barclay in London,	34
The storms encountered by the Missionaries,	41
Perils in the British Channel,	42
Missionaries in Malta,	48
Arrival of the Missionaries in Jerusalem,	58
Dr. Barclay's Journal,	66
London,	73
Valetta,	103
Beyroot and Mount Lebanon,	111
Sidon,	124
Tyre,	128
St. Jean D'Acre,	135
Jaffa, ancient Joppa,	145
Jerusalem entered,	157
The first Converts,	165
Valuable additions to the Church,	179
Letter to Dr. Barclay, No. 1,	183
" " " " 2,	186
Dr. Barclay's Report to the Virginia Co-operation,	192

CONTENTS.

	PAGE.
Dangerous Illness of the Mission Family,	200
Report to the A. C. Bible Society,	203
Dr. Barclay and the Polish Converts,	212
First Annual Report of the Mission to the Board of Managers,	217
Dr. Bacon and Dr. Barclay,	238
The Jordan—a Baptism there,	245
Wady Farar,	264
Arrival of Supplies,	269
Mrs. Barclay's Letter,	273
" " Portrait,	6
Persecution at Bethlehem,	279
J. Judson Barclay on the Architecture of Jerusalem,	292
Perils at Wady Farar,	305

THE

AMERICAN CHRISTIAN MISSION

IN JERUSALEM.

DR. BARCLAY'S OFFER OF HIMSELF AND FAMILY AS A FOREIGN MISSIONARY.

On the 5th of October 1848, Dr. James T. Barclay addressed the Corresponding Secretary of the American Christian Bible Society a letter, from which the following extracts are made:

"Deeply deploring the comparative inefficiency of the churches, and ascribing it alone to the want of general organization, I hailed with no ordinary pleasure, the call for a general meeting of the brotherhood, 'for to consider this matter,' and promised myself no little pleasure in attending its deliberations. Sorry am I indeed therefore to forego the pleasure of enjoying 'the feast of reason and the flow of soul,' which I doubt not will characterize the proceedings of the convention.

"Should your deliberations result in the establishment of a Foreign Missionary Society, or department, or should it be deemed expedient to engage seriously in the cause of foreign missions, on any Scriptural plan, which the good Lord grant,"—Then (beside promising pecuniary aid, he thus writes):

"For in my estimation the time has come when we not only *may*, but *should*, and *must* attempt immediately to disseminate the truth as it is in Jesus, among the benighted pagans, both by colporteur operations and regular foreign missions. Would that I had the wealth of a Crœsus to convocate to this all-important enterprise! But of silver and gold I have little—very little—yet have I a heart to attempt whatever such feeble instrumentality can be expected to accomplish; and should we organize as a missionary body, as I trust we will, and some be found in our ranks willing to 'hazard their lives' for the purpose of declaring the name of the Lord Jesus Christ to them that 'sit in darkness and in the shadow of death,' cheerfully will I say, '*Here am I, send me.*'"

"J. T. B."

LETTER TO THE BOARD OF THE AMERICAN MISSIONARY SOCIETY, CINCINNATI, BY BROTHER BARCLAY, ETC.

The following communication was addressed to the Board of the Christian Missionary Society, immediately after its organization:

CINCINNATI, Oct. 30, 1849.

To the board of Managers of the
American Christian Missionary Society.

BRETHREN:—Prompted by an ardent desire to be as useful as possible, and believing that I can be more usefully employed in communicating the Gospel to those who are entirely destitute of its blessings, than by any service that I can render in this land of Gospel privileges, I have determined, after mature and prayerful consideration, to offer myself to the church, as a missionary to the heathen. And being comparatively unknown to you, it becomes both proper and necessary for me—even at the expense of some apparent egotism—candidly to communicate to you such information as may enable you to determine whether my qualifications are such as will justify you in appointing me to that responsible office.

I have been a member of the Church of Christ about ten years, and during the greater part of that time, an elder; but have only been engaged in the public proclamation of the Word during the past year. To be able to "endure hardness as a good soldier of Jesus Christ," is deemed an indispensable requisite on the part of him who would lead the self-denying life of a missionary of the Cross, and I bless my Creator and Preserver, that though I am now in the forty-third year of my age, my health is uniformly and unusually good; being blessed with an excellent constitution and great powers of endurance. I have some acquaintance with the Latin, Greek and French languages, and such an aptitude for the acquisition of foreign tongues, that no insuperable obstacle exists on this score. I am a regular graduate of the medical profession; and although I have not been engaged in practice for some years, yet, but little application would suffice to qualify me as a practitioner of medicine again. My acquaintance with the arts and sciences is quite extensive; and with some of them intimate—

both theoretically and practically—possessing great artistic and mechanical tact. I mention this, because such attainments on the part of the missionary, are esteemed very desirable, inasmuch as they tend to procure a favorable access to the heathen.

My wife, whose mind has long been exercised on this subject, cordially dedicates herself to the cause of missions, so far as her influence can be appropriately exerted.

"The children whom God hath graciously given us," consisting of two sons—the one aged eighteen, the other fifteen, and a daughter only thirteen years of age—desire also to "go unto the heathen" with us, and thus be fellow-helpers to the truth in their respective spheres. Having long since made our God their God, and our people their people, it is natural that they should desire to go where we go, lodge where we lodge, and die where we die; but so far as can be ascertained, they seem to be actuated in making such a choice by higher motives than those that spring from mere filial affection. Their education having been early commenced, is now nearly completed on a somewhat liberal scale; and I am happy in the assurance that they possess far more than an ordinary share of piety and zeal, and are perfectly willing to do whatever they can, either now or hereafter, in behalf of the perishing heathen.

Such a statement I deem due, alike to you, to the cause, and to ourselves.

It must be understood, however, that though willing, and anxious to carry the glad tidings of salvation to Jews, Mahometans or Pagan idolaters, the tender of our services is only made in the event that no others can be found possessing greater promise of usefulness, who are willing to "hazard their lives for the name of our Lord Jesus Christ;" for our willingness to embark in the missionary enterprise, proceeds from no desire to expatriate ourselves and forego the endearments of home; but from a sincere regard to the glory of God and the welfare of the poor benighted pagans, "sitting in the region and shadow of death, perishing for lack of knowledge." And therefore if the services of more competent brethren can be obtained, cheerfully will we consent to "*tarry by the stuff*" in our own American Zion, and contribute to their maintenance among the heathen—content to serve in any capacity whatever, in a cause so glorious as that of the conversion of the world.

May He who is "excellent in counsel and wonderful in working," direct you in all things, to the glory of His name and the advancement of His cause; "working in you that which is well pleasing in His sight, through Jesus Christ," to whom be all the glory, for ever and ever. Amen.

With sincerest Christian regards,

Dear Brethren,

Yours, in hope of life eternal,

JAMES T. BARCLAY,

Of Scottsville, Albemarle county, Virginia.

JERUSALEM PROPOSED AS THE FIELD FOR THE FIRST FOREIGN MISSION.

This anonymous article, containing valuable information, was published in *The Christian Age*, to act upon the minds of the Board, and the Brotherhood at large. Dr. Barclay is understood to be the author of it.

WHERE SHOULD WE FIRST ESTABLISH A FOREIGN MISSION?

Our Missionary Society being now fully organized and ready for action, it becomes necessary to select its field of labor, and designate a place for the establishment of a Missionary Station. And truly the quarter of the globe, or the particular nation first claiming the missionary efforts of the Brotherhood is a matter of no little interest and importance. Let no one say—"the field is the world"—and therefore it is immaterial where we commence—for although it is true that the whole unevangelized world is the field, any part of which we may of right occupy; yet many considerations enter into the correct decision of the question—What part of this wide field, is it most important first to occupy and cultivate? If immediate fruit of missionary culture be the prevailing object, irrespective of a wide-spread influence with a view to ultimate success, we should thrust in "the sickle" of truth wherever the prospect of early reaping seems most cheering: and hence the conversion of such a people as the Karens, though neither numerous nor influential, should be first attempted. Should we address ourselves to the task of cultivating the largest field, the followers of Confucius and the devotees of Fo, inclosed within the wall of China, composing as they do, nearly a third of the human family would present by far the strongest claim. If ignorance and wretchedness, combined with deep depravity, be allowed to exercise a controlling influence, then ought we to go to Idolaters alone, with reference not only to their spiritual but temporal condition. Should responsibility be the prevailing consideration and extent of privilege be the measure of responsibility, then should some of the civilized and semi-christianized nations of Europe be entitled to share largely in the benefits of our earliest efforts. If contiguity of situation or facility of access constitutes the strongest claim upon our evangelizing operations, then should we first plant the standard of primitive Christianity in the wilds of our own Aborigines. And if—as some contend—the mission ought to be located where "Christ has never yet been named," still we have a choice of fields varying in size and character, from the most insignificant islet of Oceanica up to populous and polish Japan itself.

But the dictates of a discriminating judgment and sound policy plainly indicate that our first efforts should be expended more in reference to permanent effect and extended influence in order to ultimate success, than to immediate results: and hence our labors should be devoted to that nation which when evangelized will exert the most powerful and wide-spread influence — the indications of Providence being always observed. If this be a sound rule of action, we should send our missionaries at first, neither to the myriads of secluded

Chinese, nor to the feeble and inert Karens, nor to the illiterate and impotent Red-men of our forest, nor to the debased and stupid Idolaters of Africa and Polynesia, nor to any of the semi-christianized nations of Europe, already blessed with so many privileges, nor yet to the besotted Polynesians or isolated Japanese, although they never yet have heard the glad tidings of salvation; but the first offer of the "ancient Gospel" should be made to the ancient people of God.

"Say unto the cities, Judah, behold your God :—
Zion — thy God reigneth!"

The general neglect of this interesting people, on the part of the friends of missions, can only be accounted for by ascribing it to the prevalence of the belief that they are so judicially blinded as to be precluded conversion without miraculous interposition— than which no dogma can be more absurd or unscriptural. But notwithstanding this strange neglect on the part of the church, they are still beloved for their fathers' sake, and no nation on earth presents so strong a claim on our consideration as this noble race—none for whose conversion such strong inducements are presented—none, of whose recovery such glorious consequences are predicated. O! Israel,

"Blessed is he,
That blesseth thee."

In the special promise of their conversion (according to the most sure word of prophecy whereunto we do well to take heed) and in the glorious issue of their reunion with the "true olive branch," we find all that the most ardent imagination or heart could conceive to encourage us in attempting their regeneration: "for if the fall of them be the riches of the world and the diminishing of them be the riches of the Gentiles, what shall the receiving of them be but life from the dead!" "Wherefore then should the heathen say—where is now their God?" Nor should it be a matter of indifference with us that to this most noble of all races we are indebted, not only for the "living oracles" of the Old Covenant but for Christianity itself. Indeed, to no people on earth are we so indebted as to the Jews, and nothing less than a great missionary effort in their behalf can cancel the obligation resting upon us that "through our mercy they may obtain mercy." Should we not, therefore, esteem it a sacred duty, as early as possible to adopt the measures necessary for removing the vail of "blindness which has happened in part unto Israel," that they no longer abide in unbelief but be grafted in again into the true olive tree!

Even if the Bible did not contain such exceeding great and precious promises in connection with the conversion of the Jews, it would still be evident from considerations of human expediency that the evangelization of no people on earth would promote the interests of Christianity so much as that of these "lost sheep of the house of Israel." In more senses than one, is it true, that "salvation is of the Jews." And if the views of many eminent theologians be true, we need look for no great ingathering of the nations until "the tabernacle of David which is fallen down be built again that the residue of men might seek after the Lord, and all the Gentiles upon whom his name is called." Were they once converted to Christianity, what a noble army of missionaries would their circumstances and natural endowments constitute them! Judah and Benjamin to the lapsed churches of Greece and Rome, within whose territories they are principally dispersed, and the other ten tribes to the Mohammedans and other Pagans among whom they are scattered. Any one at all acquainted with this remarkable people, can bear record that they still have a zeal worthy of any cause. Their hatred of idolatry, their wealth, intelligence, and energy still characterize them most signally. And with the most jealous care have these librarians of the world ever guarded and preserved the living oracles, of which they are the appointed conservators. With such missionaries as these, the curse inflicted at Babel, would scarcely be felt as an impediment to the universal diffusion of truth; for it is as true now as when Luke announced it to be a fact, that there are Jews dwelling in every nation under heaven; and yet not reckoned among them, though speaking their language, as well as their own divine vernacular—for there is no language nor speech where their voice is not heard. So that were they converted, every nation and kindred, and tongue, and people, might at once hear in their own language the wonderful love of God, without the delay, difficulty and uncertainty attending the ordinary acquirement of languages. Neither could there be any better substitute for the spiritual gifts of the first age of the church desired, than the well attested providences of the Lord toward this singular people; and their wonderful dispersion and preservation for so many ages and under such adverse circumstances, as a separate and peculiar people, would procure a Hebrew missionary a successful introduction to the nations, where we Gentile Christians would fail of access. Indeed in all that pertains to missionary qualification, no people in the world can compare with the Abrahamic family.

The signs of the times are altogether auspicious too, for the immediate fulfillment of the glorious prophecies relating to this once covenant people of the Lord. Tired of looking for another Messiah, they seem at last, willing to investigate the claims of Jesus of Nazareth to the Messiahship. According to recent accounts there are many of these outcasts of Israel who have arrived at the conclusion, that the once despised Nazarene is indeed the Son of God. It is an augury full of hope to Israel, that they are everywhere paying more attention to literature, and less regard to the Talmud and Rabbinical tradition.

Then verily if we have rightly discerned the signs of the times, God hath not utterly cast away his people whom formerly he acknowledged; and neither should we. So much interested were the apostles in behalf of the Jews, that even after having preached the Gospel exclusively to them for twelve years, when they were at last specially summoned by the Holy Spirit to the work of Foreign Missions among the Heathen, we discover that it was still their uniform practice, wherever they found Jews, first to propose the Gospel to *them*. And so important did they deem *their* conversion, that after they had been fifteen years thus engaged in missionary operations among the Gentiles, they still deemed it expedient to send special missionaries to the Jews. The first three years of Paul's missionary career, were devoted to one branch of the Abrahamic family, and the last we hear of him, he is still pleading with God's chosen people. Perhaps we could not do better than to imitate this example of the apostles, in their decided preference for the seed of Abraham. Did an apostle feel such great heaviness and continual sorrow, that he could even wish himself accursed for his brethren, the Jews! and shall we feel no peculiar interest in this noble race to whom pertain the adoption, and the glory, and the covenants, and the giving of the Law, and the promises; whose are the Father's, and of whom as concerning the flesh, Christ came, who is over all, God blessed forever? The evangelization of Israel becomes invested with tenfold interest, when it is considered, that without their conversion, vain are our hopes with regard to the consummation of many of the great events, so dear to the friends of Zion. But slight them as we may, this much is certain, that let what will happen, the conversion of God's ancient people is clearly predicted, and must be accomplished, and that too, as an event preliminary and indispensable to the general prevalence of the empire of Truth. An additional reason for making the Jews a special object of missionary effort is found in the fact that other nations, when evangelized, may be speedily enslaved or even exterminated by some more powerful nation, or like the South Sea Islanders, and some of our own Indian tribes, dwindle to nothing, and thus their auxiliary agency be lost to the cause of missions; but this peculiar nation is absolutely indestructible by all the combined powers of earth, because preserved by the arm of Omnipotence for the wisest purposes. Many a Gentile will doubtless yet be glad to take hold of the skirt of the despised Jews, saying, "we will go with you, for we have heard that the Lord is with you."

Admitting that the Jews are the people to whom we should first send the Gospel, where should the mission be located for their benefit? for they are found dispersed abroad "in every nation under heaven." Perhaps they are to be found in greater numbers in Salonica, than in any other city in the world; and, (as we learn by the late arrivals), "these (inhabitants of Salonica) are more noble than were those of Thessalonica, (its ancient name) in that they search the Scriptures," and throwing aside their antiquated parchments, receive, as genuine, the Old Testament, which the colporteur of the Bible Society has carried them. They are also very numerous in Constantinople, Smyrna, and other Mediterranean cities; yet without doubt the Holy Land is the place where we should first establish a mission, for their special benefit, for the Jews there, are very accessible, and a blow struck on this great center of sympathies would be felt much more sensibly than anywhere else. They are there found congregated in various cities in sufficient numbers to justify the settlement of a missionary among them, and are composed of such as are most interested on the subject of religion—are the least money-loving, time-serving, and over-reaching; (for it is not to be concealed that being almost invariably disfranchised and persecuted by the Gentiles, too many of them have attempted to compensate their civil disabilities by the acquisition of wealth obtained too often by "wiles not justified by honor"). They are already quite numerous in Palestine—that glory of all lands—and now that many long-existing obstacles to their return are removed, and they are permitted by the sultan to build a temple on Mount Zion, they will doubtless soon be found there in greater numbers than in any other quarter of the globe. Believing, as they universally do, in their literal and speedy restoration to the Land of their Fathers, and ardently desiring to return thither, the removal of that despotic embargo which for eighteen centuries has been scattering them to the four winds, will cause them to flock to Judea, "as doves to their windows."

The Mohammedan portion of the population of Judea, are very generally impressed with the belief received by tradition from their fathers, and riveted by their doctrine of fatalism, that the "Franks," as they term Protestant Christians, will soon possess that country, and indeed, all the Ottoman Empire; and the Ishmaelitish part of them especially, ardently desire it, as we learn from the reports of late travelers. Perhaps no event whatever, furnishes a happier augury for the speedy triumph of Christianity, than the present attitude of the Turkish government toward the Christian religion : for whereas, but a few years ago, there still existed that obstinate bigotry and unrelenting spirit of persecution which had ever characterized the followers of the false prophet, there is now perfect toleration! Even twelve moons ago, apostasy from Islamism to Christianity, was punished with death and confiscation—*now* such encouragement is offered to "Franks," as almost to constitute a premium for Christianity. The "Crescent truly is rapidly waning," and "the Euphrates fast drying up!" Here then is a great and (must needs be) effectual door opening (through the sublime Porte) for the establishment of a mission, in reference to Mohammedanism. The last sands of the prophetic period assigned to the Moslem Desolater, are now running out! The "Little Horn of the East" shall gore no more ! and no more shall the desolating abomination "practice and prosper!" "Lo! what God hath wrought!" Mr. Thompson, who has recently returned from the Syrian mission, remarked at a late missionary meeting, that "just before embarking for the United States, he had preached before a congregation of Arabs, at their own request, in Joppa." * * * * * *

The place whence the Gospel started on its westward mission to us eighteen hundred years ago, is now waiting for us to send it back to its inhabitants. When he was about to leave, they came and threw their arms around his neck, and told him to tell Christians in America to pray for them, and send them missionaries. Some of them followed him several miles on his journey, and bathing his hands with their tears, begged that missionaries might be sent. They do not ask for our money, but they want our sons and daughters; "and somehow," said Mr. T., "I thought they ought to have them!" From what part of Heathendom does there come such a Macedonian cry as from these swarthy sons of Ishmael, residing at this old port of Jerusalem? Surely we should not be indifferent to the fact that the Father of the faithful—the friend of God, prayed so earnestly for these Bedouin "dwellers in the desert," in the person of their progenitor Ishmael—"O! that Ishmael might live before God"— a prayer too, that the Lord has promised abundantly to answer!

Beside the Turks and the descendants of Abraham by Sarah and Hagar, the Maronites and Druses also exist in considerable numbers; the latter of whom, if we can credit accounts recently received from Mount Lebanon, are ripe for missionary effort and ready to press into the kingdom of heaven. How long shall "that goodly mountain Lebanon languish?" "Behold, how beautiful upon the mountain the feet of him that bringeth good tidings!" Is it not also due to ourselves and to the oriental churches, so many of whom are represented in the Holy Land, degenerate as some of them are, to present to their consideration the principles of reformation and Christian union, among the very first acts of our missionary movement? Who can read without deep emotion the affecting appeal of that interesting Christian sect on the other side of Jordan? Who knows but that numbers might come out of calculated to engage the affection and enlist the *esprit du corps*, as well as the prayers, contributions and co-operation of the Christian Brotherhood, as one to the Holy City!

Let it not be supposed by any one that Jerusalem is already pre-occupied as missionary ground, and that therefore we had better carry the gospel to some more benighted place, where Christianity has not yet been preached—for it is a great mistake to suppose that the city is monopolized, or fully occupied by any missionary society, even if the gospel preached there of late was identical with the ancient gospel which we propose to restore to its down-trodden inhabitants. True it is that the American Board of Commissioners for Foreign Missions, and the London Missionary Society have made some demonstration in behalf of that devoted city, but their missionaries—strange as it may appear—distinctly disclaim all intention of calling their converts out of their present corrupt associations—and of course all their efforts must prove entirely nugatory. It is also true that an Episcopal palace is now in progress of erection on Mount Zion, designed to be the residence of the Bishop of Egypt, Mesopotamia and the Holy Land (!!!), but it is well known that this See is sustained by Prussia and England not for religious but political purposes merely. With the above exception, the only exhibitions of Christianity made in Jerusalem are much better calculated to disgust and deter, than to allure, edify and engage the idol-hating Jews and Mohammedans; being a mere parade of senseless superstition and idolatry—a perfect contrast to the simplicity of primitive Christianity—for what is Romanism, and the mummery practiced by most of the other religious communities there, but christianized Paganism—a mongrel compound of Heathenism and Judaism, with a mere spice of Christianity!

Is it not a little singular, considering the great importance of Jerusalem as a missionary station, that it should have been so greatly neglected by the various Protestant denominations engaged in conducting missionary operations. And yet, perhaps, it is not so strange that it had been thus overlooked, inasmuch as none of them could, without sacrificing their identity and virtually unchurching themselves, adopt the phraseology, and conform to the usages of the Acts of the Apostles—a practice that seems particularly incumbent upon those who would preach the gospel in places consecrated by the labors of Apostles, but which can be adopted fully and in good faith by none except ourselves.

With us, however, it should perhaps be less a matter of regret than surprise that it has been thus neglected, while other places far less important and interesting, have been fully occupied. For to those whose "fear toward God is not taught by the precept of men,"—who dare be "valiant for the truth upon the earth," and venture, amid all the obloquy of a degenerate age, to declare the truth just as it is in Jesus, "holding fast the form of sound words" and "rightly dividing the word of truth"—there is not, in all the world, a more important and interesting spot than the Holy City!—

once the cradle, but now more like the grave of Christianity! Yet "this is Zion, whom no man seeketh after!"—"Zion, the city of the Great King!"—"The joy of the whole earth!" How affecting—that in this age of missions, we should be constrained to take up the language of inspiration and ask—"Who shall have pity on thee, O Jerusalem—who shall bemoan thee, or who shall turn aside to ask thee how thou doest?" But though thus sadly neglected by man, yet the "Lord hath chosen Zion; he hath desired it for his habitation; this is the hill which God desireth to dwell in; yea, the Lord will dwell in it forever. Thou shalt be called, sought out—a city not forsaken." How delighted a mission for those whose exalted vocation it is to "restore all things," "as they were delivered to us by the Apostles," to "seek out," Zion as the first act of our foreign missionary efforts, and there establish another model church for Jew, Gentile and Apostate! Then "shall God arise and have mercy on Zion, for the time to favor her, yea, the set time, will have come, when her servants take pleasure in her stones, and favor the dust thereof: So the Heaven shall fear the name of the Lord, and all the kings of the earth his glory!" "O, that the salvation of God were come out of Zion!" Is it nothing to us that the fairest portion of the earth—the garden of the Lord in whose fertile soil and genial clime grew the Rose of Sharon and the Lily of the Valley—whose pure Apostolic Christianity once flourished in all its glory, is now in possession of the "worst of the Heathen?" Has not Jerusalem long enough been "trodden down of the Gentiles?" Are the mercies of the Lord toward his once favored land and people clean gone forever? No, he is waiting to be gracious. How long shall it be, then, before the fountain again be opened to the house of David and the inhabitants of Jerusalem for sin and uncleanness? Are the pools of Jerusalem and the waters of Jordan no more to be the emblematic grave of the penitent believer?—Shall the institutions of the Church in her primitive beauty and excellency never be restored to the land, where they were first ordained by the great Head of the Church?—the land of patriarchs, prophets and apostles—the land of Messiah! Guided by the Holy Spirit in our march, under the banner of the Lion of the tribe of Judah, we are fully able to go up and possess the Land! Let us, then, arise in the name of Emmanuel, and without delay, "prophesy to the dry bones of Israel that they may live." The God of Heaven—He will prosper us! "For thus said the Lord of Hosts, I am jealous for Jerusalem and Zion, with a great jealousy; and I am very sore displeased with the Heathen that are at ease." Who then can abide in his tent and refuse to come up to the help of the Lord against the mighty hosts of Heathen besieging, "the Mount Zion which he loveth," when the watchmen on Mount Ephraim are crying—"Arise ye, and let us go up to Zion, to the Lord our God, for this is the year of recompenses for the controversy of Zion."

And now that the "cloud" (after abiding so long upon our tabernacle) is at last "taken up," and we are authorized to leave the camp, journeying on Canaan-ward to act aggressively against the spoilers of Zion, may the God of Israel grant us the guidance and blessing which He vouchsafes alone to the true "Israel of God!" May his good Providence, as well as his Word and his Spirit, lead us in the day, "as by a cloudy pillar, and in the night, as by a pillar of fire, to give us light in the way wherein we should go!"

The memorial above is respectfully submitted to the consideration of the Executive Board of the American Christian Missionary Society. May "this service for Jerusalem be accepted of the saints." N.

THE FIRST MISSIONARY IMPULSE IN THE MINDS OF THE BARCLAY FAMILY.

HAVING given the reader the propositions of Dr. Barclay, made to the Missionary Board, in regard to the employment of himself and family as missionaries, and his views in regard to the proper field in which to commence labor, it may not be uninteresting, at this point, to inquire into the causes of the remarkable consecration of a whole household, not merely to religion, but also to its highest, most responsible, and most perilous services. How came a whole household not only to be believers, but also to be missionaries or assistant missionaries? The compiler is not informed of the early history of this devoted family, but it seems certain that a love of missions early possessed the hearts of Mr. and Mrs. Barclay, as their two sons are named after two of the most remarkable missionaries, Gutslaff and Judson. The subjoined sketch credited to the pen of Mrs. Margaret Thomson, in the Christian Sunday School Journal of July, 1852, assumes, without naming the parties, to give an account of the immediate occasion of this startling expatriation of a whole family, and their settlement, perhaps for life, on the man-made-desolate shores of Western Asia, among nearly the same representatives of the wicked world, that stood around the inspired fisherman "at the beginning," with the apostate Greek, Roman and Armenian Churches added, to fill up the measure of hostile influences.

A SKETCH.

One lovely evening in the June of 1849, a family group was seen on front of one of those beautiful vine-trellised cottages so common in the eastern parts of Virginia. It consisted of a lady, who read aloud from the divine volume, her husband, who was seated near by, their only daughter, whose head rested on her father's knee; and, on the green sward at some distance, two boys, engaged in the erection of a bee-house, completed the family. The gentleman seemed somewhat fatigued, having just returned from visiting a patient at some considerable distance. The daughter, as already mentioned, seated on a low stool by his side, raised her head on hearing a gentle sigh escape from his lips; and, putting aside the glossy curls that had fallen around her face, she observed an expression of sadness on that beloved countenance, which caused a momentary uneasiness.

"Do you consider Mrs. L—— dying, or dangerously ill?" she inquired.

"No, my daughter; on the contrary I consider her convalescent. But what makes you think of Mrs. L—— at present?"

"Dear father, it was the sigh which just now escaped you, and something in your look, that betrayed a weight on your mind."

"You have judged rightly, Mary; there is a subject that has taken deep root in my mind; a subject of intense interest, which as yet I have communicated to no one. My dear wife, you look very much surprised; but from you I have received the idea which now pervades my mind, and, next to my own salvation, lies nearest to my heart. But I see the boys putting away their tools. Let them be seated, and you shall hear, for we are all interested.

"My sons, I hear the clock strike the hour for worship; but we will defer it awhile this evening. Your mother has just been reading one of her favorite chapters to your sister and myself, and has thereby called up in my mind, emotions that are uncontrollable. The chapter that was read, is the 11th of Romans. You know what it refers to. Our constant prayer is for the fulfillment of the promises contained in that chapter. I have been reflecting on the question, Whether we can pray with confidence for anything which we are not willing to lend our aid for the accomplishment of? or whether the bringing in of God's ancient people, the Jews, is a solitary exception in the case?—whether that event is to be brought about by the performance of a miracle, without the instrumentality of Christians; or whether there is not a deeper responsibility resting upon us than we are at present aware of? Many seem to think, or at least to act, as if they thought that nothing is required at their hands in the matter. I think differently; chiefly for this reason, that the Apostle asserts that " it is to be through our mercy that they are to obtain mercy." We having received our mercy through them, what so fitting to show the gratitude of the repentant younger son, as to assist in reconciling his elder brother to their mutual parent. It is true, all attempts of this kind have hitherto proved unsatisfactory; but it seems to me that the reason of the failure is this: Those who have engaged in the work have always been disqualified, in some way, for its successful performance; either they have been encumbered by the splendors of will-worship, or bound by the trammels of a scholastic theology, whose metaphysics it is as impossible for the Jew to comprehend, as it would be for him to apply them to any practical purpose. How weighty, then, is the responsibility resting on us, who have only to exhibit facts, based on testimony, and call for the obedience which the belief of these facts naturally induces, in order to turn the feet of the wandering Jew into the paths of righteousness and peace.

" But I perceive, by the earnestness of your intention, that you anticipate me. I have brought my mind to this conclusion:—We have all been praying for the conversion of the Jews; yet no one has stepped forward to engage in the work. If the end is to be gained, some one must commence the undertaking. Shall I, if I obtain the cheerful co-operation of my family? Yes! May I, then, expect that co-operation? I leave the matter for your deliberate consideration and reflection. The Brethren of this Reformation have established a Missionary Society. Shall we, as a family, offer ourselves to proclaim the glad tidings of salvation in the ancient city of Jerusalem? Weigh the matter well before you reply. If I can read your countenances aright, the affirmative is there indicated, with a will. But are you prepared to make the sacrifices necessary? My sons! perhaps the fondness of a father's heart makes me think that you give promise of talent in no mean degree. Are you prepared to give up all those prospects of competence and distinction that are within your reach? And you, my daughter; I well know the charms and allurements which are presented in the world to one of your age, doted on as you have been by relatives and friends, and courted by society at large. Are you prepared to forego all, in order that this work of God may be forwarded? Are you willing to leave our beautiful home, surrounded as it is by affectionate friends and brethren, to encounter the difficulties and trials of a missionary life? I would not have you sit here under the shade of this acacia, snow-white with blossoms and perfuming the air around, and dream of what poets call the Land of the East; for you will find that the page of romance and the realities of the missionary life are altogether different. We must not expect our way to be strewn with purple heart's-ease, or perfumed with ottar of roses, if we would render ourselves useful in the service of Christ. No! There are stormy seas to be crossed, rude deserts to be traversed, peopled only with ruder man. Pining sickness may be our lot, in the midst of strangers, in a far-distant land; our society, not the educated and refined, but the poor, the ignorant, the barbarian. Our only expectation of reward in this life—the consciousness of doing our duty and of the Divine approbation resting upon us; and our fullness of reward, all in the future, when the Lord shall descend with the heavenly Jerusalem. From these premises, my dear children, you must judge for yourselves, and make up your minds resolutely; for no one, having put his hand to the plow and looking back, is fit for the kingdom of heaven. To-morrow is the first day of the week, and when we assemble for our morning worship, let those who have made their decision, record it on the blank page of this volume."

The group separated, to retire, but not to sleep. Their thoughts were too overpowering. The more they realized the greatness of the undertaking, the more ennobled they felt to be engaged in it. They tried to weigh the adverse circumstances which their father had presented to them, but they seemed lighter than vanity. They longed for the night to pass away, that they might have an opportunity of recording their decision. Nature, however, at length prevailed, and they sank into slumber.

On the morning, when they awoke, a few moments

sufficed them in preparation. They hasted to the place where the family Bible was accustomed to be put after worship was over; for what purpose the reader already anticipates. There the boys met their sister. She, like the Mary of another morning, had risen early, and by the dawn of day had subscribed her name before her brothers had arrived. The crimson roses bent their beautiful heads in at the open casement where they seated themselves, and tears of joy dropped into their leaves, to mingle with the dew and the fragrance they shed around, while their sacrifice of praise ascended with an odor sweeter and richer than the perfume of roses.

Having individually recorded their determination, this devoted family proposed to their brethren the mission over which they had been deliberating, and to which they were prepared to consecrate their lives. The chord which was struck by the thought thus presented, vibrated in unison with a long pent-up feeling in the hearts of the disciples; the response from all quarters was nearly universal. Their proposal was accepted, the church became awakened from a state of apathy in regard to missions, a holy emulation was excited between different regions as to who would have the honor of doing most for the support of the work. As for the members of this lovely family, they have already encountered dangers, privations and sickness, but none of these things move them; they persevere with their work, bearing up with a cheerful courage, having respect to the recompense of reward.

DOCTOR BARCLAY IN LONDON.

This letter shows our missionary to be most actively engaged in the great objects of the Jerusalem Mission. His heart is in the work. He is also as much distinguished by an enlightened frugality, as by the ardor of his zeal. He supremely realizes that he is a trustee of the funds placed at his disposal, and he most obviously keeps a conscience void of offense in their management. Under such auspices, the mission, with the blessing of God, may be expected to do much good. Such a man will raise friends to himself and his cause, wherever he goes.

London, Oct. 28, 1850.

My Dear Brother Challen:—" The good hand of the Lord our God being upon us," we reached this city on the 4th instant, after an unusually short passage of twenty-one days, which though so rough as to cause us much sea-sickness, and deprive me of the privilege of preaching more than once, was yet, through the great kindness of Captain Hovey, (the excellent commander of the Devonshire,) a very pleasant one.

I thankfully acknowledge the receipt of your prompt and kind favor of the 17th ultimo, which came to hand a few days after my arrival.

Anxiously desiring to enter the field of my future labors, and wishing to tarry here barely long enough to accomplish the object of my visit, one of the first matters that engaged my attention was to secure a passage to Beyroot, or some of the neighboring parts; but finding no vessel for the first few days, destined to any port nearer than Alexandria, I applied at the office of the Oriental and Peninsular Steam Company, in hopes of being able to engage our passage in one of their Southampton steamers, two or three of which ply regularly every month, between that city and various ports of the Mediterranean. I found the rates of charge however, so exorbitantly high, that I was compelled to decline taking passage in that line: nor are the Liverpool and Alexandria steamers materially lower in their charges. I therefore, took the cheapest lodgings that could be found of a respectable character, and determined to wait awhile in the hope of obtaining a more reasonable, and perhaps direct conveyance: nor was it long before I had the pleasure of finding a vessel advertised to sail directly for Jaffa, (the ancient Joppa), and though I learned, on application that it was not to leave for about a month, yet the accommodations were tolerable, and the fare so moderate that we deemed ourselves very fortunate in finding it; and though so anxious to be voyaging *Zion-ward*, made up our minds to wait patiently the appointed day of sailing. Judge then of our disappointment a day or two ago, on learning from the ship-broker, that the merchant who had chartered the vessel had decided to send his son as a passenger, and would permit no others to go. There being however, two vessels in port loading for Alexandria, the one to sail on the 10th proximo, and the other day after tomorrow, I succeeded in engaging our passage in the Hebe, of Glasgow, a little brig of only one hundred and eighty-four tons burthen, in which, by the blessings of a kind Providence, we hope to reach Alexandria, by the close of the year—stopping two weeks at Malta, on the way.

For the passage and fare on board the Scotch brig, the captain asks £75, or £37 10s., if we do our own victualing, etc., he supplying fuel and water. Being able to buy provision, etc., for about eighty or ninety dollars, we have concluded to accept the latter offer, which is certainly much the lower. You must not for a moment suppose that any of us deem this adventure any hardship. So far from it we are all anxious to start, and anticipate the voyage with feelings of delight.

If, on arriving at Alexandria, I can ascertain that the monthly steamer, for Beyroot, will start in a short time, I will await its departure, unless deterred by high charges, in which event we will either take an Egyptian smack, for Jaffa; or, (which is more probable, if the cholera shall have disappeared, and the fifteen days' quarantine, at Arish, can be avoided), we will engage a fleet of "ships of the desert," and pursue the route that the emancipated Israelites were forbidden to go on account of the warlike Philistines, as far as Gaza, and then take the back-track of the Ethiopian grandee—"the way that goeth down from Jerusalem to Gaza, which is desert." The most of my articles are left here in the Queen's warehouse, subject to the order of Messrs. Ollin & Clemention, shipbrokers, who will forward them to Jaffa, about two weeks hence, by the vessel in which we are denied passage.

To our most estimable minister, Mr. A. Lawrence, I am under the deepest obligations for his kind offices. The interest he manifests in behalf of the mission is quite unaccountable.

But for his kind interposition I would have sustained a heavy expense at the Custom-House, on account of dutyable articles, and an irreparable loss, in the way of American reprints of English works — to say nothing of injury done to my apparatus, by the ruthless examination to which every article is subjected, by the vandal-like examiners at the dock. On representing the matter to Mr. Lawrence, he very promptly interposed, and addressed such a letter to the Lords of the Treasury, as induced them to pass an order to forbid the inspection of the articles at all, and to have them "roped, taped and sealed," until I should be ready to leave the kingdom, when they are to be delivered to me, duty free, except the usual rent for storage in the Queen's warehouse.

To Mr. Lawrence and his son, (who has lately been to Jerusalem), I am also indebted for valuable letters, which they have been kind enough, unsolicited, to favor me with.

I trust the very flattering reception given the Turkish envoy, in the States, will tend materially to allay Mussulman intolerance of Christians, and secure for Americans a kinder reception than it has generally been their good fortune to enjoy.

Thus far we have received the most unexpected kindness, from persons whence it might least be expected.

I availed myself of an early occasion to present to the Secretaries of the British and Foreign Bible Society, the commendatory letter of the American and Foreign Bible Society, and though their donation is quite small, (consisting of only twenty-five volumes), yet I was much pleased in my various interviews with its officers. The reason assigned for making so small an appropriation, is that Bishop Gobat has drawn on them so heavily for Bibles, Testaments, Psalters, etc.; for distribution in the Holy Land, that justice to other more destitute portions of the world, requires that they should not be too lavish in their donations, even to that interesting part of the "field."

This Society has now established depositories at Malta and Smyrna; and inasmuch as they authorize the depositories at those places to sell to me on the same terms as the present Society, I thought it best, in the absence of exact information, as to the best versions to distribute among the inhabitants of Judea and the pilgrims resorting to Jerusalem, I thought it best to purchase here, only about one-third of the amounts appropriated by the American Christian Bible Society, and the co-operation of Eastern Virginia, and order the balance from Smyrna, after a personal examination of the field shall have enabled me to form a more correct estimate of its wants.

I have purchased, and received a donation, from the Church of England Jewish Society and from the British (Dissenters) Society, for the Propagation of the Gospel among the Jews, a good many small works, such as "the Prophecies relating to the Messiah," portions of the Gospel, etc., in Hebrew and Judeo-Spanish, which with upward of two hundred and fifty volumes of the entire Bible and the New Testament, will require some considerable time judiciously to distribute. Should an effort be made to dispose of any of them by sale, or must they all be given without money and without price? Please favor me with your opinion, if you cannot speak officially.

I had the pleasure of receiving, a few days ago, your esteemed letter forwarded from New York, containing a substantial proof of the regard entertained by the superintendent and pupils of the Sunday School, attached to the Christian Congregation of the First Chapel, Cincinnati, for the children of the Jerusalem Mission.

Be so good as to convey to Dr. Leslie and his interesting charge, our thanks for this flattering proof of their interest in the Mission, and assure them that their offering is highly appreciated. Our best endeavors shall be made, so to apply it as shall seem most promotive of the interests of the erring young lambs of the House of Israel, and the juvenile followers of the false prophet, and most likely to impress their minds with a sense of the superior excellence of Christian instruction over Rabbinical and Mohammedan.

I have not yet been able to obtain my consent to the arrangement you suggest, in relation to the twenty-five dollars, for constituting my son Robert a life-member of the American Christian Bible Society. Just let the matter remain as it is. I trust the Lord will enable me not only to make all my children life-members, by annual subscriptions, but to continue my contributions afterward ; the effect, therefore, will only be to postpone the membership of each of them for one year. Many thanks, however, for the intended kindness.

In relation to your inquiry about the future transmission of funds, allow me to say, that I know of no place more expeditious or safe, than the remittance of bills of exchange to the house of Messrs. Baring, Brothers & Co.

I had an interview with one of the firm a few days ago, and he informed me that whenever such a bill is transmitted to them, they will immediately advise me of the fact, and send me a letter of credit, which will be available at Joppa, Beyroot, and Alexandria, and probably at Jerusalem. Such an arrangement I found it impossible to effect at New York: and hence the absolute necessity of visiting London. It will however, always be a somewhat losing business: when I came over I had to pay ten and a half per cent. for a sixty days' draft; and then to submit to a further discount of about one-half per cent., in order to have the draft cashed. Nor would the operation have resulted more favorably, had I purchased sovereigns in New York, all things considered. Learning that the Hebe has nearly cleared, I must abruptly conclude, as I yet have some business to transact.

With love unfeigned, yours in the good nope,

JAMES T. BARCLAY.

THE STORMS.

Our Missionary encountered severe weather in the British Channel, but was mercifully preserved. The storms were remarkably violent, doing great damage to the shipping. We have much cause of gratitude to our Heavenly Father for his mercies to those whom his providence has set forth as the representatives of the cause, in the ancient realms of Israel. Brother Crane, the successor of Brother Challen, kindly furnished this letter:

PORTSMOUTH HARBOR, ENGLAND, Nov. 27, 1850.

MY DEAR BROTHER CHALLEN:—When I inform you that we actually sailed from London on the first inst., as I intimated to you in my last that we would, you will doubtless be no little surprised to hear from me again from these shores—when you are no doubt expecting a letter from me at Malta.

We have encountered two most terrible storms, the last of which we took refuge from in this port thirty-six hours ago. I intended to have written to you in full, but find that I now have only a very few minutes to address you—a pilot having come aboard, and the wind all at once abated and shifted to a favorable point. Praise the Lord, my dear brother, for our marvelous—our providential escape; and especially for his sustaining grace these trying times, and the great spiritual blessings we now enjoy. Bless the Lord, O! my soul.

I shall write in detail by first opportunity. The newspapers will give you some idea of the sad devastation among the shipping on this coast. Wrecks all round us!

These trying times have served to develop qualities and attainments in our little band which I had not ventured to hope we possessed.

What a blessing to have such trying scenes sanctified to our good. Again I say, bless the Lord!

I need not invoke you to rejoice with them that do rejoice.

By-the-by, I must just say, that the pilot is waiting to sail lest we may yet be cast away—that beside the specie I have on board, I got a letter of credit from Baring & Co., for £200, which in the event of our being taken to the Jerusalem above, in place of the Jerusalem below—might be lost to the Board, without your possession of this information.

In great haste, your most affectionate brother,

J. T. BARCLAY.

PARTICULARS OF DR. BARCLAY'S PERILS IN THE BRITISH CHANNEL.

THE subjoined lengthy extracts from a letter to John Tyler, Sen., of Virginia, will impress our minds more fully than the short one to the Corresponding Secretary, of the greatness of the peril to which Brother Barclay was exposed. We extract from the Intelligencer:

JERUSALEM MISSION. 43

FALMOUTH, ENGLAND, Nov: 25, 1850.

MY DEAR BROTHER TYLER:—I had not designed writing to you until I reached Malta; but the events of the last few days brought me to a different conclusion; and I then decided to write a few lines and keep them by me in the hope of coming close enough to some America-bound vessel to throw them aboard; this evening, however, affords me an opportunity of addressing you directly from England. But I must necessarily be brief, as a change of wind may enable us to launch forth again on the mighty deep in a very short time.

We left London on the 1st inst., in this ship, the Hebe of Glasgow, Capt. Watson, but owing to adverse wind, were compelled to take shelter at Deal, a town in the Downs, where Julius Cæsar first attacked our illustrious Druidical ancestors. After weathering this storm for eight or ten days, we again put to sea; but another gale overtaking us, we were compelled to put in at Dungeners, a roadstead on the coast of England, where we remained four or five days; and having recruited our supplies, for you must know that we are furnishing our own stores, etc., we again spread our sails to the *inviting* breeze. On last Sunday morning, however, there was such ominous signs of a storm, that we had to intermit our *public* religious services. You will be pleased to learn that we not only enjoy the privilege of family worship and the eucharistic supper in our own stateroom, but on the Lord's day have preaching in the cabin, for the benefit of all. As I was about to say—the appearance of an unusual meteor in the heavy swells of the sea, induced our forecasting captain to prepare for a storm; and sure enough, it burst upon us in fury that night. O! such a storm! The Capt. says, he never witnessed such a one before, and that we might spend our whole lives at sea, and never encounter such another. The waves soon washed over the deck, not only the main deck, but the higher quarter-deck above the cabin and staterooms, with such irresistible fury as to break the skylights, and pour down in torrents into the cabin. Our own room was occasionally deluged—the surf tumbling like a cataract down the gangway. The first mate and two of the sailors were washed overboard; but fortunately a returning wave brought them back again. Fortunately, only one barrel of water was washed from its lashings, though it was thought for some time, that all was gone save the reservoir below. The only sail we could carry was the stay-sail, reefed to steady the ship. Whenever any of the large sails were hoisted, they were torn into tatters instanter. Chain and spars gave way, but fortunately our bulwarks were but slightly injured. The jibboom falling on our stove-pipe, carried it away in the early part of the gale, and hence we have been without fire ever since, though the beds of Robert, John, and Sarah being considerably wetted by the spray, have very much needed warming and airing. The milk of human kindness that courses so richly through your sympathetic heart, would almost have curdled had you seen the state of anxiety in which our good captain was thrown, when the storm was at its height. O!

what tumultuous rushing of the mountain-like masses of waters! One of the sailors declares, that whenever he saw one of these mighty ingulfers coming "all his bowels would jump right up into his throat." These awful breakers would fairly thunder, as they spent their fury on our noble craft. Our trunks and other articles jumped and rattled about like dice in the shaken box, until we procured ropes to lash them securely. To add to the horror of the scene, the flash of lightning was not wanting to add its lurid glare. I made out to get on deck once or twice, and though the storm was not at its height, yet to all human appearances it did not seem that we would be able to live a single minute. But "thanks to Him, who alike commandeth and raiseth the stormy winds, and who maketh the storm a calm, so that the waves thereof are still," we were graciously spared, and the storm began to abate about the time of the evening sacrifice—your Wednesday evening prayer-meeting. Julia remarked, that you were all then at prayer-meeting, and was vain enough to believe that you might at that very time be interceding for us! But we were doomed to pass through another stormy ordeal, scarcely less terrible than the first. We had scarcely entered the Bay of Biscay, on last Friday night, when we were overtaken by another furious gale, and after buffeting it for three days we find ourselves at last blown back to the British Channel, the scene of the former storm, and fortunately descrying a pilot near shore, were glad enough to be conducted to this port, Falmouth, about dark. We thus find ourselves, on the twenty-fifth day of our voyage, instead of being at Malta as we had hoped, only about two or three hundred miles on the way! As it is an act of Providence, however, it is all right, and therefore, we murmur not, though exceedingly anxious to reach the point of our destination. Our escape has been almost marvelous! Some of the shipping officers from the city have just boarded us, and report that about thirty vessels have put in here in a state of distress—some with most all their rigging gone—one entirely without water for four days; three have been totally wrecked, as already ascertained, and many accidents reported; so that, you perceive, we have great cause of thankfulness to our Heavenly Father for the preserving care he has been kind enough to exercise over us during these tremendous gales and hurricanes. An evil wind, they say it is, that blows good to no one. We have the happiness of realizing that though our stomachs were so deranged that we "abhorred all manner of meat," and our bodies were tossed and rolled about till they were sore even unto bruising, yet it was to us a kind of heaven below! Those tempests served to develop in our little circle, qualities and characters which I had scarcely ventured to hope were possessed by any of us. Our room was a little Bethel, the whole time. Why did not Death enter? There was no fear of him there. We cannot but indulge the pleasing hope that the Lord has preserved our lives for extensive usefulness. Certainly a more fitting preparative for the responsible and arduous task which may soon devolve upon us, could not well be devised.

Believe me, my dear Brother, how apparently anomalous and paradoxical, that we never were happier or more heavenly-minded than during the prevalence of the most impending danger. But still, when you send out Mary and Willie, don't let them take the coast of England in their route during the months of November and December. "No: *that I wont*"—says Mrs. Tyler. But then you must send them in the Spring, my dear sister—and let it be the spring of their lives as well as the spring of the year: for according to the signs of the times the Lord has a great work to do, and but a short time to do it in. I hope you don't claim any dispensation in this great work either for yourself or children. Who then can forbid that my dear sister should even now forsake the sweets of home, and among Jews and Mussulmen spend the balance of her life in playing lady Priscilla, lady Phœbe, or lady Claudia? Julia says, "Tell Brother Tyler, he has no idea how well I can cook, and how I fatten upon a seafaring life." Indeed we are all in very fine plight. But I have used up three-fourths of my sheet without mentioning a word about the matter that induced me to tax you at this time; so that I must rein in my thought, and devote the remainder of it only to that subject.

* * * * * *

Bro. Tyler, please offer thanksgiving to the Lord for his preserving care of us during the storms, and especially for the great spiritual blessings so richly conferred upon us.

But I must conclude, in order to avail myself of an opportunity to send up to the Post-office.

The blessings of Almighty God, richly rest upon you all.

Most affectionately, your Brother in Christ,

JAMES T. BARCLAY.

DOCTOR BARCLAY AT MALTA.

FROM the subjoined excellent letter, kindly furnished me by Brother Crane, it will be perceived that Brother Barclay stood, at the time of writing, upon the ancient Melita, and nearly in the same condition as the good Apostle of the Gentiles; for though he was not shipwrecked upon its coast, he got safe to land, with great difficulty. He was in perils oft, yet the good Lord delivered him out of them all. Even during his great trials, he was busy as an evangelist, and in fitting himself and his for future evangelical work.

VALETTA, January 11, 1851.

VERY DEAR BROTHER:— I addressed you a very hurried note from Falmouth, by a pilot, who had boarded us just as we were leaving the harbor, (into which we had retreated in distress); but fearing that you may not have received it, I write you again, at the earliest convenient moment, after reaching this city, in order that my letter may be dispatched by the first westward-bound steamer. It was my intention to have written to you in detail, from Falmouth, but by the time I had written a letter or two on business, the boat was sent to town, and I availed myself of that opportunity to replenish our supplies, (then somewhat exhausted and damaged), intending to write on my return; but our damages having been repaired sooner than was expected, and the wind suddenly decreasing, and becoming favorable, we set sail before I had an opportunity of doing so. Lest I should forget it, I will mention here, (which was the main object of my hasty note, and without which information, the Board, in the event of a shipwreck, would be considerably the loser), that beside the specie which I brought with me, I bought from Messrs. Baring, Brothers & Co., Bishopsgate, London, a circular letter of credit, or general draft, for £200.

Having completed my business, and made all necessary arrangements, we left London, in the brig Hebe, of Glasgow, Captain Watson, on the 1st day of November. Beside the heavy gales, from which we took shelter at Deal, the spot where the invading army of Julius Cæsar first effected a landing on the British coast, and at Dungeners, a roadstead in the British channel, we encountered no less than six storms in the first five weeks of our voyage, two of which were of such severity and long continuance, that our veteran captain declares he "never saw the like before," though he has been a sailor forty years. The damage done to our ship during the first four or five storms was quite inconsiderable, though so many other ships were either seriously injured or entirely lost; but that sustained during the three days' continuance of the last, is quite considerable in extent, though it is thought, not very serious, unless the fissure in the rudder should extend. At the height of the storm, so severe was the wind, that not a single soul could stay on deck, except the helmsman, whose only safety consisted in being lashed to the wheel.

No canvas could be carried but the stay-sail, any other being immediately blown into shreds or torn away. Such was the tumultuous rushing of the overwhelming waves, that an anchor, weighing nine hundred pounds, was *seen to swim* from the bow of the vessel, half way up its entire length, and thence back again, over the bulwarks, (four or five feet high), into the sea, where it remained suspended by the chain cable! But the tossing of the ship must have co-operated with the surging billows, to have produced such an astonishing effect. The first mate and two of the sailors were washed overboard, but fortunately, brought back by a re-current wave, and lodged in the rigging! The mate declares that at one time, the whole of the main deck was submerged in the space of ten minutes, and concluding that the ship was gradually sinking, he came to summon us to the lifeboat; but happily, the noble Hebe, maid-like, emerged from the whelming deep, and bore us triumphantly along. So exceedingly high did these tremendous mountain masses of water rise, that ships, only one or two hundred yards distant, would, at one time, entirely disappear, and seem to be ingulfed in the abyss of "the deep," and at the next moment, when riding on the tops of the waves, seemed to be floating in the atmosphere! "They go up to the heavens, they go down again to the depths." Then tumultuous avalanches of water would come rushing with such impetuosity as to break the sky-lights, pour down into the cabin, and smashing the companion door, tumble down the stairway like a cataract, deluging our state-rooms! During two of the storms, the cooking stove was rendered entirely useless, the caddy being upset and smashed; the cabin stove being also rendered unavailable at the same time, by the fall of the mizzen-boom, our discomfort was greatly increased, for it was uncomfortably cold. Our bedding also required drying, having been considerably wetted by the briny surges; and we were reduced almost entirely to a diet of crackers and cheese. At length the gale increased to such a violent hurricane, that the tops of the waves were cut off, and falling into the intermediate gulfs, the sea became "as smooth as a millpond," to use the expressive language of the helmsman.

It was at this critical juncture, amid the war of elements, when "all hope was taken away that we should be saved," that "He, who hath his way in the whirlwind, and in the storm, and the clouds are the dust of his feet; who commandeth and raiseth the stormy wind, which lifteth up the waves," and who, in his good pleasure, "maketh the storm a calm," was pleased to say to the raging sea, "thus far shalt thou come, and no farther, and here shall thy proud waters be stayed." And yet, my dear brother, notwithstanding the terrible ordeal through which we passed, we never, in all our lives, realized a higher order of pure enjoyment. The Lord was with us for a truth; and we felt it was good to be thus tempest-tossed, in sight of the jaws of death, yawning, as it were, just at the door, for days and nights together; for we felt all the time, that we were quite on the verge of heaven. 'Tis true, at first the bud was bitter, but " sweet has been the flower." May this chastening act of Providence be so sanctified as long to yield the peaceable fruits of righteousness! A better preparation for engaging in the responsible work assigned us in the Canaan below, or for entering upon the joys we hope to realize in the "Canaan above," could not well have been devised; and I must be permitted to add, that those light afflictions have served to develop qualities of mind, heart, and body, very desirable in the Missionary, but which I had scarcely ventured to hope, were possessed by our little, feeble band.

The destruction caused by these disastrous gales, (both of life and property), must be immense. Before we left Falmouth, it was ascertained that thirteen or fourteen vessels had been wrecked, within a short distance of that place, before the occurrence of the severest storm; and at that time, only a small portion of the English, and none of the Spanish or French coast had been heard from. And no doubt many vessels foundered at sea, one of which, water-logged, abandoned, and apparently about to sink, we passed, but were unable to board, as it was in the roaring forties, (40 deg. 40 min.), a latitude celebrated for its tremendous swells.

Under all the circumstances of the case, we can but regard our escapes, in our old, crippled, and overloaded vessel, from all the perils of the deep, as altogether providential: and venturing to regard it as an intimation that the Lord has something for us to do, and designs to smile propitiously on our Mission, we cannot but rejoice "with joy unspeakable, and full of glory!" In this view of the matter, will you not also "rejoice with them that do rejoice?"

I am thus minute in this account of our voyage, in order that the Board may profit by the information, when it shall send forth more laborers in this part of the foreign field—which, I trust, it may soon do. I was entirely too late in commencing the voyage. The dangerous coast of France and England should never be visited in the winter, or even in the fall, without absolute necessity; and as navigation is so much more dangerous and disagreeable in winter, than in spring and summer, in all regions, the voyage ought to be timed accordingly.

But, having made arrangements with the universally known house of the "Barings," there will be no occasion, henceforth, to send Missionaries via London. The great British and Foreign Bible Society, too, has now, or will soon have, depositories of all its versions, in, or on the outskirts of all the Heathen lands, more convenient and accessible than the parent Institution, at London. Had I known as much as I now do, I would have embarked at New York, for Gibraltar, Marseilles, or Malta, from each of which places there is regular communication with Alexandria, and occasionally with Beyroot, and, with the ordinary blessing of Providence, I would, doubtless, by this time, have been settled in my appointed field, at an expense considerably within the amount appropriated by the Board for conveying me there. But I dare not regret either the delay, expense, inconvenience, or dangers to which we have been subjected, assured that " there is a destiny that shapes our ends, rough hew them as we may." "A man's heart deviseth his way, but the Lord deviseth his steps." The cheapest, as well as the most expeditious route, would probably be by a fruit vessel, to Syria or Smyrna, and thence to Jaffa, by an Austrian or Turkish steamship. The departure of these fruiterers from New York, can be relied upon with great certainty, at certain seasons of the year. By-the-by, ought not the Board to have a regular agent in that city?

Never have we been in better health and spirits. Whether at sea or on land, we spend our time very pleasantly, and we trust not very unprofitably to a few others, as well as to ourselves. Having purchased some Arabic works in London, we bestow a good deal of attention on that language, and also give some attention to Greek, Latin, Italian, and French. In proclaiming the truth to the officers and sailors, as I am permitted to do, not only privately, but in public discourse, on the Lord's day, I have occasion to bring certain strange things to their ears; and yet they all admit, that however contrary to their preconceived notions, it is all in exact concordance with the teachings of the Spirit. Whether they will embrace it gladly, is yet to be seen. One only, as yet, has requested to be inducted into the kingdom. The captain being religiously disposed, opposes no obstacle whatever, in the way of our religious exercises.

We reached this city, on Friday last, and have spent part of our time on shore, in order the better to "refresh ourselves," preparatory to re-embarking. Should we meet with no better conveyance, we expect to proceed in the Hebe, a few days hence, for Alexandria.

Having entertained very serious apprehensions, that the Susanna, of Montrose, by which my apparatus, medicines, books, etc., were shipped, had been lost in the last severe gale which we encountered in the Bay of Biscay, we were no little pleased, on reaching this place, to learn that her excellent commander, Captain Findal, had anchored before the city, ten days before our arrival, and sent in to make inquiries after us.

This is, by far, the most interesting and lovely spot that I have ever visited. No wonder that the Phenicians and Carthaginians, Romans and Greeks, Turks, French and English, should all have fought so desperately to possess and retain it.

The climate is so mild and equable, that umbrellas are more necessary for protection against heat than rain.

The markets are abundantly and cheaply supplied with new potatoes, green peas, radishes, tomatoes, oranges, lemons, pomegranates, watermelons, and other vegetables and fruits, for which you occidentals must either sigh in vain, or patiently wait until summer's scorching heat shall mature them.

The fortifications around the city are stupendous, and one would suppose perfectly impregnable, when properly manned.

Such a succession of palaces I never before beheld! There is no portion of London, itself, that will compare with it in point of architecture, picturesque beauty, and cleanliness. Every house is built of stone, flat-topped, and chimneyless, in true Oriental style. This letter is addressed to you from the lofty terrace of what was, probably, a palace of a knight of St. John. But to be known, Valetta must be seen, or else conceived of, from scenes described in the "Arabian Knights;" indeed, the "*tout ensemble*" is so unique as to be insusceptible of satisfactory conception through any other medium than the eye. The blight of Romanism, however, rests upon the whole isle, and the Maltese are proverbially ignorant, superstitious and idolatrous, and very like the Cretans of old! Oh! how my spirit was stirred within me, when I visited a few of their three hundred and nineteen churches, chapels, and oratorios, where, beside the exhibition of the most unmeaning and disgusting, heathenish mummeries, indulgences ("*indulgenza plenaria*,") are openly and unblushingly advertised for sale!!! I ought to mention, that when put to the test by Mr. Dunmore, who accompanied me to St. Paul's, they refused to sell to us—probably, because we are heretics. Their churches far exceed in splendor, and everything else, except dimensions, the boasted St. Paul's, and Westminster Abbey, of London. It is truly lamentable that the bigotry of the Maltese, judging from the few efforts I have been able to make in their behalf, is entirely unassailable!

I have felt so sustained, in the hour of peril and trial, by the assurance that many brethren in Cincinnati, and elsewhere, were interceding in our behalf, that I cannot conclude without most earnestly soliciting a continuance of their interest in behalf of our infant Mission, assured, that however important the object, and feeble the agency appointed for its accomplishment, the fervent, effectual prayers of the righteous will avail to render it efficient. You will also excuse me for asking you to mention my name in the most fraternal and affectionate manner, to the few brethren, at least, with whom I am acquainted.

Believe me, dear brother, in perfect sincerity,

Yours, most affectionately,

JAMES T. BARCLAY.

P. S. JAN. 17.—The foregoing has been written several days; but ascertaining that no mail would leave for the west for a week or two, I retained it, for the purpose of adding a postscript, should anything occur worth communicating. I am now enabled to state, that I shall, in all probability, embark to-morrow morning, in the iron steamer Brigand direct to Beyroot, at an expense rather less, I think, than the route via Alexandria and the Desert would cost. The good Lord direct me. Setting a high estimate upon your intercessions, I again invoke them.

DR. BARCLAY ARRIVED IN JERUSALEM.

OUR beloved Missionary, and his devoted Family were, at the date of the subjoined letter, at their place of destination, in "an upper room" "near the Damascus gate." Like Peter, they came "from Joppa," on their mission. In the route they stood repeatedly on ground consecrated by memories of Paul and Peter, and now they stand where once stood all the apostles with their Master at their head.

The influence of Brother Barclay upon the captain and crew seems to have been very marked, and it is to be regretted that opportunity did not serve, to administer the Gospel to those who had become enamored of it.

JERUSALEM, February 28, 1851.

MY DEAR BROTHER:—At length, after encountering so many dangers and delays, I have the happiness ("the Lord being merciful unto us,") of addressing you from this ancient city, the bourne of my travels. Learning, unexpectedly, that we could reach our destination more expeditiously and cheaply by a steamer, which touched at Valetta, while we were there awaiting the sailing of the Hebe, than by pursuing our intended route via Alexandria, we took passage in her, and in six or seven days, had the pleasure of landing at Beyroot.

It was with much regret, however, that we left the Hebe, for great preparations were just being made to assemble, on the next day, the English and Americans, then very numerous in Valetta, to hear the ancient Gospel proclaimed under the "Bethel flag." It was all, however, unknown to me until the hour of my departure, as was also the fact that the captain and second mate had decided to be baptized; of which I was not apprised until our fare had been paid, and the very moment of our embarkation arrived, when it was certainly too late to administer the ordinance. One of the *sailors* had previously requested me to baptize him; but such was his ignorance of " the truth as it is in Jesus" (Episcopalian though he was) that I had come to the conclusion not to administer the ordinance until we should reach Alexandria, by which time he would have been sufficiently well "instructed in the way of the Lord," to obey intelligently and satisfactorily, and, as I confidently believe, would have been accompanied by others. I have seen so much evil both to the cause of truth and to the preacher, result from hastily thrusting into "God's building" improper materials of "wood, hay, stubble," that I am perhaps too much afraid of precipitancy, and acted with too much caution in this instance.

But still, whether or not we should "baptize the same hour" that application is made, must, in my opinion, depend somewhat upon circumstances. Will you favor me with your views on this subject?

It was five days after our arrival at Beyroot, before arrangements could be matured for prosecuting our journey to Jerusalem; for it unfortunately so happened that the usual regularity of the steamers was just at that time interrupted; and we were compelled either to take the land route, or remain there at heavy expenses awaiting the arrival of the next onward-bound steamer, which was not expected for some weeks. We, therefore, selected that course which promised to be attended with the least delay, and expenses, and starting from Beyroot on horseback on the 30th ult., we traveled along the sea coast via Sidon, Tyre, Ptolemais, and Jaffa; thence by Romly and Lydda to the Holy City, where, notwithstanding rains and bad roads, we arrived in nine days, exclusive of Lord's day, which we spent in Sidon. We were treated with no little consideration and kindness by the American consulate at Beyroot, and at other places where our country is represented; we are also under great obligations to Mr. Eli Smith, Mr. Whiting, Mr. Thompson, Dr. Vandyke, Dr. De Forest, and Mr. Williams, missionaries of the American Board of Commissioners for Foreign Missions at or near Beyroot; to Dr. Kelly, who has been much persecuted by the Roman Catholics, and to many of the American and English residents at Beyroot; but especially to Mr. Manning, a "Friend" indeed, long a missionary to the Jews of Palestine, who, though a Quaker, is under the patronage of the London Society for the Propagation of Christianity among the Jews. Indeed, whereever we have been, we have met with the kindest of friends, and in gratitude to the "Author and Giver of all good," I desire to record the fact. To Mr. Murad, our consular agent at Jaffa, and his excellent brother Lazarus, who happens to be spending some time in this city, we are under the deepest obligations for valuable services. After spending three days at the Latin convent, I succeeded in renting the upper story of a house near the Damascus gate, where we are now quite comfortably situated, and assiduously studying Arabic, under the tuition of an excellent teacher, who also serves us, when occasion requires, as dragoman.

We are all in good health, and highly delighted with the City of the Great King; but if I may credit what I am told on all hands, there is no worse missionary ground on all the earth than this same city; but I forbear particularizing at this time, lest the Board should be needlessly discouraged. I can assure you, however, that I am not in the least disheartened, knowing, as I do, that the "truth is mighty and will prevail," and surely if there is a spot on earth where the Lord will be pleased to bless the means of his own appointment in answer to prayer, that place is Jerusalem! O that all the holy brethren would strive together with us in prayer, that the word of the Lord may again go forth in Jerusalem in its primitive purity and power!

I yearn over this benighted people, and ardently long for the time when I can proclaim to them, in their own language, the truth as it is in Jesus; and I cannot bring myself to believe that it will be two years, according to the unanimous opinion of the missionaries and others, before we can converse freely in their native language, confessedly difficult as it is. Could I believe that half that time would be required to speak their vernacular, I would earnestly beg the Board to furnish the means of speaking to them through a dragoman, who would also assist in the judicious distribution of the Scriptures, etc. So high is the estimate put upon colporteur operations, that the Episcopalians, although they have several ordained missionaries here who speak the language fluently, have also here, and in other parts of Palestine, some half dozen native colporteurs, whom they give from 150 to 200 pounds sterling per annum, simply to distribute tracts and the Scriptures—a sum, however, entirely too high. But surely there is no place on earth—strange as it may seem—where the diffusion of truth is more needed than this very spot where it first emanated. I was prepared to find all the ignorance, superstition and bigotry which I have witnessed among the Mohammedan portion of this people; but for the bitter hatred of everything called Christian, on the part of the Jews, and for the groveling superstition and degraded idolatry (in what else can their Maryolatry and other saints, and demonolatry be termed), which I am constantly pained to see among all the lapsed churches of the East, I was by no means prepared, and still less was I prepared to find such a wide departure from the simplicity and purity of the faith once delivered to the saints, on the part of those not only styling themselves Protestants, but claiming succession from the Apostles! Believe it if you can—for it is even so—that there are those here whom "it grieves exceedingly that there is come a man to seek the welfare of the children of Israel!!" Now, were those persons of the same category with Sanballat, Tobiah, Geshum, and Gashum, I could make some allowance on the score of ignorance and prejudice; but they are "Protestants" professing the greatest regard for the welfare of the Jews—men too, whom I told, in answer to their inquiries, that the great Protestant principle, as avowed by Chancellor Chillingworth, was our grand motto, and strictly construed would give them a perfectly correct view of our theology.

By another clerical *friend* (not a Protestant though) I have been seriously advised to join the Anglican church if I would escape persecution! But that precept which enjoins the "wisdom of the serpent, and the harmlessness of the dove," admonishes me to forbear: nor would I drop these few hints, but to stimulate your prayers and efforts, in behalf of this interesting and important spot, over which the blessed Savior wept and lamented so pathetically, and where, I think, it has been so wisely determined to make our first effort for the foreign propagation of the truth. I have not had the pleasure of hearing from you since last October; and so you may well imagine, I am not a little anxious to be greeted with a sight of your ever welcome autograph. The postal arrangements of this country, I fear, are neither very ample nor reliable.

A mail, I am told, will be forwarded to-morrow to Beyroot, per post-walker; and it is for this mail that I am hastily addressing you to-night. Had I time and space at disposal, I have many facts and incidents to communicate, but straitened and restricted as I am at present, I must necessarily omit their relation. Dr. Bacon, of New Haven, who, together with his son, is on a tour of visitation to the Missions of the American Board of Commissioners for Foreign Missions, has just called to see us, and expresses the opinion that the safety of Franks (and especially missionaries), in every part of Turkey, is much endangered by the late disturbances in the divan at Constantinople, which have necessitated the flight of the liberal-minded Sultan (it is reported) from his capital to Cairo. But I hope better things, and feel everything but fear, trusting, as I do, in him who is Ruler among the nations, and will not permit to fall unnoticed, a single hair from the head of those who put their trust in Him.

Please address me by way of Beyroot, to the care of the American consulate of that place. By-the-way, Mr. J. Horsford Smith, our estimable consul at that place, is a member of a commercial house in New York; and I was told by Dr. Vandyke, who called to see me a few days ago, that instead of making remittances through the round-about medium of the Barings, the most economical, direct, and, in every respect, best way, would be to remit through that firm. It is in that way that the American Board accomplishes its remittances to its Syrian missions. I do not know the exact style of the firm, but will communicate with Mr. Smith, and let you know the result.

Our articles shipped from London, per Susanna, I was happy to inform you, arrived safe at Jaffa, notwithstanding the great peril to which, I learn, the ship was exposed, and our fears, in relation to our trunks, furniture, etc., shipped from Beyroot, per Arab vessel Ibrahim, are also at last happily relieved by letter from the British consul at Jaffa, stating that after consuming twenty-one days in a passage which ordinarily occupies two or three days, they are at last safely landed at that place, and together with the other packages will forthwith be forwarded here by camels or mules. Great, indeed, would have been our loss, had this vessel, as was believed, been lost; for, having to bring along with us our tent, canteen, etc., in our overland journey, we were only enabled to take one small trunk, and a few carpet-bags. Will you do me the favor to present to the holy brethren of Cincinnati, as well as accept for yourself, my warmest Christian salutation? My wife and children also desire to send their best greetings.

The fervent intercessions of the brethren, in behalf of our incipient labors, I must earnestly invoke—striving together with us—that "our hand may be strengthened for this good work."

With love and esteem that gather strength, rather than suffer abatement by lapse of time and space, believe me, my dear brother,

Most sincerely yours,

JAMES T. BARCLAY.

DOCTOR BARCLAY'S JOURNAL.

"Lord, we commit ourselves to Thee,
As guardians of th' expansive sea;
Preserve us on the trackless main
To praise thee on the shore again.

Especially preserve our souls
From sin's destructive rocks and shoals;
From quicksands ever casting up,
Our progress in thy way to stop.

O may we keep the mark in sight
Where there is everlasting light;
And in that light, O Lord, may we
Our calling and election see.

All consecrated be each heart—
And every hand—to do its part—
Directed by Thy holy will,
The great commission to fulfill."

Sept. 11, 1850.—After spending ten days in New York, the anxiously desired hour at length arrives, when, through a kind Providence, we are to set sail for the shores of old Canaan. Cheered by such hope, and animated by such joy, as that which now bounds in our bosoms, never did Crusader or pilgrim set face Zionward with greater buoyancy of spirit.

12 o'clock, M.—Boom! roars the signal cannon! Plash! splash the paddle-wheels of the huge steam-tug, Ajax, as he puffs, puffs, puffs! from his iron lungs; and our "good ship Devonshire," with her thirteen hundred tons of freight, and fourscore passengers, is soon towed to Sandy Hook, where, spreading her ample sails, she scorns the further aid of her

renowned Grecian escort, and, rapidly gliding along the coast of "sea-girt Long Island," soon

"Leaves Columbia on the lee,"

while these very words are echoing to the notes of the sweet-toned guitar in the cabin below. Swiftly and joyously we go on the wings of the freshening breeze; but Neptune begins to drive furiously. How soon is our elasticity of mind, body, and soul, palled by depressing and distressing nausea! O this qualmishness of the stomach! Better qualms of the stomach, however, than qualms of the conscience! Never felt more conscious of being in the path of duty: never happier.

SEPT. 12.—So prostrated with sea-sickness as scarcely to be able to make this short entry.

*　*　*　*　*　*　*

MONDAY, SEPT. 30, 1½ o'clock.—"Land! ho! land!" Aroused by the stimulus of the above joyful cry, I creep up on deck to enjoy the pleasing sight; and now again resume my Notes, which, for seventeen days, have been suspended by sea-sickness, or the scarcely less disagreeable lassitude of body and mind consequent upon this subduing affection. Little or nothing, however, has occurred in the interim worth recording. The monotony of sea-travel has been occasionally relieved by the cry of "Whales!" "Porpoises!" "Sharks!" "Ship! a-hoy!" "There goes that leviathan!" etc., etc. Calms, squalls, and thunder-gusts, we have had in their usual variety. Occasionally, a storm-driven land-bird has enlivened us by a visit; glad to find, even among such fellow-bipeds as sailors, a resting-place for the sole of its foot. From our excellent commander, Captain Hovey, we have received the most unexpected marks of attention and kindness; and with our fellow-passengers of the cabin, our intercourse has been very pleasant; and with some of those in the steerage, I hope, quite profitable. Great indifference to spiritual matters, however, seems to characterize almost every soul on board, being very averse to religious conversation, especially if of a personal or controversial character. Strange to say, those in the steerage, though many of them are Romanists, infidels, and irreligionists of the worst caste, are much more accessible than the refined and (some of them) professing cabin passengers! Have had the pleasure during the voyage—though the while, "reeling to and fro, like a druken man, at my wits' end"—to save one of the crew, a poor English sailor, from a drunkard's death and a watery grave—a distressing case of *mania a potu*.

Truly sorry that, owing to utter incapacity the first Lord's day of the passage, and the state of the winds and waves the last Lord's day, I have only preached once on shipboard. This is the more to be regretted, inasmuch as no little interest was manifested on that occasion; and truths that are deemed altogether contraband in lands (self) yclept orthodox, were regarded as entirely evangelical on these high seas. It is a little singular, that while I have suffered so much from sea-sickness myself, my wife and children have suffered but little, or, at least, but for a short time: and I may truly say, that, sea-sickness to the contrary notwithstanding, we never have spent our time more profitably, and in a most important sense, *pleasantly*, than during this voyage. Truly can we say, " it is good for us to be here." The true secret of this enjoyment is, perhaps, that self-examination, when conducted with nothing but a thin barrier of wood between us and eternity, is apt to be more faithful, thorough, and searching than under ordinary circumstances on *terra firma*.

The land which has just been espied, proves to be the group of Scilly isles, a short distance from that noted projection of England termed "Land's End."

A few hours' sail have brought us to " Lizard's Point," the extreme south end of England; owing, however, to the nature of the coast and the narrow sinuosities of the British Channel (which is as *sinuous* as it is *strait*), we shall yet have to sail more than four hundred miles, in so large a ship as this, before we can reach London.

At 9, P. M., opposite Plymouth, we pass within a short distance of the blazing light of Eddystone lighthouse, so famous for its surge-repelling powers, and its immense cost. Just opposite, are the world renowned tin mines of Cornwall, over some of the submarine ramifications of which we may now be sailing. Can this be the "Tarshish" of the Scriptures, whence the Israelites and the Phenicians derived their supply of tin ?* If it was here that the Romans first caught

---

* The WHEREABOUTS of Tarshish is a matter that has sadly puzzled modern and medieval geographers. Is it not highly probable that there

a glimpse of the chalky cliffs of England, the propriety of the cognomen they bestowed upon "Angle Land," is obvious enough. "Album," (Albion"), was, no doubt, the word that immediately escaped from many a lip. And truly some of these lofty white cliffs are very imposing. Our good ship is now almost embraced in the arms of her illustrious *alma mater*, the old shire of Devon.

At sunrise, on the first day of October, find ourselves quite near the Isle of Wight. O how refreshing the sight of its green hedges, cultivated slopes, and neat farm houses! Learn from the pilot, who has just boarded us, that "her most gracious majesty, Victoria Alexandrina, and his royal highness, Prince Albert," with the royal nursery of princes and princesses, have just left this, their favorite residence, for Buckingham Palace, in London. Mayhap we may be so fortunate as to get a peep at some of these royal

---

are two places of that name, inasmuch as it has been the custom in all ages of the world to assign the same name to cities and even countries far remote? It is evident, at least, that the Tarshish to which Solomon sent a fleet triennially along with King Hiram's navy, was approached through the Red Sea and Indian ocean, and answers well to the British East Indian possessions; while it was on the Mediterranean that Jonah embarked to reach the Tarshish, to which he wished to flee, precisely in the opposite direction, and in the direct route to these distant capes. Who knows but that the timid Prophet imagined, could he once ensconce himself in the depths of these mines, he would be concealed from the all-searching ken of the Omniscient, and evade his perilous mission. Be this as it may, many an ancient place has been identified from the similarity of its ancient to its modern name, by an analogy far less striking than that which exists between "Britannic" and "Baratanic," or Tin Land of the Phœnicians. But whither am I wandering in the undefined regions of speculation?

wights! The wind being high and adverse, we are compelled, at 9 P. M., to cast anchor before the far-famed town of Dover. Have just been gazing at the splendidly illuminated front street; but while thus admiring the splendid achievements of the "Hermetic Art," by which the chemist delves down into the pitchy regions of darkness and transforms the jet-black carbon into such resplendent light, a bright meteor shot athwart the heavens, just over the town, and seemed to say, " how insignificant are the most brilliant achievements of man compared with the merely incidental works of God." 'Tis thus, the heavens declare the glory of God, though only on a small scale. And, thanks to his condescending kindness, we are permitted to glorify Him too, by "letting our light shine." Though but twenty miles from France, she is illuming the track of the benighted mariner of these seas, by the cheering beams of her conspicuous light-houses. May we all shine as lights in the world, holding forth the lamp of life, admonishing and instructing, by word and deed, our fellow-voyagers over the ocean of life.

Some of the passengers, tired of "life on the ocean wave," and preferring the undeviating track of the locomotive to the trackless path of the Devonshire, here take leave of us, for town, via railroad.

Oct. 2.—Pleasantly rocked in our huge cradle by the joint agency of Æolus and Pluto, Orpheus himself could impart no sweeter repose than that which we have enjoyed during the past night: our unwonted rest being entirely uninterrupted until the first gleamings of Aurora admonished our watchful pilot that we might safely weigh anchor, and pursue the uneven tenor of our way. Rise betimes to get a good view of the renowned Dover Castle; but am greatly disappointed in its appearance. Learn, however, that all its beauty and strength lie in the interior of the hill on which the castle is situated, being perforated and intersected in every direction, like the far-famed fort of Gibraltar. The Duke of Wellington is reposing for a time, beneath his laurels, (but it is to be feared, not on a bed of roses), at one of his splendid mansions just above the town, as we learn from the flag which now gracefully waves its folds over this splendid edifice of the great Napoleon-whipper.

We are now threading our way very cautiously through the shoaly "Downs," while forty or fifty ships in full view are anxiously contending with wind and tide, to gain an entrance into this same narrow channel. Had no idea that access to the Great Emporium is so obstructed by bars, rocks, shallows, and narrows. How like the way to the great city—New Jerusalem! "Straight is the gate and narrow the way!" The wind is so unfavorable, and sailing so dangerous, that our prudent captain had just concluded to *hove*-to, and cast anchor again; but meeting with a steamer, has engaged her services to tug us to the mouth of the Thames; and there is now a reasonable probability that we shall see the great metropolis to-morrow, instead of being locked up here some days, in what the captain styles the most dangerous coast in the world. Compelled to pursue a route so far east that we are now opposite the south-western corner of Belgium, and nearly ready to "fetch a compass" for the Thames. Having met with another steamer, the captain has engaged its services also; but fearing lest we should run foul of the quicksands, cast anchor for the night.

OCT. 3d.—At early dawn weigh anchor; and escorted by "Hercules" on one side, and "Sampson" on the other, speedily reached the mouth of the Thames. How delightful to be within a stone's throw of land! and such a land as this! What exciting scenes delight the eye! What soul-stirring recollections crowd upon the mind as we wend our way amid thousands of ships that throng the river, with castles, hospitals, monuments, factories, and hundreds of strange and interesting objects in view! But who can write amid so much to distract!

LONDON.

[A HIATUS.—The account of London, which occupied some space in the Journal, was mislaid by the printer, and though diligent search was made, was not recovered.]

AT 12 o'clock, reach that wonderful depot of the productions of all climes—the St. Catherine Docks, after a quick, and, in many respects, delightful voyage of three weeks. What just matter of devout gratitude to Him "who holds the winds in his fists and measures the waters of the ocean in the hollow of his hands."

By dint of hard begging, we obtain leave of the stern custom-house officer, who came on board as soon as we touched the wharf (and two of whose

Argus-eyed *subs* had taken possession of the ship at Gravesend), we were permitted, as a special favor to take on shore a few pieces of clothing, after submitting them to a keen examination. Take lodgings at Randall's private boarding-house, King-street, Cheapside, centrally situated between the Post-office, Exchange, and St. Paul's Cathedral.

> " At length we launch again
> Upon the mighty deep,
> Do thou, O Sovereign of the main,
> Our souls and bodies keep.
>
> If hardship and distress
> We should be called to bear,
> O let thine all-supporting grace
> Preserve us from despair.
>
> Be Thou forever nigh,
> That we may hear Thee say,
> ' Be not afraid, for it is I,
> To guide you on the way.'
>
> Then come whatever will,
> We nothing have to dread,
> When Christ continues with us still,
> And says, " Be not afraid.' "

Nov. 1, 1850.—Having accomplished the various objects which rendered it necessary to take London in our route, we leave the city of smoke and fogs (having engaged passage in the Scotch brig, Hebe, Capt. Watson), the first available opportunity of re-embarking for the regions of the " pleasant land," presented during a four-weeks' sojourn among the " Cockneys!" Discharging our steam-tug at Gravesend, and parting *sans ceremonie*, with our most vigilant custom-house officer of the school of Paul Pry, we spread sail before a fresh south-western gale, under an experienced pilot, but are soon compelled to take refuge under the walls of the Castle of Deal, where we are surrounded with more than a hundred ships of all classes, glad enough to cast anchor in these roads, and await the subsidence of the waves and winds. Find to our sorrow, that during our month's tarry on *terra firma*, we have lost our sea-seasoning for the sea. Our anchorage, though far from being pleasant, is regarded as quite safe for so near a vicinage of the much-dreaded "Goodwin Sands"—this fatal Syrtian shoal being just opposite, and the beacons on either end in full view. The ominous wreckers, in numbers, make their appearance, and very *politely* offer their services to pilot us into safer anchorage at Ramsgate; but the exorbitant price demanded for what they call such a hazardous service decides the captain to ride out the storm where we are now moored.

SATURDAY MORNING, Nov. 9th.—The wind which has been blowing a gale for the last eight days, having at last abated, and veered to a more favorable point, late last night, we are aroused very early this morning by the clattering of the windlass and anchor chain; and going above are greatly delighted to observe the bustling scenes all around us in our naval forest. How changed the scene! The forest of summer is not more unlike that of winter, than is the present appearance of our fleet unlike that of the last eight days. The hundreds of denuded masts in the Downs, so much resembling a winter's forest, are now clothed with their various riggings ready for sailing, presenting a most animating appearance, instead of the gloomy aspect that has pervaded it during the week that it has been compelled to furl all sails and ride at anchor in this dangerous strait. Many of the ships surrounding us have at various times, ventured out, but, after a few hours' buffeting have been glad enough to put back into this anchorage, insecure as it is. Our long delay here, though rather trying to our patience, has at least afforded us ample opportunity of examining the battle-ground of the first action between the Romans and Britons; for it was at this identical spot that Julius Cæsar, nineteen hundred and four years ago, landed from Gaul. The cliffs of Dover, a mile or two below, being the nearest point to his Gallic conquest, "*La belle France*," and very conspicuous objects, he doubtless steered directly for them; but finding them inaccessible, at least when defended as they then were, he was compelled, by the nature of the coast, to come around into this little bay; and here it was that his landing was so bravely disputed by our warlike ancestors. How very different the condition of the present polished inhabitants of this isle from that of their savage, naked, tattooed ancestors! How wide the contrast between the mean mud huts and stockades of that day, and the splendid mansions, castles, and forts of the present! Nor is the difference in their physical condition more striking than that of their spiritual; how surpassingly superior to the Druidical religion of our ancestors, even in its merely humanizing tendencies, is Christianity, even in its Anglican form, polluted as it is by union with state government and human invention.

The country hereabouts is not particularly inviting, even when its murky, smoky, hazy, misty, foggy atmosphere allows it to be seen to the best advantage; and it was doubtless the tin, lead, iron, and copper of this remote island that tempted the horse-leech-like cupidity of the insatiable "Mistress of the World" to invade it. How emblematic of the atmosphere of her moral and political condition, is the condition of her natural atmosphere! The state of religion, not only in the Established Church, but among dissenters of all denominations, is far—very far—too low; her numerous and well-sustained benevolent institutions to the contrary notwithstanding. Judging from what I saw of her preachers in private, the charge of wine-bibbing, which has so often been brought against them, is but too well founded. I was no little disappointed and mortified to find the Hon. B. N ——, who is certainly one of her most pious and enlightened ministers, so benighted upon so fundamental and plain a subject as that of *faith*—so plain, as plain, as "certain also of her own poets have said,"

"That none by reason could it plainer make."

Candor compels me to confess that the worshiping assemblies of the United States are not so well behaved in all respects as those of England, nor apparently so devout. The church-goers of England, however, would deserve more credit for their devotional deportment, were it not for the fact that they are compelled to keep still and behave themselves by a richly cos-turned band of semi-ecclesiastical officials. This, at least, is the case at the cathedrals that I visited. Nothing struck me more forcibly nor disagreeably, than the prominent part taken in worship by a set of graceless-looking boys, unless it were the affectation of her priests, and the drawling incantation of her whining choirs:

> "O wad some power the giftie gie us
> To see oursel's as ithers see us—
> It wad fra mony a blunder free us,
> And silly notion;
> What airs in dress and gate would lea' us,
> And e'en devotion."

Another thing that struck me with force, though not with much surprise, was the universal distrust that prevails among all classes of English society; and the great want of delicacy that exists among the females, at least, in the middle walks of life, is absolutely shocking to American sense of propriety. One might suppose that long ages of spiritual despotism and political tyranny had, at last, reconciled the people to the yoke; but it is far otherwise; great dissatisfaction prevails on both scores. The onerous system of taxation entailed upon the English by the failure of many of her avaricious schemes of aggrandizement, has engendered a spirit of discontent which cannot long be smothered. These down-trodden people are taxed to the eye-brows; and that, too, without any hope that their burdens, temporal or spiritual, will be lightened, except by such a radical change in Church and State as few of her statesmen seem now to apprehend. Hence, the multitudes, and among them some of her best population, are preparing to emigrate to Columbia's happy shores! Yet there are many who affect to glory in the immense national debt beneath which they groan. It is truly lamentable to see how the leaven of Oxford tractarianism is fermenting the whole lump of English society. And many of her nobility as well as commonalty, not satisfied with Puseyism, tarry but a short time at Oxford, and then go directly over to Rome! All this, however, is but the legitimate tendency of Harry-the-Eighth-ism, and might readily have been predicted as the result of the concurrence of existing circumstances. Although their mode of living, their manners, customs, etc., differ so widely, in many respects, from those of their transatlantic brethren, yet nothing, I think, will strike the American traveler with more surprise and disgust than the vexatious regulations of the English custom-house. With Paul-Pry-like curiosity, her Vandal officers seize on your trunks, empty their contents, and rummage every article, charging a most immoderate price for such impertinent officiousness! But for the kind interference of our Minister, the Hon. Abott Lawrence, who kindly procured an order from the Lords of the Treasury to have my packages put under *seal*, my apparatus, medicines, books, etc., would scarcely have been worth repacking, after passing the ordeal of the custom-house examination. The sad fate of the Alexandrian library is that of many a trunk of books that enters the custom-house; and the fiendish pleasure with which they burn up such of our books as they are pleased to term "*piratical*," seems expressly designed, however poorly calculated, to force our Government to pass an international copyright act. But notwithstanding all this, I must still say, with one of England's exiled sons,

"England, with all thy faults, I love thee still."

I love her because she is throwing the ægis of her protection over God's ancient people; I love the "Lion Isle," for the sake of the third lion emblazoned on her significant escutcheon, said to have been placed there by Richard Cœur de Lion, after his brilliant career in the Holy Land, as emblematical of "the Lion of the tribe of Judah." I love her, because I can but think she is designed by Providence to play a most important and interesting part in the great events soon, perhaps, to occur among the nations; for I know not how to withhold my assent from that interpretation of the prophecies which makes England the Great Lion, and "the Merchants of Tarshish" (whose merchants, even the mighty East India Company, and "princes whose traffickers are the honorable of the earth"), at all events the possession of Babelmandeb, Aden, and other strongholds around Moab and Ammon,—the late governmental reconnoissance of the Holy Land, and the influence which Great Britain already exercises over her population, will enable her to make "Moab and Ammon a covert" for the gathering flock of the lost sheep of the house of Israel." But whither am I wandering!

At last we are underway. A spirited rivalry existing between so many ships starting at the same time, all sail is crowded upon the Hebe, and we come to the conclusion that she is at least a fair sailer; but the wind chopping around again and blowing very fresh in our faces, we are compelled to " tack," and thus stemming both wind and current, make very slow progress, as we soon discover. The first tack taken by the Hebe, after going as near the French coast as the shoals would permit, brought us up to the town of Folkstone, in the county of Kent. This beautiful place and surrounding landscape, we were anxious to transfer to our portfolio of drawings, not merely for the sake of its beauty, though it is a very romantic and picturesque spot, but mainly because it is the birthplace of Dr. Harvey, the discoverer of the circulation of the blood; a discovery which the *orthodox* doctors of the seventeenth century as pertinaceously opposed as do many of the "*doctors of divinity*" of the nineteenth century, truths equally obvious and vital in theology, as that was in physiology. The winds bore us away so rapidly, however, on our back tack, that we had not time to finish the details of the sketch; and as the scene faded away from our view, we were regretting that we should see Folkstone no more; but on our return tack, where should we again approach the English shore (in consequence of the opposing tide and wind) but just a few fathoms *below* Folkstone! and this retrograde movement was so often the result of our tacking, that we not only had time to complete the view of Folkstone, but might have taken quite a panorama of the coast of that vicinity. The wind in the meantime increasing to a gale, we are glad to seek **covert from the angry surges of the rolling deep, under** the projecting point of Kent, called Dungeness, whither we are allured in company with at least a hundred other ships, by the cheering light of its lofty "Pharos," having advanced only twenty miles during eighteen hours' hard sailing!

TUESDAY EVENING, Nov. 12.—The wind having again become favorable, we now witness such a scene as we never saw before nor expect ever to see again. The ships which have accumulated at Dover and Deal during the last few days, brought thither by steam from London, and pent up during the late blow, having first experienced the change of wind, are underway, and almost upon us, while all our fleet have also spread sail except the Hebe, whose captain is on shore. We are thus advantageously situated midway between about four hundred and fifty ships in full sail, somewhat in battle array, the crescent end of one fleet nearly touched the wing of the other, disposed in amphitheatrical form. Compared with this immense fleet, what was the sight of the hundred and thirty ships of the boasted "invincible Spanish Armada," once on these shores, which occupies so large a space on the page of history! It is true, we hear not the roar of cannon, nor see men plunging into the liquid element, there to seek a less painful death than in the igneous element which consumed so many thousands on that dreadful occasion, when Philip sought to crush Elizabeth at a blow, but we see what is far more delightful to behold, the gorgeously tinted sky vividly emblazoned by resplendent clouds, reminding us of that glorious day when the Son of Man shall descend in like manner as he ascended, and the "sea shall give up the dead that are in it, and death and the grave shall deliver up the dead that are in them."

Though four miles from shore, our provident captain has wisely improved his leisure time by replenishing his stock of water and provisions; and as *we* have been detained ten days longer on the coast of England than we expected, it was deemed advisable for two of our party to go on a purveying expedition to a neighboring town, in order to replenish our own stores.

Nov. 13.—Sailing very pleasantly down the English Channel—having first the coast of England, then that of France looming up before us. Cannot help speculating on the impending destiny of that "broad street" of mystic Rome, which seems to have occupied so large a space in the vision of the Seer of Patmos. What countless myriads of the sackcloth prophesiers against spiritual despotism, stain the soil of that Romanized country with their blood, and cry aloud for vengeance!

THURSDAY, Nov. 21.—Bay of Biscay. The sea was observed to be laboring under a commotion so unusual even in this turbulent bay, the weather being serene and the sky ominously red *—that our ever-watchful captain could not refrain from auguring a forthcoming storm. A broad iris around the moon, and a very uncommon meteor in the heavens concurred to strengthen

---

* "A red sky at night
Is the sailor's delight;
But let them take warning
If seen in the morning."

this prediction; hence, the ship was kept in trim for a storm, and the usual public Lord's day discourse was omitted, in momentary expectation of a gale. Nor was it long before our worst apprehensions were realized; such a storm ensued, as the captain declares, he never had witnessed before—not so much for its extreme violence as for its protracted continuance.

> "The ocean yawned, and rudely blowed
> The wind that tossed our struggling bark."

That such tumultuous rushing of mountain masses of water should be produced by an agent like the atmosphere—so attenuated as to be invisible—is surely one of the most wonderful works of God! "They that go to the sea in ships, these see the works of the Lord and his wonders in the deep." Never while memory does her office, shall I forget the wild revel of the winds and the howling scowl of the tempest's roar! During most of the storm the stay-sail was the only piece of canvas that could be carried, any other sail being torn into tatters almost as soon as hoisted. Fortunate indeed, was it that our wary captain had razeed the main top-gallant mast, and taken care to keep at a most *respectable* distance from land. Hundreds of times did our noble old craft "ship" the heaviest "seas" with impunity, the waves not only totally submerging the main-deck, but rolling furiously over the quarter-deck, and breaking the skylights, rush madly down into the cabin, or tumble like a cataract down the companion-way, despite of every effort to bar them out. The first mate and two of the sailors were washed entirely overboard, but fortunately brought back and lodged on board by another wave, but how they know not. The only security for the helmsman during many a fearful hour, was to lash him to the wheel. The mate declares, at one time, the whole main-deck was totally submerged for at least *ten* minutes; and concluding that it would never emerge again, actually came to summon us to take to the long-boat. To add to our calamity, the main-boom had fallen in the early part of the storm, and carried away our stovepipe, so that thenceforth we had neither fire to warm ourselves nor dry the bedding; the door of the kitchen had also been crushed in by the waves, and the cooking-stove rendered useless; so that our bill of fare, scanty enough at best, was no little curtailed; this, however, was matter of small moment, for although we had considered ourselves perfectly acclimated to "life on the ocean wave, and a home on the rolling deep," yet during that trying time "our souls 'almost' abhorred all manner of meat." Having been unable for several days to take the necessary observations to ascertain our longitude and latitude, we were in constant dread of running in contact with the coast of England or France, or some of the neighboring islands; and for this apprehension, the thick mists for which the capes are so remarkable, contributed no little. Drenching rain, pattering hail, and the lurid glare of purple lightning, all concurred with the thundering avalanches of water that made our ship quiver from stem to stern, to render the scene terrific, awful, and sublime in the extreme. But just when "all hope that we should be saved was taken away," the hoarse voice of the second mate was heard to exclaim in joyful tones, " The gale is broke."

Never shall we forget that storm! Bless the Lord, O my soul! Never were we so near the confines of eternity, in the very purlieus of heaven! Never had we enjoyed so realizing a view of the omnipotence of the Lord, nor so firm and consoling an assurance of enjoying the divine acceptance and blessing. We felt of a truth that Christ was in the bark, and we smiled at the storm. This memorable occasion served too, to develop qualities and attainments which I had scarcely ventured to hope were possessed by our little band.

FALMOUTH, TUESDAY MORNING, Nov. 24.—Have been tossed about in the channel and bay by another storm scarcely less violent than the preceding, but being descried by a pilot near the Lizard last evening, were safely conducted into this beautiful port of Cornwall. Awful as the storm appeared to us at sea, we were yet not fully impressed with a sense of our danger until we actually saw in port some proof of the damage done by these awful gales. And grateful as we felt to our kind heavenly Father for his signal protection, yet never can we sufficiently thank Him for this great deliverance from death and the fear of it; especially as we can but regard our escape as an intimation that Providence is sparing our lives for future usefulness. Our deliverance is signal indeed, when we consider the violence of the storm, the dangers of the coast at this season, and the overloaded state of the vessel, now waning in the eighteenth year of her age. Sad indeed, was the injury inflicted on some of the shipping that effected a retreat into this port; but far worse was the fate of many others that were unable to find shelter. The total loss of thirteen vessels is already ascertained; and generally all on board perished; and as yet but a small part of this coast, and none of that of France has been heard from!! Although we have been out twenty-five days, and have progressed but three or four hundred miles, we are at least as far advanced as some other vessels that started two or three weeks ahead of us, but have been compelled to put back in a state of distress. The injury sustained by the Hebe being but trivial, is soon repaired; and now, having replenished our stores of provisions, are nearly ready to put to sea again.

Nov. 25.—Through a kind Providence we are again under sail in pretty good trim. But we are never exempt from danger. Returning from Falmouth, last night, in a small boat, a fight ensued between the drunken sailors and an officer, during which we were in the most imminent danger of capsizing, and being run over by a ship in full sail. But what threatened at one time to be worse than all our misfortunes combined, was a mutiny, in which a majority of the sailors were found to be implicated more or less, but was fortunately discovered in time to be suppressed and counteracted in a great measure.

MONDAY, DEC. 2.—Had another severe gale, commencing Friday and ending Lord's day morning. Sea still exceedingly rough. This bay, indeed, is said never to be at rest. Fit emblem of the state of the wicked!—" there is no peace to the wicked, saith my God, they are like the troubled sea when it cannot rest, whose waters cast up mire and dirt." A dismantled and forsaken ship, which we were unable to board, together with floating spars and other portions of ship-riggings apprise us that other vessels have not been so fortunate as ours. The mist suddenly clearing away, this evening, about 4 o'clock, our position is fortunately (*providentially*) revealed to us just in time to effect our rescue; for we are running directly on the St. Agnes Island, one of the *Scilly Group*, esteemed so very dangerous, (where three men-of-war were wrecked in the course of one night). All hands are immediately summoned to " bout ship;" and now we beat off toward the coast of France. Wind again increasing in violence. Young Leviathan, as if to show his superior locomotive powers in his own element, and his entire independence of that element that tossed us about like a thing of nothing, has been escorting Madame Hebe, cutting all manner of fantastic capers, and refusing to leave us; until pelted by pieces of coal he finally makes his puffing, snorting salaam, and disappears in the "vasty deep." Have seen some very curious creatures " in this great and wide sea, wherein are things creeping innumerable, both small and great;" and of the former, truly, nothing is more marvelous than the phosphorescent phenomenon which we have had occasion so often to admire, supposed to be produced by marine animalculæ. These globes of fire rolling through the sea in the wake of the ship, or sparkling like brilliant gems at its sides, especially when contrasted or rather harmonized with the dalliant chatoyant play of "the moonbeams dancing on the sea," are a sight as beautiful as it is unique.

> "Poor wanderers on this stormy sea,
> From wave to wave we're driven."

MONDAY, DEC. 9.—Have had another storm, the sixth since leaving London, beside the two which we evaded at Deal and Dungeness. The last, which was of several days' continuance, and severer than any which we have yet encountered, has considerably, and yet not very seriously, damaged our noble craft—the principal damage being sustained by the bulwarks, stanchions, chains, yards, sails, and rudder-beam. Some idea of the violence of the storm may be inferred from the fact, that the large cast-iron anchor weighing nine hundred pounds, was seen to *swim* from the bow to the middle of the ship, and thence back again beyond its original position, *over* the bulwarks (five feet high) into the sea, where it swung suspended by the cable chain!! Tell it not to the marines! The good captain remarks that this is the only piece of iron he ever heard of swimming, except the ax of the sons of the prophets. Such, however, was the violence of the waves that washed over the decks as actually to cause this large piece of iron to change its position; but this astonishing circumstance must, of course, be ascribable more to the wild tossing of the ship than to the force of the waves. Our kitchen was again upset and smashed; and having exhausted our stock of cold meat, we lived several days on crackers and cheese, spiced by some little nicknacks that we had stored away, in case of sickness. As to making use of our cabin stove—that was entirely out of the question—so exceedingly were we tossed. The helmsman declares that the hurricane raged so excessively at one time that the wind cut off the tops of the waves, and throwing them down in the intervening valleys, made the sea as "smooth as a millpond." The door of the "companion" was again broken by the violence of the waves, and the cabin and staterooms deluged with water.

SATURDAY, DEC. 14.—Off Cape Finisterre, the north-easternmost land's end of Spain. Wind still from the south-west, as it has been almost ever since we left London.

DEC. 16.—Last evening, in lat. 40 deg. 40 sec., lon. 10 deg. 30 sec., just as it was growing dark, a ship was discovered a little way to the leeward, tossed about in a sinking condition, and apparently abandoned. We immediately bore down to her as closely as we dared venture, exhibiting a blazing turpentine light, and hailing her; but received no reply nor signal of any kind. We would have made an effort to board her immediately, but it was evident from all the circumstances of the case, that there were no human beings on board; and nothing short of a reasonable hope of saving life could justify an attempt so hazardous. She was a very large ship, and very tempting as a prize; but our ship is already overloaded, and our crew insufficient for the navigation of two ships, even if she could be kept afloat in her present water-logged condition. So we are compelled, very much in opposition to the officers and crew, to abandon her to her fate. The probability is that she had sprung a leak in the late gales, and was still buoyed up by lumber or light goods, and that her affrighted crew had prematurely abandoned her, and made for the coast of Spain, in the life-boat. How much better to have remained on deck! for there is scarcely more than a bare possibility that they could succeed in reaching the land, in this latitude of the "roaring forties," so celebrated and dreaded for its roughness. Such tremendous *swells* of the sea, I have never witnessed in any other part of the ocean that I have visited. For the last few days we have been sailing nearly due south, at the rate of about two degrees per day, and are now very evidently in a different climate from that of ever-beclouded England. The temperature is so pleasant that we have no occasion for fire, and sleep comfortably under a single sheet. While each successive day becomes shorter to our less locomotive friends in the United States, to us who are journeying southward they gradually increase in length. Temperature very uniform and delightful. Music on board by moonlight! What a contrast between our condition now, and what it was but a few nights ago!

FRIDAY, DEC. 19, 12 M.—Sailing rapidly before a south-east wind, opposite the island of St. Leon: Cadiz, the ancient Gades, in view, and very conspicuous, owing to its snow-white buildings. At 2 o'clock, we pass near Cape Trafalgar, the spot so celebrated for Nelson's naval victory over the French and Spaniards. Forcibly reminded of the memorable remark of the brave admiral, which is said to have produced such an effect in animating his sailors and marines, and "*determining*" them for victory — "England expects every man to do his duty!" And does Heaven expect anything less of its soldiers in the great crusade against the world and the devil? O that it might be said of each soldier of the Cross, "he hath done what he could!" Then would the Great Captain of our salvation immediately gain the final triumph over the "Prince of the power of the air, that now worketh in the children of disobedience.

> "O that each in the day
> Of His coming may say,
> 'I have fought my way through—
> I have finished the work thou didst give me to do.'"

Great numbers of old-looking Spanish fishing-smacks around us. At 3, the coast of Africa distinctly in view. Land of Ham! Poor, injured Africa! When shall her dark, benighted children cease to be the servants of servants unto Shem and Japheth? And when shall "Ethiopia stretch out her arms to God?"

> "O when shall Afric's sable sons
> Enjoy the heavenly Word,
> And vassals, long enslaved, become
> The freemen of the Lord?"

The two "Pillars of Hercules," gradually rising into view. We are now entering upon highly mythic and classic ground. The "Herculis Columnæ" were supposed, by the ancients. to have been once united, but torn asunder by Hercules, as the crowning act of his marvelous doings, in order to unite the waters of the Mediterranean and Atlantic. The African pillar, formerly called "Abyla," is known under the less classical appellation of "Apes Hill." We were not near enough to get a peep at their *apeships*, but are assured that this eminence is still a favorite haunt for these cousinsgerman of the Algerine Arabs. "Calpe," the European pillar, is nothing more nor less than the world-renowned rock of Gibraltar—so called from the Arabic, *jebel* or *gibel*, a hill, and *Tarik*, the name of its Saracen owner. The term Gibraltar is certainly a great corruption of *Jebeltarik;* but nothing is better established than this etymological derivation of the word. Such abbreviations, perversions, and corruptions abound throughout the *old world*, where places received their arbitrary names before the principles of orthography were at all established.* We ran so far off, it was 8 o'clock, before we found ourselves opposite this impregnable fortress: viewed by the light of a full Mediterranean moon, (no contemptible light), it resembled very much a colossal lion wading waist-deep into the ocean—no very inapposite emblem of the grasping cupidity of the "Lion Isle," for foreign plunder. Just before reaching this part of the strait, we witnessed a very interesting and extraordinary phenomenon—a double lunar rainbow! the colors

---

* There is certainly better foundation, both upon principles of reason and analogy, for the derivation of the name "Britannia" from Baratanio, the Phœnician term for Tin land, than for the name Gibraltar from Jebeltarik.

of the iris were not at all brilliant, but what was very singular was that all the archway of this *complete semicircle* was radiant with a uniform *white* light: and what excited the liveliest emotions at the moment was, that one end of the arch rested upon Papal Spain, and the other upon Moslem Morocco! the rainbow of hope spanning the sea connecting two continents and resting, the one end on Romanism and the other on Mohammedanism! Who can help believing as well as praying, that the light of heaven shall soon irradiate the lands of both these debasing superstitions, and fill the whole earth, as the waters cover the deep! I was very anxious to get a sight of Tangier, Ceuta, and other places in Morocco, of which my venerated grandfather had written a history, and particularly of the latter, where he resided when he negotiated a commercial treaty with the emperor, which has accomplished so much for humanity, civilization, and commerce; but the wind compelled us to keep near the opposite shore. How preferable civilization is, even under the greatest disadvantages, to *barbarism* is evidenced by the splendid towers and other buildings on the Spanish shore, contrasted with the miserable huts and tents on the Moorish coast.

The average width of the Straits is fifteen miles, and at no point is it less than seven or eight. How very fortunate that this grand canal, the highway of the nations, through which flows so much of the commerce of the world, is too wide to be commanded by gunpowder! The Pillars of Hercules were not only the *ne plus ultra* terrestrial point of the ancients, but most fortunately the terminus of the nomadic Arab. It is pre-eminently the spot of mystery, superstition, and poetry. It was here, too, that there was to be seen in quite modern times, on the Mauritanian side, just opposite Gibraltar, a monument in Phœnician characters, with this inscription, "We are *Canaanites* fleeing from the face of Joshua, the son of Nun, the *robber*." It was here, too, according to all mythology of the early ages, that Atlas stood up and supported the world on his shoulders. So very unique are these two columnar masses of rock that it required but little stretch of the imagination on the part of the superstitious worshipers of Hercules, to convert them into commemorative Ebenezer: and accordingly a temple once stood near Gibraltar, where this famous hero was worshiped. It was no unmeaning device in Charles the Fifth, considering the great commercial importance of the Straits, to enstamp on his coin a representation of these awe-inspiring pillars; and hence, the Spanish pillared dollars are to this day, the best currency in the world. But these Straits are very interesting in themselves, apart from any sources of superstition. Had this passage been much narrower, so great is the evaporation from the Mediterranean, and so inadequate its supply of water, that this vast reservoir, the scene of so many interesting events, both in profane and sacred history, would have been reduced to a second Lake Asphaltites, or perhaps to a mere desert plain of salt. But happily the occurrence of such a calamity is now prevented forever, inasmuch as the capacity of the Strait is sufficient to supply all loss by evaporation. But if there be a deficiency of water in the Mediterranean, as is here assumed, and as is amply susceptible of proof, it may be asked: Why does it constantly send a current of water through the Strait *into* the Atlantic? Nothing is easier than satisfactorily to account for this apparently paradoxical fact, which has so long puzzled the world. The inflowing waters of the Mediterranean, by reason of evaporation, become much more saline than those of the Atlantic, and hence possess greater specific gravity; of course, when they come in contact, the water of the Mediterranean will occupy the bottom of the Strait, and the Atlantic the top, which being above the level, will naturally flow in to supply the deficiency, and restore the equilibrium. And in exact accordance with this theoretic view, two opposite currents have actually been found to exist—the one flowing outward into the Atlantic at the bottom, the other inward at the top, into the Mediterranean, the latter, of course, possessing much the larger volume. This, no doubt, is the true explication of this anomalous phenomenon. The city of Gibraltar is said to be rapidly retrograding, in a commercial point of view, and is remarkable for nothing but its redoubtable fortress, unless it be the smuggling, said to be permitted in the very mouth of the bellowing cannon, and even to receive their sanction. Great Britain regards this rock as the apple of its eye—the very biggest gem that Johnny Bull owns; but it is said to be very like the Indian's gun—" costs more than it comes to." And so thought that astute politician and destroyer of the nations—Napoleon Bonaparte. When asked if he did not intend to take it away from the British, he archly replied, that it was no business of his to relieve England from such a burden, "it shuts nothing, it opens nothing, it leads to nothing, and only serves to secure to England the undying hatred of Spain."

DECEMBER 20.—Driven furiously by a stormy northwesterly wind we have made rapid progress along the coast of Spain, which is here very abrupt and mountainous, and appears to be still more so in the interior—the snow-capped tops of the higher peaks of the Sierra Nevada and La Mancha, though distant, being very conspicuous. We are now, at noon, between the capes De Gath and Palos, and when we make the latter, near Carthagena, will steer—Providence permitting—due east for the island of Pantelaria, within a short distance of the Sicilian coast, where we will diverge to the south directly for Malta. During the last week the weather was so warm that we could scarcely sleep under a single sheet, but the vicinity of snow-clad mountains, has rendered it quite uncomfortably cold during the past day. Progressing eastwardly at the rate of a degree or two per day, our watches require changing every day—the sun rising five hours earlier in this longitude than it does in central Virginia. The many ships and steamers with which we meet, indicate the vast amount of trade and travel for which this sea is now so remarkable.

CHRISTMAS DAY, 25.—On last Lord's day we were becalmed in rather uncomfortable propinquity to the

Algerine coast; but on Monday a Levanter (Euroclydon) sprang up, at whose mercy we have been tossed about until this morning, when it terminated in showers of rain and hail—the latter of which, being in large lumps, was joyfully *hailed* as a condiment to our insipid water, and gathered as a very acceptable Christmas gift. It is observable that while these east winds are prevailing below, a counter westerly current traverses the skies, as indicated by the course of the clouds above. On Tuesday evening about three o'clock, a curious and unaccountable phenomenon was observed in the east. A number of rays were observed, radiating from a point, apparently as far below the horizon as the sun was above it in the west. The appearance was very much like that presented when the sun is about to rise or set in the midst of fragmentary clouds; and was such as would be supposed could only proceed from some powerfully-illuminating body. What could it be? "The oldest inhabitant," and most veteran tar, had never seen the like before. The captain at once pronounced it a "weather brewer," and prognosticated a blow. A vaticination, however, which every uncommon circumstance is sure to suggest, and which is just as sure to be verified sooner or later; but certain it is, we have had a most uncommon succession of squalls, hailstorms and warm showers of rain. During these gusts, coming as they did from every point of the compass, sometimes carrying us toward the Barbary coast, sometimes to the Spanish, we lost our reckoning, and were entirely ignorant of our position, except that we were sure we had lost ground, until an observation to-day, (December 25,) places us in latitude 36 deg., 48 sec., and west longitude 10 sec., nearly opposite New Granada, just about where we were three or four days ago. Observe numbers of tortoises floating about on the surface of the sea, apparently asleep.

JANUARY 1, 1851.—Lat. 38 deg., 26 sec., E. lon. 4 deg., 10 sec. The close of the year is a season calling so peculiarly for fasting, humiliation and prayer, together with thanksgiving, self-examination, and forming of new resolves, that we could by no means think of omitting a practice from which we had so often derived both pleasure and profit. We, therefore, observed the closing day of the year, as usual; and God was with us of a truth; and never before did we enter so fully into the spirit of that beautiful hymn—
"Come let us anew our journey pursue."

Query: Do the brethren at home observe the *ordinance* of fasting, as frequently and rigidly as they should do? As there were some demons that could not be cast out without the aid of this powerful auxiliary, may it not be the case that there are some evil propensities of which we cannot be exorcised without the observance of this effectual means of bringing under the body! It is much to be feared that the abuse of this means of grace by others has nearly led to its private disuse among us; and that it is one of those matters of which it may be affirmed that, "in coming out of Babylon we ran past Mount Zion,"—to use the language of an eminent brother.

The new year is ushered in by a bright *May-day*,

and brings with it a very fine westerly breeze, the finest wind with which we have been favored since we started. And now Madame Hebe is nimbly flitting along with a grace and celerity of movement worthy of the "goddess of youth." This is now the sixty-second day since we left London, and though, "no small tempest lay on us" several times, and we have had much to contend with in various ways, yet we are still in the enjoyment of excellent health and spirits. Thanks to Him "in whom are all our springs, who holdeth our souls in life, and crowneth our days with loving-kindness and with tender mercies." It is not a little singular that the voyage, thus far, though so unusually protracted, seems to us unaccountably short, despite the dull monotony of seafaring life. This is ascribable, no doubt, to having something to do. The fare in the steamers being so exorbitantly high as to preclude all propriety of taking passage in them, and no packets or other vessels designed for carrying passengers, being in London, bound for the head of the Mediterranean, we were compelled to equip and victual ourselves. This gives us all something to do in the various departments of our household arrangements. But our habits being very simple, and our wants few and easily supplied, our culinary and domestic operations are plain and easily performed. But though this mode of living is so very different from that to which we have been accustomed, the inquiry has not yet been started, "What is the cause that the former days are better than these?" for we have learnt (if not in *what*soever state we are—at least in *this*) to be content—and indeed are more than content—for we are as happy as it is good for mortals to be. We rise with Aurora, or with Sol at the latest; and as soon as family worship is over, dispatch our breakfast, dine at two, and sup—if we feel like taking a third meal (which owing to the habit we acquired in London is not often the case)—at six. Then after evening service, spend several hours on deck, in exercise and conversation with the crew; or retire early to bed. The intervals between meals is mainly devoted to study; Greek, Latin, French, Italian, and Arabic receive daily attention, and Hebrew occasionally. On the first day of the week I preach once to the crew either on deck or in the cabin, and have one or two other services among ourselves. Situated as we are we have been enabled regularly to observe the ordinance of commemoration every Lord's day, until week before last, when, unfortunately, our cruse of wine was broken. There being no wine on board the vessel, and desiring only to keep the ordinances, "after the due order," "according to all the rites, and according to all the ceremonies thereof," " as they were delivered unto us," we could not think of omitting one of the appointed symbols, or substituting anything for it; so that we have twice foregone the privilege of breaking the loaf, nor shall we be permitted to enjoy it again till, in the good providence of the Lord, we shall reach Malta. We find no seasons more interesting than our little prayer-meetings; the weekly one on Wednesday evening for general purposes, and one monthly, (on the first Monday evening,) the special object of which is to pray for the conversion of the world. Our own embryo mission, of course, is the object of unceasing prayer. O! that all the holy brethren would "strive together with us for the furtherance" of its great and glorious object!

JANUARY 9.—Alternations of calms and squalls have characterized the last week, and hence we have made but little progress. A fine breeze has, however, at last sprung up, and brought us off the Sardinian coast, around which we have been so long hovering, and we are now rapidly sailing opposite Carthage, but not sufficiently near to see this famous spot, once the rival of the "Mistress of the world." The Cape Bon in Africa, the bold coast of Sicily and the towering Pantelaria (the enchanted Isle of Calypso!) all in sight at the same time. And soon we hope to see the coast of Gozzo, which claims also to have been trodden by the feet of Telemachus; and what we anticipate with far greater delight—be permitted to put foot on her sister isle, whose soil has doubtless been impressed by the footsteps of the great apostle to the Gentiles. The latter part of our voyage has been as remarkable for fine weather and smooth seas as the former was for coarse weather and rough seas.

FRIDAY, JANUARY 10.—The dawn of day reveals to us close at hand, on the right, the bold, beautiful, fertile and picturesque Island of Gozzo (the ancient Gaulos,) which is separated only by a narrow channel from Malta, the goal of our anxious efforts for the last seventy days. Coasting along the shore of this celebrated island (the Melita of Luke, so called on account of its exuberant production of honey, and truly the very sight of it was mellifluous to us), we pass quite near St. Paul's Bay, the spot where the Maltese confidently affirm, the apostle was wrecked; and whether or not this be the identical spot, the tradition is at all events rather better sustained by circumstances than most Romish legends; for all the conditions indicated by Luke's narrative, are so well fulfilled by the facts of the case, that the tradition cannot at least be disproved. At 10 o'clock, drop anchor in the "great harbor" of Valetta. "Bless the Lord, O my soul,"

"Through many dangers, toils and cares
I have already come,
'T is grace has brought me on thus far,
And grace will take me home"—

to Jerusalem, my happy home—both below and above!

The apprehensions which I could but entertain for the fate of the Susanna, on board which my books, medicines, apparatus, etc., were shipped from London, are happily relieved on hearing, as soon as we are at moorings, that her excellent commander, Captain Tindal, had anchored before the city ten days previous to our arrival, and sent in his boat to make inquiries after us, and to offer us a passage directly to Jaffa—the Supercargo passenger who had deprived us of a passage in the brig, having been so alarmed in the late gales, that he insisted upon being put ashore in order that he might return to London.

Delighted once more to have a little elbow-room on *terra firma* we lose no time in reporting ourselves, per passport, at the health-office, and fortunately escaping quarantine, we no sooner obtain *pratique* than we climb the numerous rock-hewn flights of steps, by which alone the city can be reached, and walk about her beautiful precipitous streets, marking particularly the mighty bulwarks that crown the lofty cliffs of this renowned military stronghold. And in order the better to "refresh ourselves" and recruit for the remainder of the voyage, we leave our little domicile in the harbor, where we are so much incommoded by the discharge of the cargo, and take lodgings in the city, in a large, airy, castle-like building, on Strado San Dominico, which was formerly the palace of one of the Knights Hospitalers. Spend half a day very pleasantly in wandering through the spacious aisles and chapels of San Giovanni (St. John's) admiring its mosaic flowers, its escutcheoned walls, its splendid sculptures, beautiful arabesques, rare marbles and precious stones, and, in spite of their misplacement, its gorgeous guilding, rich tapestry and splendid mausolea. But oh! how painful to witness—instead of that pure spiritual worship and service which alone can please the Lord or profit our souls—such veneration of relics, invocation and adoration of pictures, images and saints, confession to priests, kissing pictures, statues, hands, floors and relics, crossing of bodies, and other acts of will-worship as amount, some of them at least, to absolute idolatry in the eyes of Him who has declared himself "a jealous God." How various are the costumes, complexions, and tongues that arrest our attention as we walk the streets of this modern Babel. Judging from the naval and military appropriations annually lavished upon this place by the English

Government, Johnny Bull is desirous of emulating the Knights of St. John in the warlike appearance of this famous spot. Go where you will, you encounter the paraphernalia of Mars. Drum and fife, cannon and mortar, fosse and rampart, horse and dragoon, men-of-war, arsenals, armories. In vain would Bonaparte have invested this citadel city, but for his silver balls and golden bombshells, with which he bombarded it. Gold possesses rather greater specific gravity than lead and iron! Pelf is more powerful than powder, and well did Napoleon know how to deal out this article to his *sappers* and *miners!* Surely, "money answereth all things." The rich soil with which this once naked limestone rock is covered, was brought from Sicily, and, fostered by this equable and genial clime, furnishes the markets with the finest vegetables and fruits the whole year round. Fish, flesh and fowl are also very abundant and excellent.

The *mediterranean* situation of this island, between the three old continents of the world, has always invested it with a high degree of importance in the estimation of every commercial and warlike people; hence it has been a bone of contention from the earliest times down to the present day. Phœnicians, Carthaginians, Etruscans, Greeks, Romans, Goths, Vandals, Saracens, Crusaders, Turks, Arabs, Normans, Barbary Powers, French and English, have all, in their day and generation, been lavish of blood and treasure in its capture and defense. The whole island being one entire rock, it was very natural for the Phœnicians to change its original name, Iperia, to that of Ogygia (stone), the name of one of the fabled daughters of Niobe and Amphion. Such splendid piles of architecture, of all orders and ages, I never saw grouped together before. The magnesian limestone rock, of which the houses are built, being so abundant, easily quarried and sectile, is, of course, cheap; hence the Maltese are lavish of architectural ornament. Everything combines to render this island one of the most delightful spots on earth. But, alas! the leprosy of Romanism infests the whole island, and rests as an incubus upon the minds, hearts and bodies of the people; and the scall is even visible upon the walls of the houses! And yet it is the constant boast of the Melitan Church, that their forefathers were every one converted by Paul in one night, (a fact which Dr. Lucius entirely forgot to mention), and that to this very day they are "followers of Paul, even as he followed Christ, keeping the ordinances as they were delivered unto them!" Alas! for such converts! If the great apostle so scarified the foolish Galatians for commingling a little Judaism with Christianity, what would he say of this people who not only compound with it a good deal of Judaism, but heathenism, (without saying how much), and philosophy, falsely so called, *quantum sufficit* to please the taste of even the infidel himself? The Maltese are proverbially ignorant, indolent, poor, superstitious, bigoted and I had well nigh said, *idolatrous*.

No Christian can visit any one of their three hundred and nineteen places of worship without thinking and feeling as Paul did about the Athenians—"too superstitious"—wholly given to Demonology, Maryolatry, etc.

I offered a Bible to "mine host," but though he confessed that he knew little or nothing of its contents, with many apologies for his *apparent impoliteness* he refused it, alleging that he would be compelled to confess it to the priest, that it would make him angry, he would then compel him to do heavy penance, and it might utterly ruin him! What a pity that such should be the consequence of reading that book which the Eternal Word commands us to search, of which it is affirmed that it is able to make us wise unto salvation, to build us up in the most holy faith, and will assuredly judge us at the last day,—milk, honey and meat—yet must not be tasted by babes or adults! Indulgences ("*Indulgenza Plenaria*") are unblushingly advertised for sale on the church door! A missionary of the American Board of Commissioners for Foreign Missions (Mr. D.) with whom I visited "St. Paul's Church," made application for one of these precious documents, but the wily priest was not to be caught by a customer so Protestant-looking, and evincing so much of the spirit that animated Elijah in his interview with Jezebels, Tetzels of yore.

There are a great many Phœnician antiquities and other artificial as well as natural objects of curiosity on this interesting isle, which we expected to have ample time to visit; but a steamer having called in, on her way from Liverpool to Beyroot, an opportunity of reaching the Holy Land more expeditiously and cheaply than per Hebe, via Alexandria, the Desert, etc., is thus presented, which we gladly embrace, and therefore prepare post-haste, to depart. But though anxious to reach Jerusalem as soon as possible, we left the Hebe with much regret; for we learn on going to take leave, after our baggage was put on board, our fare paid, passport "*visaed*," and the hour of departure actually arrived, that preparations were on foot for me to preach to-morrow, under the Bethel flag, to the numerous English and American sailors in port, as well as many visitors and residents, who, it was thought, would attend, and that two of the Hebe's officers had then made up their minds (as one of the sailors had done some days previous,) to "become obedient to the faith." Circumstances, however, were imperious, and we were compelled, most reluctantly, to leave under these interesting circumstances, counseling and commending our friends, as best we could, to Him on whom they believed and whom they wished to obey.

MONDAY NOON, JANUARY 20.—After screwing our way for forty-eight hours, calmly yet rapidly, under the watchful care of Captain Walker, gracefully plowing the main,

" Europam Lybiamque rapas ubi dividit,"

we catch the first glimpse of Candia—the Crete of Acts of Apostles (and Caphtor of Old-Testament times), the wind from whose snow-capped mountains—one of which is the classic Ida—is somewhat chilly, but not enough so to render fire necessary to comfort. No spot on earth is said to be more abundantly blessed **than** this "ninety cited" island, yet "in vain with

JERUSALEM MISSION. 109

lavish kindness the gifts of God are strewn"—the present Moslem population are said to be every whit as debased as its inhabitants two thousand years ago, are represented to have been, by Polybius, Callimachus, and Epimenides, indorsed by an apostle— mendacious, gluttonous, addicted to debauchery, piracy, and all manner of wickedness—"always liars!" This island is, perhaps, more celebrated as the birthplace of Minos, the great lawgiver and creed-maker of the Greeks, than for anything else. But what rendered it particularly interesting in my sight, was, that it had been visited by Paul, Luke, Aristarchus, and other Christian worthies. Cape *Salmone* is, perhaps, visible, but we are too far off to discern the "Fair Havens nigh unto which was the city Lasea." We also find ourselves " running under a certain island called Clauda" in Acts of Apostles, but which now is known in common with several other islands as Gozzo and at one time Gaulos. Oh! how much more pleasant is our voyage than that of those holy brethren, upon whom " lay no small tempest" as they sailed along these shores eighteen hundred and six years ago! How superior, too, are the accommodations of our steam screw-propeller to those of the indifferent galley, in which they were crowded along with more than two hundred wicked idolaters! Enjoy much religious conversation (although of a controversial character), with the learned Dr. Bacon, of New Haven, who, in company with his son, is on a tour of visitation to the various missionary stations of the

American Board of Commissioners for Foreign Missions in the Levant.

WEDNESDAY AFTERNOON, JAN. 22.—Distant view of dark Cyprus, one of the "Isles of Chittim." This island—so celebrated of old for its copper (whence its present name from *cupros*), and so interesting to the classical scholar, as the favorite abode of the goddess of beauty and love, and the theater of so many fabled events in mythology, is yet far more interesting to the Christian as having been the birthplace of Joses Barnabas, the Son of Consolation, and the scene of the conversion of Sergius Paulus, the first idolater converted to Christianity—from which, doubtless, and not because the apostle was so small that Chrysostom calls him " a man of three cubits in height"—" Saul was called Paul." A mist and vapor of darkness hovers over the whole island, from Paphos to Salamis. How emblematic of that "mist and darkness" that fell upon Elymas, who sought to turn from the faith the "*prudent*" consul, the portion of all who like this speculating sorcerer, oppose Christianity or even " pervert the right ways of the Lord." Here lived Mnason — that good " old disciple;" and it was here, too, that the pure, uncorrupted word of the Lord was first " sounded out in the regions beyond " the Holy Land, by the first foreign missionaries of the Church — Paul, Barnabas, and John Mark. And now, after the elapse of eighteen centuries, it is about to be brought back and proclaimed in its original purity, in the same region, whence this great light first emanated. May the joyful tidings of redemption through the sin-atoning Lamb, soon overspread the whole earth—

> "Waft, waft, you winds, his story,
> And you, ye waters, roll,
> 'Till like a sea of glory,
> It spreads from pole to pole."

THURSDAY, JAN. 23.—Fearing lest we should run ashore on the Syrian coast in the dark, we have been standing off during the night; but having made greater headway than we supposed, find ourselves, this morning, when the anxiously desired light reveals our position, in full view of "that goodly mountain Lebanon," and almost within the Bay of Beyroot. What overpowering recollections, reflections and anticipations take possession of our minds! But who can control his hand to write, when first his eye rests upon "the glorious Holy Land?"

SATURDAY, JAN. 25.—No sooner had we, yesterday, dropped anchor in the open roadstead, a few hundred fathoms from the shore, than several boats emerged from the foaming surge, which was breaking in wild confusion on the beach, and despite opposing wind and wave were soon alongside the Brigand. Into one of those we entered as soon as *pratique* could be obtained; and though the heaving sea broke uproariously upon the rockbound coast, yet so anxious were we to set foot on "*terra sancta,*" that we soon effected a landing. Our feelings of joy and gratitude were unbounded; and well might they be; for after many toils, perils, and privations, we had at last reached our desired haven—having safely passed over the width of one mighty ocean, and traversed the entire length of another—a distance of eight or ten thousand miles! We had at last put foot upon the "delightsome land," land of Palestine, and at this interesting spot, too, so rich in classic as well as Biblical reminiscence—the Berothai of the Scriptures, where once was worshiped Baalberith, and the Berytus, and "Julia Felix," of the Greeks and Romans. Equally impelled by a sense of duty and pleasure, we were not long in raising an Ebenezer to the Lord, for thus safely bringing us to "Emmanuel's Land"—the glory of all lands, which, in the hope of benefiting its present benighted inhabitants, and hoisting anew the standard of Primitive Christianity, I had so long wished to make the land of my adoption, and the final resting-place of my bones.

The first exhibition of the manners and customs of our Moslem and Christian boatmen, was not such as to impress us with a very high estimate of their sense of delicacy; for no sooner were we securely sheltered behind a ledge of rocks than some of them divested themselves of every article and particle of clothing, save one scanty, unavailing piece! and wringing out the sea-water, (with which we were all pretty well saturated), put them aside to dry, with as much nonchalance as though there were no ladies in all the land! We took lodgings at the delightful house of Demetrio, "*La Belle Vue sur la Mer*," and with light feet and gladsome hearts paced its long, flat roof, until we had formed quite an acquaintance with the gigantic cactus, richly adorned with its golden fruit, the stately palm forcibly recalling "Judea Capta" to mind, the Kharob tree of prodigal-son memory, the fig, pomegranate, mulberry and citron, (the apple of Scripture), and other neighboring trees and shrubs, for which this prolific soil was wont to be so celebrated in days of yore, by the sweet singer of Israel and other Hebrew bards and seers. So new to our occidental eyes is everything around us that we see nothing scarcely to remind us of our own happy land, except the sparrow and the house-fly. In this oriental region we are evidently in a very different clime from that of our sunset land. The cow appears to be of a species very different from that of the west. Hogs, there are none, they say, in all this land of Islamism and Judaism. The unsightly camel, the stupid ass, the lugubrious donkey, and the patient ox, usurp, almost entirely, the place of the noble horse. The sheep, while its countenance very much resembles, in bland innocence, the American species, differs from it so widely in its huge, broad, adipose appendix as scarcely to admit of classification among the ovine genera. The sylva and the flora—for, even during this midwinter season, there are flowers in Syria—are so totally different from what we have ever seen, that we seem to know nothing of the vegetable kingdom. Even the faithful dog and the indispensable domestic fowl, here wear an aspect, and *speak a dialect* so different from their fellows of America, that we are compelled to regard them more in the light of curiosities than as members of the same great families. But in nothing, perhaps, do the occidental and oriental worlds stand in more striking contrast than in that wonderful biped of the genus "homo." In color, dress, manners, religion, language—everything—how different from the Anglo-Saxons! That lady—so shamefully rude—how widely does she differ, not only from the chaste daughters of America, but from her own companion by her side, with face so muffled and vailed that no mortal eye can see how pretty or how ugly she is! What a striking contrast, too, between the humble, modest Jewess, clad from head to foot, in pure white robes, and the haughty Druse dame, with that singular silver horn; the badge of matrimony, so highly exalted that she must needs stoop to enter the door. The women here, universally, " wear the pants," and the boots *to boot!* Has Memucan no fears lest this custom be transplanted beyond the seas? How different our large, well-filled stores from the little five feet square cells of the dark bazaars, where the Syrian merchant sits cross-legged all the year round, without doors, windows or fire, selling his armful of wares to his customer, who has to stand in the street while making his purchases. The American mechanic, in his spacious and well-arranged shop, would laugh at the articles of Syrian manufacture, and, perhaps, ask in derision, "if they grew in the woods." But his derision would be turned into admiration, when he learned the disadvantages under which he works. The carpenter sits upon the plank to plane it, and holds it between his fingers and toes to saw it; the smith sits down, or stands in a hole thigh-deep, by the side of his anvil on the floor, "raises the wind" by a goat-skin for a bellows, sits down to file the iron, which he holds in his hand, for a vise—for old as *vice* is, the hand was first made, (hands, they say, were made before knives, forks and spoons, and hence they never use such inconvenient implements), and when he wishes to grind an article, he holds his little grindstone between the toes of his feet, while with one hand he holds the metal, with the other he pulls the strap, thus turning the stone, first backward and then forward. Even the turner sits to work at his little upright lathe. To sit down and smoke the everlasting chibouque, seems to constitute the *summum bonum* of this stationary Medo-Persian people. Wonder if the Moslems sat to perform their various avocations, when their national emblem was progressively *crescent*, gibbous and full, as they now do when it has waved so much, and is still so manifestly decrescent? Guess not.

Our first view of Lebanon was quite captivating—indeed, any mountain seen rising out of the sea, (as all appear to do in the distance), is interesting; but notwithstanding the high encomiums bestowed upon it by the Great Lawgiver of Israel, a nearer inspection began to create a disagreeable kind of suspicion that Moses had spoken more after the manner of an enthusiastic poet, than a sober statesman and prophet. At all events our near approach to Lebanon, forcibly reminded me of the poet's declaration:

> "'Tis distance lends enchantment to the view,
> And robes the mountain in its azure hue."

And by way of apology for the son of Amram, I began to frame the plea that he had supposed himself to be imposed upon by some visionary poetical traveler; for in truth, notwithstanding its snow-clad ridges and cloud-capped peaks, its straggling plantations of pines, its olives, vines and villages perched here and there upon its sides, it had too little of living green, and too much of the characteristic dead white of the limestone, whence it derives its name — to please the eye. But a change came over it with the setting sun that was almost enchanting. We were perfectly wrapped in admiration, and no longer wondered at the fame of that "goodly mountain." Its whole aspect became rubescent; the dull, somber gray of the base was now exchanged for a lively purple; the sides presented every variety of hue, producible by the harmonious combination of blue and red, the latter predominating on the ridges and the former strengthened by black, in its yawning chasms; while the glittering snow, and fleecy white clouds on the tops, presented that delicate, pure and charming roseate hue, to be seen nowhere but under a Syrian sky: such a phenomenon I never had seen before.

Broken columns and entablatures of the Corinthian order, together with exposed patches of tesselated pavement remind us that we are treading on ground once called Roman and Grecian; though certainly the descendants of Abraham have rather the best deed, coming as it does, directly from the "Maker and Possessor of heaven and of earth," and dating back to the year 1921 before A. D., many hundred years before the Romulus founded Rome, or Cecrops, Athens. Numbers of Mohammedans, apparently very devout, are observed to select the most conspicuous places along the sides of the street or road skirting the sea, and after performing their ablutions and spreading their handsome mats, rugs or shawls, they go through their (not altogether unimposing) routine of genuflexions, manustretchings, caput-tossings, down-squattings, and other indescribable kinds of bodily exercise. How very different is the service of those who worship God in spirit and in *truth*, from that of these poor dupes of Mohammedan delusion—the pomp, circumstance and parade of whose every act of devotion, forces upon the mind the irresistible conviction that it is all done to be "seen of men." It should be remarked, however, upon the principle of "rendering to all their dues," that in all these latitudes the Mussulman stands higher in point of honesty than the native Christian.

Pay a visit to the American Consulate, where, in the absence of our highly respected Consul, Mr. J. Hosford Smith, we are very kindly received by the other excellent members of the Consulate, and form a most pleasing acquaintance with the amiable and hospitable Mrs. S. Through the kind offices of Mr. Walcot, the accomplished Vice-consul, and Mr. Armuney, the polyglottal interpreter of the office, we were greatly refreshed and rejoiced by the various letters and papers, which, though scattered about among various officers and merchants, through their exertions we were enabled to get from their various depositories.

These, despite the interesting scenery and circumstances, by which we are surrounded, we spend the balance of the day in reading; and at a late hour we retire to rest with the most grateful emotions that had ever swelled our hearts; having spent one of the most delightful seasons that had ever fallen to our lots to enjoy.

Having formed the acquaintance of the various excellent missionaries who permanently reside in the city, as well as various others who are transiently here, preparing for settlements in other parts of the east—to one of whom, Mr. Manning, a missionary of the Quakers, I am under very special obligations—and made such other arrangements as are necessary to secure the transmission of letters, etc., between the Holy City and this place, which is now regarded as its seaport, we hasten our departure for Jerusalem; and learning that the arrival of the downward-bound steamer is very uncertain, and that we can probably perform the journey altogether by land, as expeditiously as to wait and take the steamer to Jaffa, we send our goods and most of our baggage by an Arab boat, to Jaffa, and determine to go up to Jerusalem altogether by land.

THURSDAY, JAN. 30.—At an early hour, this morning, our dragoman makes his appearance with his imposing cavalcade—a very passable horse for each of us, several mules for transporting the tent, canteen and trunks, a beautiful little donkey for occasional riding, a muleteer for each of the horses under side-saddles, and a splendidly caparisoned Arabian charger for himself. Thus equipped we take up the line of march, wending our way in Indian file through the narrow streets of Beyroot, and leave, not without regret, that ancient and now flourishing city that reposes so beautifully upon one of "the roots of Lebanon," at 9 o'clock, with the hope of spending the night at Sidon. Soon after leaving Beyroot, pass through immense mulberry orchards, and occasionally a lemon or an orange grove; we then traverse a sandy plain several miles in extent, with nothing to relieve its dreariness, save here and there a solitary palm, or a small grove of "candle trees." Having no recollection of ever having heard of the existence of such a Saharan desert in the midst of the land that once flowed with milk and honey, we were quite startled, and could only resolve it into the curse under which this devoted land has been so long laboring; and had it been anywhere in the vicinity of the Kishon would have dubbed it "Meroz." The mountain, too, within a few miles of which we are traveling, appears to be very sterile; and is either entirely destitute of vegetation or clad with very scanty herbage, and has a very desolate appearance.

At 1 o'clock, take lunch at Ghaffa khan, glad to shelter ourselves from the rain, though in the midst of growling camels, braying donkeys, and querulous fellahs. The rain somewhat abating, we resume our journey, but again considerably increasing, we are compelled to take lodgings for the night, at Neby Yunas, (Prophet Jonas), a small Mohammedan village, consisting of the prophet's tomb, and half a dozen other houses. It rained so incessantly during the remainder of the day, that we were denied the gratification of examining the battle-ground of Ptolemy and Antiochus the Great, as well as the sepulchral excavations in the neighboring mountains belonging, doubtless, to the ancient city of Porphurion, some remains of which are still to be seen in the immediate vicinity. A slight examination, however, of the topography of the shore was sufficient to produce the conviction that the tradition (whether of Rome or Mecca, I know not) which assigns this as the place of the recreant prophet's *debarkation* is egregiously at fault, or else the nature of the coast is materially altered, for it seems now utterly impossible for "a great fish to get *near* the dry land." Several other places on the Syrian coast dispute with this, the honor of receiving the recusant missionary; but the precise spot, if ever known, is now lost. May the rich lesson conveyed by the conduct of Jonah not be lost upon *me!* and may the good Lord enable me, unterrified by difficulties and dangers, faithfully and effectually to " preach the preaching that He bids me preach," without vacillation. We were the more disposed to lodge at this place of entertainment because we were told that it is the best khan in all Syria. Judge, then, of our lugubrious forebodings of future lodgings when we discovered that this celebrated tavern had neither bed nor table, nor seat nor rug—nothing, whatever, but the naked room, and that, too, without a single pane of glass or even a bolt to the door; we soon, however, had a "fireplace" *brought in;* and having been pretty well dried and smoked, we cooked and ate a hearty meal on the floor "a la Turc." Some Mohammedan ladies having called on us, and seeming rather averse to religious conversation, we proposed, after they had gratified their curiosity by a most critical examination of our clothes and persons, that they should favor us with a song. And with this request we were soon gratified to our hearts' content. It seems that the word made use of by our dragoman, means a dance as well as a song, and accordingly, suiting the action to the word, they commenced a regular, or rather a very irregular demi-semiquaver kind of quadrille!! Deeming this rather a poor business for a Christian missionary to be patronizing, I endeavored to stop them; but so well were they pleased with their performance, that they turned a deaf ear to my earnest request, even when enforced with sharp remonstrance. Finding logic and homilies on ethics utterly unavailing, at least through the medium of an interpreter, I then tried the virtue of a few words that I had learned in Arabic; and no sooner had I pronounced the word "*buckshish*," accompanied by a few significant *passes* of the hand, than they appeared to be under the mesmeric influence of that potent word. Exhibited in broken doses of a few paras, this panacea, that "answereth all things," acted like a charm, and forthwith quelled the tumult. With the plastered floor for our bedstead, a hired mat for our downy bed, and a cloak or two for comfortables, we soon enjoyed that sweet repose to which the pampered epicure is such an utter stranger.

Friday, January 31.—Rise at early dawn, and soon dispatch the simple meal which our dragoman had already prepared in his simple, primitive *kitchen*, which, though it had so often taken the tour of the Holy Land, could still render excellent service. The bread generally made use of in Syria is made of wheat pounded in a stone mortar, or about as closely ground in a rude hand or horse mill, without undergoing any effectual process for the separation of tares, dirt, and other impurities, or any process whatever for the separation of the bran; the cakes, somewhat leavened, are more than a foot in diameter and about as thick as leather; indeed they look and feel very much like a large round piece of leather, but are not quite as tough. To do the Syrians justice, though, I must say that when they use the French flour (which is imported into this country at great cost), they make a kind of pastry that will compare advantageously with the "fixings" of the very best Frank cook. It is amusing to see them (as all may do—for they cook as well as do everything else on the side of the street), take a piece of dough about half the size of the hand, and with great adroitness and delicacy of manipulation, hurl and twirl it upon an oiled table until in about half a minute it dilates to the size of an outspread parasol, or even that of an umbrella, and much thinner than a wafer; this superroyal sheet they then very fantastically fold into a folio, quarto, octavo, duodecimo, or even twenty-four-mo., tastefully adorning every page with a *cut* of sweet meats or a douceur of rich preserves; so that any gastronomic bibliographer of good taste would pronounce it a work handsomely gotten up. Indeed the *elite* Turks are epicures and gastronomists of the first water. Our dragoman, however, happened not to belong to this category. Upon asking him whether the white, leathery, India-rubberish stuff he gave us, grew in that state upon native trees, or whether it was some kind of fruit that had been cooked, he affected to be not a little wrathy, and was evidently surprised and mortified; but upon comparing it with a passable piece of loaf bread, the question seemed to be so natural that his color at once evaported in a hearty, good-natured laugh. The fact is, Joseph Bodra (Joseph the Spendthrift—for so is his name by interpretation), was rather proud of his charge, and had done his best under the circumstances, as he boasts that he takes pleasure in doing for Americans. We were fortunate indeed in securing his services, for a better dragoman and guide, it is said, is not to be found in all Syria. He was the faithful attendant of the unfortunate Molyneux, in defense of whom he had killed and wounded several Arabs, near the Dead Sea, had been engaged in many Bedouin scrapes, and accoutered as he was, with horse-pistols, revolvers, double-barreled gun, daggers, club, etc., studiously displayed on his horse or about his person, he was truly an object of no little terror to those evil-doing marauders.

The weather being delightful we greatly enjoy the ride along the sea-coast, where the rocky spurs of the mountains do not approach the sea too closely. No road can be better than that on the beach—none worse than that on the side, or immediately at the foot of the mountain. Caravans of camels, asses and donkeys encountering us at these narrow passes, considerably impede our progress. The merchandise is all transported along the coast, reminding us that we are traversing the coast of Phœnicia—once the mistress of commerce and the mother of colonies! But now, oh how fallen! "*Sic transit gloria mundi!*" Beautiful fields of wheat varying in height from half an inch to three or four, occupy the narrow slips of land between the shore and the mountains. Orange, lemon, citron, olive, fig, and pomegranate groves are frequent, and as we approach Sidon, large; a few scattering banana trees also. The sickness of one of our baggage mules, in consequence of too free indulgence in the cool waters of the Nahrel Auli (river Bostrenus) occasions us to halt a considerable time at Saide (the ancient Sidon) and ultimately determines us to spend the night there; so that we have abundant leisure to examine the few fragmentary remains of that sin-smitten city.

Our wealthy and hospitable consular agent, Ibrahim Nuckly, hearing that some Americans had arrived, soon called upon us at our lodgings in the large French khan, and in true patriarchal style pressed us to abide at his splendid mansion on the city wall, during our stay in Sidon. Deeming it best to decline his kind invitation under existing circumstances, we, nevertheless, pay him a visit, and are very kindly and elegantly entertained. He inquired very specially after the health of Hakeen Robinson, (Dr. Robinson author of Biblical Researches), and Lewis Cass, "*King of America.*" By way of testifying his respect for the great nation of which he is so proud to be the consular representative, he insisted upon sending his son, accompanied by a Janizary, to escort us about the town; and greatly are we indebted to our young friend, who speaks French quite well, and acted the part of the cicerone very much to our gratification. Only one vessel, and that a small schooner is in this ancient and once princely mart, founded, no doubt, by the eldest son of Canaan—called "Great Zidon," as far back as the time of Joshua. What a commentary upon the greatness and stability of the works of men's hands! Estimates are so variant that nothing conclusive can be arrived at in relation to the population of Sidon; but it is generally supposed to amount to six or seven thousand. The result of our examination, is the full conviction that though Sidon is not quite so desolate and utterly ruined as it has sometimes been represented, yet that none can deny the ample fulfillment of the prophecies in relation to this humbled city.

SATURDAY, FEBRUARY 1.—After tarrying nearly twenty-four hours in this renowned cradle of arts, manufactures and commerce, we left its narrow, filthy lanes, glad enough to breathe the pure air, although dark angry clouds were frowning upon us in the direction of Tyre, and already sprinkling us as we mounted our horses. The soil in this neighborhood seems to be exceedingly rich and productive, even under its present miserable Turkish culture. A kind of lentil, and various other garden vegetables were observed to be in full bloom. The neighboring mountains are beautifully terraced in strata nearly horizontal, but principally by the hand of nature—the different layers of rock composing them gradually diminishing in extent upward. What a beautiful sight these mountains must once have presented! Lunch near the site of Zarepta—thankful that though so far from faring sumptuously, we yet fare much better than did the celebrated prophet and the poor woman, from whom the place derives all its celebrity. The great number of caves we see is continually reminding us of the time when, owing to Midianitish persecution, the Israelites were compelled, not only to occupy these natural caves, for which all this country is so remarkable, but to retreat into artificial ones. Nor could we forbear congratulating ourselves upon the fact, that though eighteen centuries ago our brethren in Christ were compelled, on account of Jewish and Pagan persecution, to wander about and hide themselves in dens and caves, the time had at last arrived when, owing to the good providence of the Lord, those professing precisely the same faith could not only profess but practice and preach it without molestation. And now that "the Churches have rest everywhere," may they be edified; and walking in the fear of, and in the comfort of the Holy Ghost, be greatly multiplied. Judging from the frequent occurrence of fragments, this plain was once studded with temples and perhaps cities. Immense numbers of camels, horses, asses, donkeys, sheep and goats are observed pasturing upon the plain. Perceiving, not far from our path, a Bedouin tent of the true Kedar hue, some of us ride up and ask for a drink of water—not so much because we wanted water, as because we wanted to take a peep into the tabernacle of a genuine son of the desert. The lords of the manor were seen standing on the tops of the distant hillocks, or some fallen column, keeping watch over the flocks; but we were received with many "bows" and "wows" of the canine sentinels. The only inmates were females; but there were both of the bipedal and quadrupedal orders, old and young, but the caprigenous portion were certainly far more decent and respectable in appearance than the swarthy ladies of the harem. Their tent presented the very picture of filth and laziness—not the picture either, but the living reality. Instead of pitching it ten or twelve yards farther on a slight elevation, they had placed it, in order to have water literally at their door, and to save the trouble of walking two rods, immediately by the side of the spring and branch where it was low and flat. The consequence is, that, notwithstanding the leaves and twigs with which the floor is thickly carpeted, the women and children, goats and kids sink almost ankle deep in mire at every step they take, in the greater portion of the tent. It was very kind, I thought, to keep under their own roof the tender kids and their dams; but why don't these considerate dames bestow upon their own offspring a modicum of that care which they lavish so profusely upon the young of their goats? Can the reason be that the one stock is profitable and the other unprofitable?

Vast quantities of sponge, the common article, as

well as some very curious varieties, are constantly thrown up on this coast, much of which we gathered for domestic purposes. This coast also abounds in beautiful shells, many specimens of which we collected as presents for distant friends, and among them are rare kinds, one of a deep rich purple color, which our ignorance of conchological science allowed us to come to a pretty satisfactory conclusion that it could be no other than the identical species of murex, from which the celebrated Tyrian purple was made in days of yore. The manner in which we see the fishermen *throwing* their nets into the sea, reminds us very forcibly of the various scripture allusions to the ancient practice of "*casting* the nets into the sea." His excellency, the newly-appointed Governor of Tyre, passing us with his fine equipage, while we loiter on the strand, is received by his obsequious subjects with great pomp, parade and demonstrations of joy. Lingering on the beautiful beach and in the environs of the town gathering shells, searching for ruins, and wondering at the immense labor bestowed by Alexander upon the construction of the mole or isthmus that still unites the land and former island, we did not enter the city until after sunset.

Monday, Feb. 3.—We have spent two nights and a day in this notable city, now called Sur; and though precluded from much investigation and inquiry that we would have made under other circumstances, yet we see in its present condition abundant proof of the truth both of history and prophecy.

We received a pressing invitation from our attentive

consular agent, Jacob Accad, to take up our abode at his residence, but being aware from our knowledge of oriental hospitality that we could much better observe the day which the Lord claims as His own, in the privacy of our room, at the khan, than at his house, all that I could do, was to promise him a call in the afternoon; for though we were not privileged, like the apostle Paul, during his visit here, to find disciples with whom we should lodge, " or who could unite with us in keeping the ordinances of the Lord's house," we yet had a very accommodating host, who, upon intimation that we wished not to be interrupted for a few hours, kindly kept out intruders. We had observed, the previous evening, a beautiful retired cave, bordering on the beach of the harbor, about half a mile above town, and it required no great stretch of the imagination to conceive that it was to this very spot that the disciples, with wives and children, brought Paul, Luke, Sopater, Aristarchus, Secundus, Gaius, Timotheus, Tychicus, and Trophimus, who "kneeled down on the shore and prayed," and there, as followers of Paul, " even as he followed the Lord," we wished also to worship. But it looked so much like countenancing that veneration for relics and holy places, so rampant and injurious in all this country, that we deemed it best, under the circumstances, to deny ourselves that gratification — assured that those who worship the Lord in spirit and in truth, can worship Him as acceptably and profitably in one place as in another. Those of us who visited the consul in the afternoon, were received with great cordiality and kindness—albeit we were compelled entirely to refuse the pipe, and to sip the bitter infusion of the Arabian berry with rather an ill grace. Our intended visit being rumored abroad, we found his divan pretty well filled with the dignitaries of the town, though it extended entirely around the room, and they continued to pour in as long as we remained, to see the strangers who had come from a far distant land. I asked them if it was not a delightful climate?

"Yes."

"Healthy, too?"

"Yes."

"Soil rich and productive?"

"Yes."

"Government liberal enough?"

"Yes."

"Ready sale for your silk, and cotton, and corn, and wheat, and fruits?"

"Yes."

"Why, then, is Tyre now such a small place, instead of the great commercial city that it once was?"

"Because God has said that it never shall be the city that it was then."

A sensible answer, certainly—and all-sufficient reason. After conversing with some freedom on religious topics, we left his hospitable abode and joined in a funeral procession, on its way to the Greek Catholic church, where, amid fuming incense, blazing candles, blasphemous invocations, anti-purgatorial incantations, and various cunningly-devised ceremonies "too tedious to mention," they sanctified the corpse, and then removed it to the adjoining consecrated ground, where, amid unearthly wailings, genuine as well as sophisticated, they committed it to the cold embrace of the mother of us all. Taking a little circuit on our way back, our attention was called to one or two gigantic, double, monolithic granite columns, once, no doubt, belonging to a very large church contiguous, and in ruins, but now forming the foundation of a common street wall. We had already noticed a great many very large and perfect pillars of red and gray granite lying in the sea, and projecting out of the banks, some few erect and apparently *in situ*. Numerous investigations are now being made in this interesting field of antiquarian research; and "antiques" of various sizes, from the Herculean shaft, down to the smallest signet of a ring, are offered for sale by pestiferous Arabic virtuosos.

Scarcely had we supped, when the Consul's flashy wife determined not to miss so good an opportunity to become acquainted with the manners, dress, and fashions of American ladies, made her appearance, and with such a profusion of costly robes and oriental compliments, as contrasted singularly enough with our republican simplicity of dress and manner. Her head-dress, consisting principally of coins and gems, cost about two thousand dollars, (40,000 piastres), and notwithstanding the drawback of such an unnatural display, she looked handsome. Beauty unadorned, they say, is adorned the most, but so think not the eastern ladies. Alas! that so few of them possess that adorning which the apostle so highly commends, and which "in the sight of God is a great price."

One of the very first things that arrested our attention, on looking around in Tyre, was an immense fishing-net spread out upon rocks to dry. Nor did it escape the piercing ken of the holy Seer, two thousand five hundred years ago, that "the dirt should be scraped" from the very foundation rocks of Tyre, which, instead of continuing to sustain the splendid structures then reared upon them, should in due time be used only as "a place to spread nets upon." Thus it was written, and thus it *must* be. Some persons, however, not well informed as to the true condition of the present Tyre, have entertained apprehensions lest the denunciations against this devoted city in the sure word of prophecy have fallen short of accomplishment, because we still find a town of that name; but surely the present miserable little village of Sur, with its three or four thousand inhabitants is no proof that Jehovah's decree, "thou shalt be built no more," has failed of execution. The few houses that have been built out of the fragments of old Tyre can by no means redeem it from its doom. For what are these paltry hovels of the present day compared with the splendid palaces that adorned her at the date of the decree, and of her prosperity and pride, when "her merchants were princes, and her traffickers the honorable of the earth." It is indeed implied by the very nature of the prophecy, that some few should always occupy the spot or its immediate vicinity, when it is declared, "I will make her like the top of the rock, it shall be for the spreading of nets in the midst of the sea." And, beside, it is evident from the topography of the main land, the mole made by Alexander (Scander) the Great, and the island, that the present Sur does not occupy the site of the ancient Tyrus. The continental, magnificent Tyre is now numbered among the things that were; it may be sought for, but vain will be the search—for it is no more. The hoary-looking aqueduct leading to it is almost the only vestige to be found—so well did Alexander, that great *sweeper* of the nations, execute his commission! What a rich mine of pillars and pedestals, capitals and entablatures, *et id omne genus*, lie entombed beneath the dust of old Tyre, with which he formed the connecting mole.

It is true that a vessel, now and then, visits Tyre, and while we were there, three small vessels were then in her port, (a very uncommon circumstance), but what are three compared with the navies of the earth that once resorted to this great commercial mart of nations! Dearly, indeed, has haughty Tyre paid for her "aha!" Let the enemies of Israel, and of Israel's God be admonished!

Form a pleasing acquaintance with Captain Peel, son of Sir Robert Peel, who is engaged in the singular enterprise of competing with several others for the honor of making the shortest tour through the Holy Land; but, judging from the crude observations of many travelers, their visits are sufficiently ephemeral without making any special efforts to shorten them.

Leaving Tyre, at 8 o'clock, diverge to the left a mile or two from the road on the beach, in order to view those wonderful fountains of Hiram, and the remains of the aqueduct that once conducted their streams to Palæ Tyre. This was undoubtedly a stupendous undertaking in its day; and in all probability, is of remoter antiquity than the time of Hiram, the friend of Solomon, and who was ever a lover of David, to whom it has been conjecturally ascribed. The more massive portions of it in the valley preserve their form entire to this day, and with pendent vines and stalactites hanging from its sides and arches, and large shrubs and small trees growing from its bottom and the crevices in its sides, presents altogether a venerable and picturesque sight. It has left an enduring record of itself on the tablet of the plain of Tyre; for in many places where there is not a vestige of its masonry remaining, large stalagmites of limestone deeply rooted in the earth, declare in characters unmistakable (though not Phœnician) its former existence. But, alas! for Tyrus! The mighty city that once boasted of her architects, "filled with wisdom and understanding, and cunning to work all work," to construct this noble fabric, and erect the far more "magnifical Temple" of Solomon, has not now a Hiram sufficiently "cunning" to mend a broken umbrella! Distant views, luxuriant fields of wheat, and occasional rows of cypress, (looking for all the world, at a distance, like the tall poplars of Virginia), forcibly remind us of the plantations and mansions of the "Old Dominion." Pass over very subtantial remains of Roman roads, bridges, etc. Prostrate milestones with long, but uncipherable inscriptions, still mark the Roman miles here and there. Hundreds of herds and flocks, with their attendant herdsmen and dogs, enliven the plains and hills—one shepherd apparently to every hundred animals. Flora, Vesta, and Ceres might well revel in the highly variegated carpets of flowers that border the fields of wheat and meadows of grass, through which our road leads. The landscape is picturesque and lovely, but the entire absence of houses, except now and then a ruined khan, or rude Mohammedan mosque or mausoleum, and of fences (except here and there a little inclosure of rocks, or hedge of cactus), strikes an American eye rather singularly and unpleasantly. Our road, this evening, runs parallel to an extensive aqueduct in fine preservation, carrying water to Acre. Thirsty and weary, we stop and refresh ourselves at an orange grove; and who would not indulge in this delightful and wholesome fruit at the rate of half a piastre per dozen—five or six for a cent! Pass within a short distance of the Pacha's Harem, where,

> "The turban'd Turk, who scorns the world,
> And struts about with his whiskers curl'd,
> Keeps a thousand wives under lock and key
> For nobody else but himself to see."

Beguiled by the beauties of the Galilean scenery, through which we are passing, we loiter so much that when we reach Acre, just before night, we have the mortification of finding her beautiful gate closed; but our faithful and persevering dragoman plies the authorities with such entreaties and representations that at last we have the satisfaction of seeing her ponderous leaves unfold.

Lodge in the upper story of a fine old building, used as a khan, and early in the morning, sally out to view this celebrated old city—the Akka of the Syrians, and Accho of the Old Testament, (from Ok its Phœnician name)—the Ptolemais of the New Testament, (after one of the Ptolemies who greatly adorned it), and the St. Jean d'Acre of the Crusaders, (from a fine church which they here erected to the Apostle John). Sorry, indeed, that there are no disciples here, whom, as the apostle did eighteen hundred years ago, we could "salute." Start out early in the morning to reconnoiter this celebrated theater of so many renowned military exploits, from the times of the great generalissimo of the hosts of Israel, to the year of the Prince of Peace, 1840, when it received such a tremendous bombardment under the allied powers—the marks of which are still so numerous and unmistakable. The walls have truly a formidable appearance on the seaside where so many cannons are planted; but if the city looked, in 1799, as it now does, on the opposite side, whence the great Napoleon reconnoitered it, I am astonished that great man-killer, city-destroyer, kingdom-subverter, and world-shaker should have failed him. What a fine place was this plain of Acre for the display of King Jabin's nine hundred iron chariots!

Start at 8 o'clock, and thinking more about the

fame of Kishon and the glory and excellency of Carmel, than of the exploits of military heroes, march rapidly over this celebrated battle-ground of nations. Arriving at the banks of "that ancient river—the river Kishon," we find our passage stoutly disputed by long lines of—not wild Bedouin Arabs, but tall, martial-looking *pelicans!* The obstinate stand that they make, however, is due rather to their tameness, than to their bellicose spirit, so, upon charging them whip in hand, they gracefully file off and leave us in quiet possession and sweet admiration of the mouth of the stream. The river must have been unusually low, being not more than fifty yards wide at this time; and I began to feel somewhat disappointed! But though not swollen with rain, as it no doubt was when it swept off the hosts of Sisera, nor red, as when it was tinged with the blood of all the preachers of the established church of Baaljezebel, yet this was indeed the *Kishon*, and being the same, larger or smaller, it was enough to know that no monkish tradition could cast a doubt over its reality. Allured by the deep interest that attaches to this stream, I wandered some distance amidst its clusters of palms, and over its strangely-contrasting sand-hills and lakes. Then passing through the thrifty village of Kaiffa, and among the venerable olive trees interspersed over its lovely plains of wheat, with numerous herds on the mountain to the left, and beautiful gardens on the right, we commence the ascent of Mount Carmel. Arrived at the top, after a tiresome walk, we are welcomed into the splendid convent of Elijah, by some not-quite-so-anti-carnal-looking monks as I expected to find the fraternity of Carmelite monks to be ; and displaying our canteen, lunch *sans ceremonie.* "*Frater Carolus*," who seemed to act as gentleman usher, though he can only speak Italian and a little Latin, like myself, pressed us very hard to drink some of the wine of Carmel.

' Non bibimus," I replied, politely declining.

' Sed hoc est bonum vinum," was his reply.

Upon persisting in our refusal to drink either wine or strong drink, he then brought forth a delicious flavored article which he represented as being a very weak cordial, restorative, pleasant, and refreshing, after climbing the mountain. Few of us, however, could venture to sip more than half a thimblefull, for every tongue immediately declared that it was a contraband article, from the distillery of King Alcohol. We were then conducted into the chapel of the cave, most gorgeously decorated with flashy tinsel and daubs, miscalled paintings, where the following conversation occurred, occasioned by a painting representing the Savior as being sprinkled in the Jordan.

" Putas ut Jesus Christus baptizatus erat illo modo?" said I, pointing to the representation of John pouring water upon him out of an oyster shell as he stands in a stream of water apparently about three feet wide and three inches deep, (a picture, by-the-by, which I once knew a lady confidently to appeal to in *proof* of Rantism, and I have heard worse arguments in its support, "I *know* sprinkling is right, for I have seen the *picture*.")

"Non fuit," was the prompt reply, accompanied with a look of surprise, "immergibatur sub aqua."

"Cur, tum, permitte tal ——" but perceiving that I was rather at a loss for appropriate language to ask him why he permitted such a caricature of divine truth to disgrace his walls, he anticipated a part of my inquiry, and replied, with the usual Syrian significant shrug of the shoulders, and an unspellable kind of pshaw "*pictura* est solum!"

"Populi in hac regione, scripturas legunt?" I inquired; but the subject was evidently disagreeable to him, and he abruptly broke off, and pressingly invited us to walk into the cave of Elijah; from whose idolized wall he chiseled off a piece of the soft gray limestone rock, and, as a special favor, presented us with the precious amulet, together with a vial or two of exhilarating perfumery from his well-supplied pharmaceutical establishment. All this kind attentention we would gladly have dispensed with, for we well knew that, in consideration of such valuable services, rather more than a valuable *quid pro quo* was expected in the shape of *buckshish;* and, beside, our faith, not to say superstition, was rather at fault, for we could see no particular reason why the Tishbite prophet should have selected as his domicile that particular cave in preference to various other caves in the mount, so much more eligibly situated. Indeed I could by no means feel assured—their protestations to the contrary notwithstanding—that I was anywhere very near the celebrated scene of the trial of Jezebel's chaplains.

Leaving the convent about noon, we pass by several ruins, of which the chief is Athlit, the great quarry for rebuilding other cities along the coast, (and is now rapidly being removed for rebuilding Beyroot), we reach Tantura, near the ancient Dora, after nightfall, the imposing ruins of which viewed by moonlight, amid the croaking of frogs and the barking of dogs, made us feel quite melancholy. There being no room to pitch our tent within the walls of the miserable little village, we were compelled to take up our lodgings in the khan, for fear of the Arabs, who are notoriously bad hereabouts. Here, all in the same room, but elevated a little higher on a bank of earth at one end, we lie down, but not to sleep, with one horse, three cows, several Arabs, a calf and donkey, fowls, cats, rats, bats, and insects oriental, whose name is legion—innumerable! Such a night! Such a night! Spotted, ring-streaked, and speckled all over, by these dreadful phlebotomizers, we gladly rise at $3\frac{1}{2}$ o'clock, and breakfasting with all imaginable haste, make our escape from that place of torment.

Ever since leaving Beyroot we have been traveling in Phœnicia, but this morning we enter the lot of Manasseh. A few hours' travel brings us in sight of Kaysayreya, Cæsarea Palestina, so dear to every Gentile, for it was here, in this identical place, that the Gentiles were first formally introduced into the Church of the living God, by the apostle Peter; it was here, too, that Paul delivered those splendid speeches that made Felix tremble, and Agrippa almost a Christian. It was here, too, that Herod Agrippa "was smitten by the angel and consumed of worms, because he gave not God the glory." Here, too, lived Philip the deacon and his "five virgin daughters who did prophecy." Large portions of its Cyclopean walls and deep fosse still remain, and it is said that a colony of Prussians will soon attempt their restoration. A few butterflies, bees, and birds were the only inhabitants that I saw in wandering over the ruins of this famous city. But, in exact fulfillment of prophecy in relation to the cities of Israel, that their "towers and forts should become dens of wild beasts," jackals and Bedouins (than whom no beast is wilder,) are frequently to be seen, and still more frequently *heard*, when not seen—the former at night, and the latter occasionally in the day, by the much dreaded report of his gun: of which latter salutation our dragoman was not a little apprehensive, for it was at this very place, that he and several travelers had engaged in dreadful combat with a party of Bedouins, from whose rapacious grasp they only escaped by superior generalship. We had been no little puzzled on seeing Yoseeph reprime his firearms, muffle up his face, and otherwise disguise himself; for though closely questioned, he answered so evasively as to give us no satisfaction; and it was not until we had passed Cæsarea, and, as he supposed, were out of all danger, that he commenced reciting the tale of his hair-breadth escape; I say *commenced*, for like the tale of

"Hudibras, the bear and fiddle,
Commenced—but broke off in the middle—"

just as he had deeply excited our sympathies, not to

say our fears, two of these wild sons of the desert are seen to issue from a bramble covert, and skulkingly take a commanding position, within gun-shot of the road; some, we knew, were a few hundred yards behind us; and the fear, amounting almost to conviction, that the Bedouin alternative—" Your money or your life"—would soon be propounded for our decision, found expression in the countenance of more than one of us. But our courageous dragoman, deeming himself a full match, accoutered as he was, not only for two but for twice two times two, dashed off after them in a moment; but finding three others in the mouth of the cave with them, and not exactly knowing how many others might be concealed, far back in the dark recesses, Hudibrastically deemed "prudence the better part of valor," and addressing them in very conciliatory and fraternal terms, wishing them, "salaam," peace, with an especial good grace.

Thus were my pleasant ruminations about Cornelius and Philip, the apostles and prophetesses, diverted to other subjects; and I felt constrained to reflect rather more than was pleasant about Herod and Tertullus, Drusilla and Berenice, and that wonderful people whose "hand is against every man." What we had heard and seen and felt, made us very willing to have a river and a very respectful distance interposed between ourselves and these predatory sons of Ishmael, as we hastened a-pace with double quick time to cross the river Kana (Nahr Abn Zehura), the boundary between the tribes of Ephraim and Manasseh. Much to our disappointment, however, we found on reaching it, that it was past fording. But between the alternative of encamping there for the night, or riding up the river a few miles, and then crossing, we were not long in deciding. So we immediately posted up the stream, and at length, found a shallow place, where we crossed one of the forks very easily; and by means of a few friendly Fellaheen to lead over our horses, and assist the muleteers in carrying over the baggage, we soon crossed the other, and, to our inexpressible delight, found ourselves in the valley of Sharon, of which this is the northern boundary. It was now late in the afternoon, and we had several miles of a pathless journey to perform before we could reach a place of any security; but speeding our way as best we could, and serenaded by the frogs of the little lakes, here more abundant than above, we reach Emkhalid, a miserable Turkish mud-hut, about bed-time. But still our situation is incomparably better than it was the previous night; for instead of being pent up in the midst of horses, cows, etc., we are now snugly stowed away in the loft above them. All the houses in this village are made of stones and mud, rudely piled up, generally in a circular form, and roofed over with mortar or piles of dirt heaped on limbs, branches, twigs, leaves, and grass in a hemispherical form.

THURSDAY 6.—Are surprised to see such immense herds of camels, donkeys, sheep, and goats, as they are driven off for pasturage this morning. The women seem to do all the labor and drudgery, and are excessively addicted to personal decoration, especially head, wrist, and ankle dresses of coins and colored glass rings. Children seem almost universally afflicted with sore eyes. Polygamy and premature marriages prevail to a fearful extent, particularly among the *ton* of the land. It is evident that these folks stand in no fear of King James and his " *Counterblast*," to tobacco; for a man " that he is so impoverished" that he owns nothing save that which he wears on his back, " whereon he also sleepeth," will yet carry about with him his indispensable flint and steel, together with his chibouque, or pipe, and well-filled pouch of tobacco; and the same may be also said of the women, so much are they addicted to the odious practice of smoking!

They can scarcely look at a Frank without drawling out the everlasting "*buckshish!*" Unlike the unfaithful steward, they are the most unscrupulous mendicants; though so fully able to dig, to beg they are not ashamed.

The sun is now oppressively hot, even before midday. In this part of Palestine, wheat is sown three several times between Autumn and Spring, and hence harvest is reaped at three different times. Forest trees are rather more abundant where we now are, a few miles from the sea, than immediately on the coast. Forcibly reminded of the wilds of the South-western portion of the United States, by the luxuriant and extensive cane-brakes with which some of the rich bottom-lands are covered.

It is astonishing that these Fellahs plow as well as they do, with the native plow, which is merely a suitably crooked limb of a tree, having one of its prongs pointed with iron, and drawn by such inferior cattle!

Can the oxen, from whose labor Solomon boasted that there was "much increase," have degenerated in the lapse of ages and change of circumstances into the present puny stock? We are now passing through one of the lots of Dan, and are frequently reminded of our own happy land, by frequent fields of fennel, sage, and other familiar plants—volunteers of this prolific soil. Birds of various kinds are here very numerous and tame. A tall, midnight-looking Abyssinian, who (in order to enjoy the protection of Joseph's flying artillery, has been journeying with us for a day or two) espying a porcupine a short distance from our path, makes chase, but, fleet and expert as he is, all that he could secure was a quill or two. Judging from two young ones that I saw, they are rather formidable combatants, perfectly panoplied, *cap-a-pie*. From what I learn of the peculiar habits of these doleful creatures, there can be but little doubt that they are the "*satyrs*" of the scriptures. How abundant rats are in this country may be inferred from the fact that in many places their subterranean villages are only a few rods apart.

Crossing several large streams over stone bridges, apparently of Roman construction, and threading our way amidst crowds of camels and donkeys, we pass between large groves of mulberries, oranges, lemons, citrons, vines, etc., reach Jaffa at 4 P. M., and, for greater convenience, take lodgings at the Latin Convent, instead of the delightful suburban villa of Mr. Murad, the American Consul, which is kindly placed at our disposal. In the absence of this gentleman,

Mr. Jacob S. Murad, we are greatly indebted to Mr. Lazarus S. Murad, his brother and assistant in the consulate, for his kind attention and valuable services. The American consulship for Jaffa has been in this excellent family for about thirty years, and I blush to say that no member of it has yet been remunerated by our Government to the extent of a single para, though the duties of the office have been so cheerfully, ably and faithfully performed. The philanthropist and "happy man," of whom Stephens gives such a pleasing account, is the grandfather of the present incumbent of the office; and Lynch has written with the truthfulness and fidelity so characteristic of the "Dead Sea Expedition," in giving an account of the amiable lady of the kind-hearted consul. England, France, Russia, Prussia, Sardinia, and various other governments pay very handsome salaries to their consuls at Jaffa and Jerusalem, while this gentleman, who, by-the-by, enjoys a most enviable reputation, and though an Armenian by nation, is thoroughly an American in principle, is consul for both places, and yet has never received the first cent of salary from our government for his truly valuable services. That it is most desirable for the United States to be represented by a consular agent both at Jaffa and Jerusalem is most obvious, and I most earnestly hope that our consular system will speedily undergo such a revision at the hands of Congress, that this worthy gentleman will receive a **salary commensurate with the services rendered the commercial and traveling community of the United States.**

Find that our articles per Susanna, have arrived, having preceded us more than a month, though starting several weeks later,) and apparently in good order, notwithstanding the dreadful storms through which they have passed. Those, however, from Beyroot, which were to have started the same morning that we left, have not yet arrived, though it is only accounted two days' sail from Beyroot to Jaffa.

In looking around the town, we tarry a long while at the reputed house of Simon the tanner, which for "four potent reasons," is regarded by Dr. Kayat, H. B. M. Consul, as the veritable house of the apostles' host : 1st. No fee being charged for its exhibition, nobody's interest is involved in the tradition ; and, therefore, it is more likely to be true, than where the reverse obtains. 2d. It is on the sea-shore, where it ought to be—which is certainly more than can be said for all the *holy sites* pointed out by tradition. 3d. That there are vats in the house such as a well-constructed tannery should have And 4th. That there is the additional convenience of a well of water on the premises. Now while it is undoubtedly more likely to be the true site, in some respects, on account of being identified with no personal interests, yet if there were sufficient foundation for the tradition, would it not be sure to come into the possession of some money-loving speculator, who would charge for its exhibition ? As far as its location on the sea-shore is concerned, there are a great many other houses equally entitled to the honor. As to the vats, they have evidently been used for dead mens bones, and not for dead animals' hides, being nothing more nor less than marble sarcophagi; and in relation to the well of water, several other places similarly situated may also enter the lists as competitors, and with equal chance of success; for while this water, judging from its taste, is too impure to be used in the process of tanning, there is at least a stream of water flowing from the country (to say nothing of other wells), which would no doubt, have answered the purpose much better than the well in question. But to say nothing of these objections nor others equally forcible, arising from the fact of the repeated overthrow of the city, there is one argument that proves to my mind conclusively that the alleged site cannot be the true one, i. e., that it is situated at the base of the steep hill, upon which the city is, and must always have been built, so as to be completely overlooked by hundreds of other houses; for I can never believe that he who had been commanded by his Master to pray in *secret* would ever give such Pharisaic publicity to his secret devotion as to proclaim it from a house-top thus conspicuously situated. But, after all, would Simon *live in his tannery!?*

Outside of the city walls they also show, but not with equal confidence, seeing that the "upper chamber" is now a cave—the house of Tabitha. But though we know not exactly *where* she lived, we at least know what is infinitely more important—*how* she lived; and if we cannot enjoy the satisfaction of sitting in her house, we can at least walk in her footsteps and imitate her holy life. It was on this shore that the floats of timber from Lebanon were landed; and here, too, the

Pilgrims from the ends of the earth generally land, and feel that here the pardon promised them by their priests for this meritorious pilgrimage is first begun to be realized. While passing through the large convent of the Armenians, we were shown the alcove in the wall, which Bonaparte honored with his divan. If it be indeed true that he commanded some of his sick soldiers to be poisoned in the desert, his well known conduct in here nursing the sick so assiduously with his own hands, is, to say the least of it, rather anomalous. A considerable trade is now springing up in this ancient seaport of Jerusalem, whose population is now rated at 12,000 and is rapidly increasing. Large quanties of wheat, maize, olive oil, susim seed, cotton, soap, oranges, lemons, etc., are annually exported, principally to England. The extensive young orchards of mulberry in its suburbs and neighborhood show that attention is also being turned to the culture of silk. Sugar-cane is also raised to some extent, but the grinders of the *jaw* are the only mill by means of which its juice is extracted. I have nowhere else seen such luxuriant vegetation, as in this apparently tropical region. Having no desire to be classed with thaumaturgists, I refrain from saying how large and cheap the oranges and lemons of Jaffa are.

The sight of an English brig in the harbor about to put out for the "isles of the gentiles," reminds me that it was from this port that Jonas essayed "to flee from the presence of the Lord." Could it be this circumstance that originated the fable of Andromeda? The rock upon which she was bound when rescued, is still shown by the credulous Greeks—and no wonder, when the marvelous adventure is so fully indorsed by Jerome, one of the most celebrated and reliable of the "*Fathers!*" This father upon whom modern sects rely so much in proof of their orthodoxy, deposeth as follows: "Near here I saw the remains of the chain wherewith Andromeda was bound to the rock until delivered by Perseus, from the sea monster." Doubtless his testimony is worth about as much in support of some of the tenets in behalf of which he is made to depose, as in this instance.

FRIDAY, FEB. 7.—At two o'clock, reluctantly leave this interesting city, which, though not antediluvian, as contended for by some, may yet have been founded, as the Jews allege, by Japheth; hence its name, according to its ancient orthography, Jap-ho; and hence too, its present Arabic name, Yaffa or Jaffa. But we are going to a city which, if not more ancient, is at least more venerable, founded by Melchisedec, the elder brother of Japheth, and the illustrious ancestor of the "Prince of Peace!" Passing between two lakes just after leaving Jaffa, we take the road to Ramley. Here Yoseeph, having no longer the fear of the Bedaweens before his eyes, discharges his whole battery of eighteen barrels in such rapid succession, that some of the frightened inhabitants, mistaking us and about a dozen others who are journeying with us for a party of government troops on a conscription excursion, flee with the utmost precipitation to their hiding-places, as we learn from one of them who becomes undeceived. We lodge to-night, as the Catholics roundly assert, in the house of *Nicodemus*. This town is sometimes mistaken for the Ramah of Samuel; at other times, and strangely enough, for the Ramah in the "coasts of Bethlehem." But though evidently neither of these places, it is the city of Joseph the rich counselor of Israel, in whose intended tomb the "Wonderful Counselor" condescended to repose in the arms of death. Bring "certain strange things" to the ears of the "Reverend Fathers" of the convent, as I discourse with them in broken Latin and Italian about the truths of primeval Christianity. But all the pearls seem to be lost. Just as well sing psalms to a dead horse as attempt the enlightenment of those who know nothing except that the *Church of Rome is infallibly right!* Belgian consul explains, but all to no purpose. He that preaches to the Roman Catholics must feel all the while that his commission reads on this wise: " Go and tell this people, hear ye, indeed, but understand not; and see ye, indeed, but perceive not," etc. Is. vi.

About two miles from Ramley is a small village that marks the site of the city where Æneas the cripple was made whole by the apostle Peter; the Diospolis of the Greeks and Romans, the Lydda of the New Testament, the Lodd of the Hebrews, and now called Ludd in the kindred tongue of the Arabs. The site of the other city, equally celebrated with Lydda (for the conversion of all its inhabitants,) though a neighboring city, and judging from its name, of no little importance, we saw not, for its situation has not yet been identified. Scenery beautiful, vegetation luxuriant and charming.

Leave Ramley at 7 o'clock, Saturday morning, in high spirits, to go to Jerusalem. Stop at the edge of the town to examine a beautiful pool of water more than one hundred feet square, the masonry of which is very substantial, and apparently ancient. Soon leave the plain of Sharon and begin to ascend the mountainous district. Find the cisterns of water much more numerous than on the sea-coast. Lunch at noon near the top of a mountain, at a lovely, cool spring. Have been often compelled to think of the description given of this country by Moses, " A goodly land, a land of brooks of water, of fountains and depths, that spring out of the valleys and hills, a land of wheat, and barley, and vines, and fig trees, and pomegranates, a land of oil olive, and honey," etc. Even in its present desolate, neglected, and denuded condition, Palestine is, in many parts, exceedingly well watered and fertile. I have nowhere seen such facilities for irrigation, which in this land is the equivalent of manure. The route we have pursued has brought us over thirty-four streams, varying in width from a few feet to several scores of yards; some of them spanned by fine stone bridges of several arches; and more than forty are laid down in the maps, upon the track that lies rather farther from the coast. The springs vary in size as widely as the water-courses. I stood beside the "Cisterns of Solomon," as they call the great fountains near Tyre, almost entranced to see the force with which their immense volumes of water are sent up. Instead of the few mills now turned by these fountains, they are capable of propelling many large factories, a fact that did not long escape the keen observation of the Viceroy of Egypt, who, during the brief space that he held possession of this land, actually commenced the construction of such factories there. Pass some splendid churches, erected, probably, by the Crusaders, though they enjoy the reputation of a much higher antiquity; some of them in such a state of preservation as to be susceptible of restoration at a comparatively small expense. Even amidst these rugged mountains there are very large and fine olive orchards, vineyards, and figyards; and here and there, flourishing pomegranate, almond, and apricot trees. Some quite thriving villages, and among these, that of Abu Ghosh, where, but a few years ago, travelers were regularly stopped and heavily taxed, and not unfrequently robbed. Roads very narrow, crooked, slippery, precipitous, and bad in every respect. There must certainly be much better sites for a road between Jerusalem and her port than this! How could the gigantic beams of Lebanon cedars ever have been transported over such roads as these?

What a variety of travel we have had since we left our own sweet home! Tugged along in the snail-paced canal packet; puffed rapidly on the swiftly gliding river; jostled in the flying car; whirled about in the rough-going stage-coach; tossed about on the mighty deep, in wind-ship, steamer, and sail-boat; borne sometimes on the shoulders of men; and now dragging the length of our caravan slowly along on horse, mule, and donkey; and sometimes quadrupedal ourselves. In all this country distance is reckoned in *time*, and not in lineal measure—an hour's distance being reckoned at three miles on horses, and nearly two and a quarter on camels. The broad and beautiful beach constituted nine-tenths of our road from Beyroot to Jaffa, the most delightful road that heart could desire. Sometimes, however, at high tide, when passing along the sides of cliffs, we have been compelled to ride in the shoal water for a short distance. Sometimes beds of shells have been so deep as to render traveling tedious; and occasionally a quicksand would be encountered, from which extrication would be rather difficult for the poor floundering horse; but generally the road has been as level as a floor, and strange to say, almost as hard, yet possessing elasticity enough in its wetted state to render traveling all the easier for the animals and the better for us. Often, however, we were compelled to leave the shore and clamber along the steep precipitous sides of cliffs, where, as the "ladder of Tyre," there is nothing but the solid rock worn into narrow channels, and frequently only a single spot on the slippery rock where the hoof could possibly hold; and missing which, horse and rider must be precipitated instantly down in "gurgite vasto," hundreds of feet below. I told a Syrian that if he would permit one of my countrymen to do it, he would soon make a level road through that soft limestone mountain, and would only charge half a piaster for traveling it.

"Yes," said he, "but if we allow you that privilege, how long before you would take the whole country?"

He had heard of Americans before!!

Though the Romans, Turks, Arabs, and other nations have pretty well driven out the rightful owners of the land, they have by no means expelled some of its original parasitic occupants. The two species of which David makes mention, when pursued by Saul on the mountains, are still found here in great abundance; and the partridges are very large and fine too, ditto the "varmints!"

As we pass from Dan into Judah we are exposed to several heavy showers, one of them accompanied with hail. Having stipulated with Joseph that we should converse freely on the subject of religion, the injunctions of his priest to the contrary notwithstanding, I had often seized upon occasions out of season as well as in season, to proclaim to him "the truth as it is in Jesus," in opposition to the "lie," that is in popery; and now, in view of soon parting with him, urged upon him the absolute necessity of Bible faith instead of Romish superstition, true repentance instead of priestly penance, and obedience to the requirements of the Gospel instead of pilgrimages, veneration of relics, and other superstitious observances of the beast. But Joseph was always fonder of crossing his breast than bearing the cross; would rather kiss a stone at any time than read the Bible! Auricular confession, invocation of saints, and almost every abomination of popery, he insisted, were not only proper, but enjoined in the Bible, and necessary to salvation. "My Testament, he says, "does not read as his," and his is in the original language in which it was written (he is a Greek Catholic, and understands something of the ancient as well as modern Greek); and in order to terminate, as he hoped, at once and forever, a controversy in which he could only boast of coming off second best, declared (and really seemed to believe it), that the Greek Testament tells us very plainly that we must never go more than three weeks without confessing to the priest, and that we must venerate relics, and do whatever the priest tells us.

He was no little nonplused when I told him I happened to have the Greek Testament, and requested him to find any passages that he thought had any such squinting: his reply was, that he was not well enough acquainted with it, to find them himself, but as sure as he lived they were there, and he would bring the priest to my lodgings, and get *him* to point them out. By way of stimulating him to bring a priest, I told him I would freely divide several American eagles between him and the priest if he could show me the passages he had quoted: and upon learning that an eagle is worth two hundred piasters, he joyfully asseverated his promises of compliance; for he had so often heard such things from the mouth of the priests that he verily believes they are to be found in the Bible! Well! *nous verrons, que nous verrons.* Finding myself so completely at issue with Joseph, that nothing could be done without the aid of the priest, I determined to leave him to his reflections, and ride ahead, in order to enjoy my own reflections on a more pleasing theme, for we were now near the Holy City. But reaching a spot from which it can generally be well seen, I found the city so enveloped in mist that only a minaret or turret here and there could be seen, and Mount Olivet entirely obscured. It so strikingly represented its spiritual condition, that the "vapors" began to becloud my vision of the past and the future, as well as the present; and I felt a rapid and unaccountable subsidence of my buoyancy of spirit. However, I soon recognized the much endeared Hill of Zion, as I approached the Jaffa gate, and many were the sentiments of its sweet Bard that rushed into my mind, and one especially—"our feet shall stand within thy gates, O Jerusalem!" I was about to quote audibly and exultingly, when half a dozen surly Turks—the guards of the gate—rushed up to us, and seizing the reins of our horses, refused us entrance without a *buckshish;* but Joseph was up to their tricks, and knowing that we had neither dutyable nor contraband articles, advised resistance to their unjust demands; and so, frowning defiance at their opposition, and putting lash to our horses, jaded as they were, we immediately escaped the grasp of these leeches, and in a few minutes found ourselves at the Latin Convent. Bless the Lord, O our souls!

It was now near sunset; and anxious as we were to see some of the interesting localities of Jerusalem, we were too wet, cold and tired to do anything more this evening, than pour out our souls' devout gratitude to that Being who has shielded us amid so many dangers, and brought us safely to our journey's end—to Jerusalem, our happy home. May he, in like manner, continue to watch over us, and at last bring us safely to the New Jerusalem.

MONDAY MORNING, FEB. 10. Yesterday, just after we had showed forth the death of the Lord Jesus, and were discussing the propriety of going, on his Holy day, to see the place where (they say) the Lord lay, we received a visit from a person whom we at once recognized, from his dress, as a Roman Catholic Priest. He had heard (*he said*) that we were American Catholics!! And this queer mistake led to a long controversy upon Romanism and Protestantism, that elicited from him some singular advice.

"So you are not a Catholic then?" he quaintly and rather sneeringly drawled out, on discovering his mistake.

"Well, I trust I'm catholic," said I, "in *all* my *views* and *feelings*."

"O! pardon: I thought you said you were a Protestant."

"Well: 'tis true I *am* protestant in principle; and protest against error, wherever I see it—both among Catholics and Protestants; but I sign my name neither Protestant nor Catholic, but *Disciple of Christ*, as you can see, by referring to the register-book of this Establishment."*

---

* Upon the arrival of a stranger at this convent, a large folio volume is presented, in which he is requested to register his name and his religion, in order, it is thought, the more effectually to make application of their Jesuitical tactics. Nearly all, somehow or other, subscribe

"Disciple of Christ, eh!!! Ah! I see, you are one of that sect spoken of by St. Paul, when he says, 'now the Spirit speaketh expressly, that in the latter times some shall depart from the faith, giving heed to seducing spirits and doctrines of devils'"—. Here he cut short the quotation, but I concluded to prompt his recollection: so I added with emphasis:

"'*Forbidding to marry, and commanding to abstain from meats.*' No sir: that prophecy can't possibly allude to the Disciples of Christ, for our great fundamental and distinctive principle is, to give heed neither to demons nor men; but to '*hold fast the form of sound words*,' and we encourage rather than prohibit the marriage of our ministers and people. I always understood *that* to allude to a certain sect mentioned in the Scriptures under the name of the Scarlet Lady. Do you know any sect that forbids to marry, and commands to abstain from meats? If you do, perhaps *they* are the sect that has departed from the faith, and given heed to seducing spirits and doctrines of devils."

"We do *not* forbid our clergy to marry, sir,"—he vociferated most furiously, beating his breast vehemently, and walking up to me in a most menacing attitude.

---

themselves CATHOLICS. Among other signatures were those of two Americans, from Boston, just entered AFRESH—" once Protestants, now Roman Catholics." As they thus gloried in their shame, we concluded that it would be right and proper for us to glory in our HONOR; and therefore that honorable appellation, " Disciple of Christ," was conspicuously written in connection with the name of each of us; and it was to this fact I made reference.

"Then you are most egregiously misrepresented, if you are a Romanist, as I suppose."

"We *are* most egregiously misrepresented—for we do not forbid our clergy to marry. I am a priest, and I remain unmarried through choice."

"Then a married man can become a priest, can he? And you can remain in the priesthood, if you were now to marry, can you?" He seemed to be almost choked with rage, at my daring presumption—pacing up and down the court, beating furiously upon his breast. Unable to extricate himself, and yet ashamed to acknowledge the error, he abruptly changed the subject, and with domineering air, tauntingly asked,

"What are you doing *here*, sir, if you are no Catholic?"

"I come here, sir, to this Catholic house, just as I would go to any other tavern."

"But don't you know, sir, that you are indebted to the Holy Roman Catholic Church for the Sacred Scriptures?"

"No, sir, I am not apprised of that *fact*. I thought the Roman Catholic Church was not very fond of giving the Scriptures to the people; as to getting the Scriptures through your church, I doubt whether you ought to claim any credit for it, even if it were so; but I am inclined to think that the Word of God had a place on the shelves of every large library on earth, to say nothing of the Waldenses, Albigenses, and other dissenting bodies and individuals, that never bowed the knee to the Pope: and it is from all these sources that we have had the Bible handed down to us, through a kind Providence."

" 'Tis not so, sir; you got the Bible from us. You are indebted to us alone for it. We are the only true Church; and there is no salvation out of it. You'd better come back to us. For now you've got the Bible, you can't understand it. You know God said he would give his Holy Spirit to be in us—*the Roman Catholic Church*—forever, to enable us to explain the truth to the world."

"No; I did not know that. Will you be kind enough to show me the place where *that* is written? I suppose you don't mean that passage in John, where the 'Spirit of Truth' is promised to the *Apostles*, to guide *them* into all truth. Nor"—

"No, no; give me a Bible, and I'll show it to you directly."

"Here's one; show it to me." Looks at it. "Ah! Protestant Bible." Turns over its leaves, examines various passages, and hands it back, saying, "this Bible is not like ours, and I can't find it *here*."

"No sir; nor do I think you can find it in the *Doway* either—as *you* quote it. For though you have substituted penance for repentance, and made various other alterations, yet I can not think your Church has taken such a liberty as that of which you speak."

"Well, sir, I'll bring it to you, and the original too, and show you that it is no mistake. Mind, too, I'll show you that it is your duty to receive the interpretation that the priests put upon the Word of God."

"Priests!! I didn't know that the Christian Church has any priests in it, except in the sense in which all true disciples of Christ are a royal priesthood."

"What! no priests?"

"No!"

"Don't you recollect where it says, 'ordain priests in every church?'"

"No. I recollect Luke tells us that Paul and Silas ordained elders in every church; but the Greek word there used is *presbuteros*, an elder; not *hieros*, a priest."

"Whew!!! look here, sir—by what society are you sent here!"

"By the Church of Jesus Christ, in the United States of America."

"Church of Jesus Christ! What—what we call our Church!"

"Ah! Show me your penny. Let me see your documents—your church books. How readest thou? I thought you called it the Holy *Roman Catholic Church.*"

"Well sir, don't you know that we can prove Apostolic succession, from Saint Peter down to His Holiness, the present Bishop of Rome!"

"No. I'm inclined to think you can't even prove that the Apostle of the Circumcision ever *was at* Rome, much less its bishop. But, however, will you come to-morrow, and prove all these things to me?"

"Certainly."

"Very well. I will not only hear you cheerfully,

but if you prove them, will readily embrace them, and I hope you will just as readily renounce them, if *you* fail to establish them, or *I* can prove them untrue. We should all be sincere inquirers after TRUTH. My own motto is, to 'try the spirits'—'prove all things, and hold fast that which is good.'"

"Yes; but my friend, you can't live here and talk as you do; and if you won't make up your mind to come into the commmunion of the Holy Apostolic Church of Rome, I would advise you to go at once and join the Anglican Church, for you will certainly be persecuted; you can't live here and do so."

"*Much obliged to you for your kind advice;* but I prefer the Church of Christ, to the Anglican, Roman, Arminian, or any other that mortal man can make. But will you certainly come with your Bible, to-morrow, and have the proposed conversation?" After many "ifs" and "ands" he gave me his word that he would certainly come.

True to his promise, the disciple of Loyola appeared this morning, but long before the specified time. In a very subdued tone, he confessed that he was rather mistaken in the meaning of the passages to which he had referred, ("though the Scriptures certainly do teach the fact!"), says he; and upon the mere mention of "priests" and "Apostolic succession," was seized with such a fit of anxiety about certain indispensable matters of business, that he could by no means stay any longer—promising, however, to call on me a few weeks hence. But I am inclined to think he has abandoned me as rather a hopeless case. I learn, on inquiry, that he is a missionary sent by the Propaganda, to reclaim the Protestants of the East; and that his zealous efforts are mainly directed (with no little success, too), toward the Church of the English Mission in this city.

TUESDAY, 11.—Find ourselves very awkwardly and disadvantageously situated without the services of a dragoman; but through the kind assistance of our excellent Consul (temporarily here), succeeded in renting a house near the Damascus gate, where we hope soon to be comfortably settled.

THE FIRST CONVERTS.

"EVERY one in his own order." "The Jew first." Such was the order of Providence in the conversions which blessed the labors of the mission family. Further success realized the remainder of the maxim— "and also the Greek."

JERUSALEM, May 1st, 1851.

DEAR BROTHER CRANE:—When I assign as reasons, why your most welcome letter of December 12, which was received early in March, has remained so long unanswered, that I had just previously written to Brother Challen, and have been waiting for some time in constant expectation of a private and safe opportunity to convey letters to the United States, direct, I trust that, though the apology may seem to need an apology, you will of your clemency excuse the delay. The postal communication existing between Asia and the United States, is so circuitous and defective, that but little reliance can be placed upon the transmission of letters; but inasmuch as yours reached me so safely and speedily, I can but indulge the hope that the three or four letters which I have addressed to Brother Challen, the former Secretary, since leaving home, have reached him. I shall, therefore, in order to avoid repetition, say nothing of matters prior to the date of my last.

We are not only contented, but perfectly delighted with "Jerusalem, our happy home." This place seems to be as remarkably distinguished, at the present day, for its polyglottal inhabitants and visitors, as it was at the ever-memorable Pentecostal Feast. But still, most of the people speak Arabic, more or less perfectly. Hence, our first great object is to acquire the knowledge of this difficult tongue, and we already begin to stammer a little in its grunting ventriloquials: yet so numerous and onerous are my other engagements, that I have as yet made no progress worth boasting of. We are truly sorry to find that so far as communication with the people is concerned, the little classical Arabic we learned from books, while in London and on our way here, is altogether unavailing—being so entirely different from the vulgar tongue. Deeming it entirely inconsistent with the object had in view in coming here, to put under a bushel *that* light which, though it emanated from this consecrated spot, has yet ceased to illuminate it for so many long centuries, I have made it my business to become acquainted with the chief men of the city, and to be much in contact with the people; this, mainly through the kindness of Mr. Sinyauke, a missionary of the London Missionary Society, and Mr. Murad, an excellent teacher, who has also kindly acted as interpreter, I have been enabled in a great measure to accomplish.

It was no sooner known that I administered medicine, than petitions poured in from all quarters—Jews, Moslems and Christians, so called, but especially the first named, requesting me to visit their sick. But so great was the draft upon my time, that I soon found it necessary to decline visiting those at a distance from my house, except in cases of great urgency. But still they bring to my door such of their sick as are not too ill; and it is no uncommon thing to have five or six patients in my office at one time.

In consequence of the increasing applications, my stock of medicines, which was already much reduced and injured while at sea, is quite broken and exhausted, so that I am constantly pained by being compelled to turn a deaf ear to applicants, for the treatment of whose cases I have not the necessary medicines. I have several times been called in to see the body (or at least one of the bodies), of an effendi (or Moslem lord), whose house opens directly into the yard of the Mosque of Omar (the temple area), and have thus been permitted to enjoy the much-coveted sight of that (tabooed) inclosure, the Harem as Sherif.

I have received numbers of visits from the effendis of the city, and the sheiks of the surrounding country, either professionally or socially, and they have uniformly professed themselves admirers of America, and have at the same time expressed their approbation of my residence among them, as did also the authorities in the seraglio, where the mission was brought to their notice by our attentive consul, who, though stationed at Jaffa, occasionally exercises the functions of his office here also.

You will be pleased to hear that one of the chief secretaries of the city government has been presented with a copy of the Bible, upon his own application. Some of the Jews have been independent enough to receive the New Testament; but the rabbis have as yet uniformly refused it, nor do I think I could gain access to them at all but for my medical services. When once acquainted, however, they converse very freely upon the subject of Christianity, and I may say without the semblance of boasting, that with all their Talmudical lore and rabbinical sophistry, it is quite easy to gain the most complete victory over them by the appropriate use of the "sword of the Spirit." With the exception of the autocracy of Dahomey and Nicholas, I verily believe that there is not in all this wide world a more tyrannical despotism than that exercised over the Jews of this land, by their "lords spiritual and temporal," holding, as it does, in the vilest durance, the minds, bodies and souls of these unfortunate outcasts of Israel. Hence, so very few of them have the courage to confess Jesus, even after they are fully convinced that he is their promised Messiah.

Although greatly disinclined to beg, I am strongly tempted—in view of the great good to be accomplished—to beg the Board to send out, as an assistant to the mission, a physician with a good assortment of medicines, to practice gratuitously among the poor of Jerusalem. To attend properly to all the professional calls made upon me, would entirely consume my time; to turn a deaf ear to them altogether would not only be entirely inconsistent with my feeling and sense of duty, but close up an open door of access to the people, and to pursue a middle course is almost impossible.—What then is to be done?

The London Jews' Society has a large hospital here, upon which it annually expends more than $10,000 (ten thousand dollars); and it is through this institution, almost solely, that its converts have been made. In order to counteract its influence, Sir Moses Montefiore, a wealthy Israelite, has established a large and well-managed hospital in opposition. The Armenians are now building one, and the Latins have such an institution already. Yet, notwithstanding this, I have applications from all parts of the city, more than sufficient to employ all my time, could I attend to them.

Should the executive committee not deem it within the legitimate scope of its functions to comply with this request, still, have the *Disciples of Christ* in the United States no wealthy brethren among them, as much devoted to the truth as it is in Jesus, as the Hebrew is to the truth as it was in Moses, who will send us that help at his own proper cost? If not, tell it not in Gath; breathe it not in the streets of Jerusalem.

We have just removed from the Christian Quarter, where we first rented rooms, and have settled in the Mohammedan Quarter, quite near the seraglio, or Governor's Palace, which occupies the site of the Tower of Antonia, hard by the Temple area. I will not tell you what intrigues were resorted to, nor by whom, lest it might cause my veracity to be questioned, to defeat our contemplated settlement on Mount Zion, where I made no little effort to procure a house.

The rent I am now paying is rather higher than what I paid for our late premises, being 4050 piasters, per annum. The price insisted upon for some time by its owner, an influential effendi, was 6000, but after long-pending negotiation, our kind consul succeeded in procuring it at the above rate, $202. It is rented for one year, or as much longer as I may choose to keep it; but as rent is on the rise, it will no doubt be found advisable to continue in it, although a tolerably decent and comfortable house of smaller dimensions, and situated in a less healthy part of the town can be had cheaper. But the increased size of our congregation rendered it very inconvenient to hold our public meetings in the reception room; and had we continued there any longer, it would have been necessary to rent a separate room for a meeting room, and also for teaching school, for we have some scholars already, and many more could be had if deemed expedient. This house, however, has in it a large hall, which answers very well for that purpose, and it is more economical as well as convenient to have them both together.

But what is a matter of prime importance, during our acclimation in this sickly place, is that it is located in the healthiest part of the city. That it may not seem unmeasurably high in your estimation, however, I will just remark that the house occupied by the American Presbyterian Missionaries, when in this city (which is in the immediate vicinity), is now rented by Dr. Schultz, the Prussian Consul, for 6000 piasters per annum.

While olive oil, doura, oranges, and many other

articles are cheap here, the articles chiefly used by Franks are very dear. I have kept an accurate account of our expenses thus far; and assuming this account as the basis of calculation, it will require at least $1000 per annum to defray current expenses. This is only about half the amount estimated by a few friends whom I consulted. Dr. De Forest, however, one of the Beyroot Missionaries, who was here a few days since, thinks that this amount, exclusive of house rent and dragoman's wages, might suffice. But I feel confident that it will be sufficient to meet all the expenses which I feel willing for the brethren to incur on our account. This amount you will understand is entirely exclusive of the cost of furniture, books, and many little articles required by every family; but which I can by no means consent to charge the patrons of the mission with. But although this estimate is considerably lower than it has been rated at by any one else, I am yet a little apprehensive, as it considerably exceeds the amount supposed to be sufficient before my departure from the United States.

I must take the liberty of mentioning the sums respectively received by several persons here, somewhat similarly situated, in order that the committee may be more fully satisfied.

The salary of Messrs. Nicholson and Eweld, stationary preachers, and of Dr. McGowan, physician to the hospital, is fifteen hundred dollars each, without any family, or but a small one, this, too, is exclusive of house rent, dragoman's hire and servants. Mr. Veitch, the principal of the Hebrew school, received (until the school was discontinued) $2000. Mr. Tinyauke, a single gentleman, missionary to the Jews of Palestine, is paid five hundred dollars, his traveling expenses when abroad, and incurs no charge for rent, hire of servants, etc. Colporteurs receive for their occasional services, about five hundred dollars. "The Right Reverend Lord Bishop of Egypt, Mesopotamia, Syria, Palestine, and the United Anglican and Irish Churches at Jerusalem" receives, in addition to six hundred dollars allowance for house rent, several dragomen, Janizaries, and perquisites innumerable, six thousand dollars!! But *Bishop Barclay* is happy in belonging to no such category!

But let me now speak of a more interesting subject. A few weeks ago I had the pleasure of introducing into the fold of the Redeemer, four of the lost sheep of the house of Israel. These first fruits of the mission, consisting of a mother and three grown children, were buried with their Saviour in baptism, near the Damascus gate, in one of the pools so abundant within and without the city, and give the strongest evidence that they have risen to walk in the newness of life. There were present at their baptism a few spectators from each quarter of the globe, who gazed in mute astonishment at this strange sight, behaving with the utmost propriety. But no sooner was it noised abroad through the city, than it excited the greatest disturbance; not so much among bigoted Jews as among Protestants—Christians! And whereunto the matter would have grown, but for the protection of their consul, there is no telling. Be it recorded to the honor of Her Britannic Majesty's Consul, that Joseph-like, he did not consent to the counsel and deed of them that convened in conclave to consider the matter, but nobly stood up in defense of the right of private judgment and independence. If ever I saw true penitent believers, this household consists of such, and their obedience to the faith has given us great satisfaction.

But uncertainty as to the proper course to be pursued in relation to several others who have applied for baptism, has greatly perplexed my mind and grieved my heart, with the exception of these cases, (Jewish converts,) the purity of whose motives there is every reason to question. In one or two instances, improper motives were so well developed, as to justify me in rejecting them after a very little investigation; but in others, while their motives may be reasonably questioned, there is yet no sufficient ground for rejecting them, without permitting mere suspicion to exercise too much sway. But beside these there are two or three persons of superior intelligence, and apparently very pious, and yet they come in such a very questionable shape, and so eccentric in manner, and singular in their views of prophecy, which they publish on all occasions, that the connection with us which they seek, I apprehend, would considerably tend to injure us. I have concluded upon the whole that, inasmuch as there is in the Scriptures neither precept nor precedent for the treatment of such doubtful cases, it is best to hold them in abeyance awhile, and recommend them to devote much time to reading the Sacred Scriptures, self-examination, etc., in the hope that Providence will make the case plain. By pursuing this course, and exercising rigid discipline over those already admitted, I hope to keep the church pure. I would gladly, in this dilemma, avail myself of the advice of the committee, but it is evident that without being here in person, and conversant with all the circumstances of the case, the genius of the people, and other matters, a correct idea of which it would be impossible for me to convey in writing, no correct judgment can be formed. But if the dear brethren cannot assist me by their counsel, they can at least render the valuable service by praying to the "Lord of the Harvest," who giveth liberally and upbraideth not, that he would endow me with wisdom and discretion, and all qualifications, requisite properly to meet the onerous responsibilities of my station. Were it merely my object to get *members* into the Church, I could soon have quite a number of respectable persons. But beside these crooked cases, there are several persons almost persuaded to become old-fashioned Christians, who would be a great acquisition, of whose complete conversion to the truth, and union with us, I trust, I shall soon have the pleasure of informing you.

Appearances are certainly very encouraging at present, but what a day may bring forth in this place, there is no divining.

Jerusalem, once called, *par excellence*, "The Holy City," I verily believe, my dear brother, is one of the most corrupt places on earth, especially the Christian portion of it. In this respect I have been greatly disappointed. From the Mohammedans, by whom I had expected to be denounced and persecuted, I have received the kindest and most respectful treatment; while from the Christians (and especially that portion claiming to be apostolic and enlightened), by whom I had expected to be treated, at least, with Christian courtesy, I have received treatment which has worked the censure of all classes. In the entire absence of all other occasions, the inference may, perhaps, be drawn that I have incurred their displeasure, by failing to present the truth in love, or what is still worse, have not commended myself to their consciences, by the proper manifestation of the truth. But, my dear brother, I must be allowed to plead "not guilty."

In the sagacity and the prudence of the serpent, I am, doubtless, somewhat deficient, but I must be allowed to lay claim to no small portion of the inoffensiveness of the dove, so far at least as they are concerned; albeit, I confess I have cried aloud, and shown Rome her transgressions. My only fear is that my great desire to avoid giving offense, has been construed into another quality of the dove, of which I am as little envious as deserving—timidity. But enough.

I must not close, however, without saying a few words on the subject of a mission school. Not only all the missionaries have large schools, but there are also associations of bodies in England and the United States, who maintain very large and well-conducted establishments, in which they educate gratuitously, all who choose to attend, old or young, Moslem, Jew or Christian; and the king of Prussia is also founding a similar institution, handsomely endowed. If, therefore, we would not cut ourselves off from the plastic mind of youth, we must have a regular school also. But the Board need not be reminded of the great importance of schools in connection with missions, as means of access, not only to children, but their parents, and indeed the community generally. Of course, as long as there are only a few scholars as at present (only five), we are fully able to take charge of them, and will cheerfully furnish books, stationery, materials, etc.

A lengthy reply at your earliest convenience, will not be only highly gratifying, but, inasmuch as this is an important crisis with us, will be highly expedient also.

Love and greetings to all the holy brethren.

I can but feel that I have not been forgotten by them; will you not all continue to commend me to God and the word of his grace?

With the highest personal esteem, as well as Christian love, yours in Christ,

J. T. BARCLAY.

JERUSALEM, May 5, 1851.

MY DEAR BROTHER CRANE:—Although I have now lying by me a letter which was written with the view of forwarding it to you by the present private opportunity, yet as the early departure of Mr. and Mrs. Sergent, to whose kind care I propose committing it, is somewhat uncertain, I have determined, by way of increasing the probability of communication with you, to commit that communication to the mail, and send by them, *this*, together with the last reports of the " London Society for promoting Christianity among Jews," which, I think, will place you in possession of some useful information, and amply compensate for its perusal.

The opposition excited by the baptism of the four Jewish converts not only continues unaltered, but has become absolutely rancorous, and it is quite obvious that nothing but the late tolerant firman of the Sultan (for which eternal thanks to the " governor among the nations,") prevents the exercise of open persecutions, which, however, I had almost as soon encounter, as the species of opposition now resorted to.

It is really as astounding as it is lamentable, that while the Archbishop of Canterbury has entered into solemn league and covenant with the Latin, Greek, Armenian, Coptic, and other apostate oriental churches, fully indorsing their orthodoxy, in his celebrated letter addressed " To the Right Reverend our Brothers in Christ, the Prelates and Bishops of the ancient and apostolic Church in Syria," etc., his clergy here should not only refuse to recognize as Christians those who take as their rule of faith and practice the Bible wholly and solely, but do all they can to injure them because they " follow not with them," but endeavor to Christianize the people just as the Apostles have enjoined! *O tempora! O mores!*

But it is well to remember that in one important respect, the Prince of Peace came not to send peace on earth. The good Lord give us patience quietly to endure, and properly to resist this ungracious opposition. O! for that wisdom that came down from the Father of Lights and is profitable to direct! Will not the holy brethren pray that in all things, we may be under the guidance of Him who is excellent in counsel and wonderful in working.

I begin to fear that from Brother Taffe's unusually long silence that the intervention of two oceans has caused him to forget us, or what I should regret still more that his labors on earth are ended! I am entirely ignorant of all occurrences among the brotherhood of Cincinnati for the last eight months, with the exception of the few lines you had space to mention in your kind letter.

Imagine, then, if you can, the pleasure with which we would read a long letter from yourself, our much endeared Elder Challen, or any of the beloved brethren. In relation to our much loved Brother Burnet, I must say that I feel strongly inclined to visit upon him the effusions of an attack of "cacoethes scribendi" just now exciting me to stir up his pure mind by way of remembrance.

With kindest regards,
Yours in the truth,
J. T. BARCLAY.

VALUABLE ADDITIONS TO THE CHURCH OF JERUSALEM.

Having published these letters in the Christian Age, the compiler prefaced this one with the subjoined remarks:

The following letter of Brother Barclay, possesses very great interest. At first, we speculated and hoped, now we believe and rejoice, though sometimes we are compelled to tremble in the midst of our joy. The conversion of Lazarus Murad will constitute an era in the history of the Mission. Last night, July 14, the Board appointed him an assistant missionary at the Jerusalem station. With his rare lingual proficiency and great devotion to the truth, he cannot fail to be an invaluable aid to Brother Barclay, putting him in immediate connection with the various nations resorting to the Holy City. May the blessing of the second Melchisedek rest upon that city now! May Abraham get that blessing in the person of all his descendants, the sons of Sarai, and the sons of Keturah; and both Israel and Esau—they are all there!

Want of room forbids any further reflections. The Missionary Board, as a matter of course, assumes the payment of all the necessary expenses of the mission, and passed an order to that effect. D. S. B.

JERUSALEM, May 14, 1852.

Brother Crane: My Dear Sir:—Since my last, we have received two valuable accessions to our little flock—Mr. Murad and Mr. Houser; and it is in relation to the former that I now avail myself of a private opportunity of communicating with Beyroot, to address you a few lines. This individual, Mr. Lazarus Murad, the brother of our consul at Jaffa, has been employed by me as teacher and dragoman, ever since our arrival here, and has for some years been a member of the Presbyterian Church. He is an Armenian by nation, but born in Bethlehem, Judah, and brought up in this city. Upon leaving the American Church to join the Presbyterian, he was dreadfully persecuted, being bound in fetters and scourged—the marks of which he bears to the present day. He speaks the Armenian, Turkish, Arabic, and English languages fluently, and Italian, German and French, less perfectly.

He has, for the last six years, been employed by the American Board of Commissioners for Foreign Missions as translator, colporteur, etc.; and, by order of the Beyroot missionaries, has lately rendered into Armenian, for the benefit of pilgrims, that queer, mystical production of John Bunyan—"Pilgrim's Progress!" Though formerly so much persecuted by the Armenians, and lately anathematized publicly, by the Patriarch, he still has influence enough with them to secure the attendance of a little congregation among them, that he addresses every Lord's day evening. He is entirely devoted to the work of the Lord; and his talents and attainments, which are quite respectable for this latitude, are such as to give fair promise of usefulness—indeed, have already proved not a little useful. He has been a constant attendant upon our services for the last three months, and though for some time he could not be convinced of all the truth as it is in Jesus, yet for some weeks he has been fully convinced, but owing to his sense of propriety postponed his entire submission to the truth until he could freely communicate with his former brethren at Beyroot. The strenuous efforts put forth to prevent his union with us, and retain him in his late connection, confirm the good opinion entertained of him on all sides.

I am thus particular in giving you his history and character, because I am very anxious—being fully assured of the purity of his motives and the integrity of his intentions—to have the Board appoint him my assistant, so that I can at once obtain complete access to all classes of Syrian population.

We have just advanced far enough in Arabic to perceive its difficulties, and be convinced that many a weary and unprofitable month, perhaps year, must pass away before I can speak fluently enough to preach publicly in this intricate tongue; and, beside it is a great mistake, as I now learn, to suppose that Arabic is a universal medium of intercourse, farther than mere trading is concerned. The present crisis demands too, that we should issue a few simple tracts in Arabic and Armenian, which with his assistance I can easily do.

I have just been conversing with him, and he is truly anxious to preach the *truth*, as he has now found it in the word of the Lord. Should the Board deem it expedient to engage his services, I suppose about $300 would suffice to sustain him; though others are getting about twice that sum from other missions, for doing less than he would be required to do as teacher, dragoman, Bible distributer, translator, etc.; but I have rated it to correspond with the estimate of my own allowance. Indeed, his services for two hours every day as teacher of Arabic would be rated at about that price.

The matter seems to be so providential, and his appointment so manifestly advantageous, that I have not hesitated to engage him on my own responsibility until I can hear from the Board. I must confess, however, that I feel no little diffidence in making this proposition to the Board after having so recently proposed other considerable expenditures. My only apology is that the importance of the crisis, in my estimation, demands it so loudly, and Providence indicates it so plainly, that my convictions of duty constrain me to suggest it.

But I have just received notice that I must make haste or lose the present opportunity, so that I must conclude as abruptly as reluctantly.

May the Great Head of the Church so direct our counsels and influence our course of action, that glory may redound to his name, and good accrue to his cause.

Most respectfully, fraternally and affectionately,
Yours, in the one Hope,
J. T. BARCLAY.

LETTER TO DR. J. T. BARCLAY, OF JERUSALEM.—NO. I.

Hygeia, Ohio, July 18, 1851.

Beloved Brother:—We have been delighted to receive your last two letters. We have blessed the Lord and taken courage. I have always feared that you would find a barren and ungenerous field, in a land which, though it peculiarly belonged to the Messiah, received him not, but hung him on a tree. The inveteracy of habit has been illustrated by no people more than by the various nations which have descended from Abraham, and among whom you have chosen to labor. While this fact serves you an important purpose, in furnishing you living examples of the manners and customs, and intellectual peculiarities of the nations most mentioned in the Bible, and is therefore a valuable commentary on the Sacred Scriptures, it stands most in the way of your success in evangelizing those nations. The mixing of races in the motley population of one city, the conflicting interests which obtain among them, but especially among the Franks, and most especially among the missionaries, give rise to a peculiar moral condition quite unfavorable to genuine conversion. The rival sects are liable to severe temptation, to unfair dealing and an unchristian spirit, in the management of the discussions which inevitably arise. This predicament operates deleteriously, also, upon the persons whose conversion to the common Christianity is sought. Distrust of piety and sincerity in those who labor for their good, naturally possess the minds of these unbelievers. But the worst of all is the exhibition of deep depravity on the part of those who would sell themselves to the highest bidder in the ecclesiastical market. It is painful to hesitate when it is proposed, by a sinner, to commence the service of God in accordance with the forms of primitive Christianity. Yet both wisdom and sad experience dictate great carefulness in the administration of the initial Christian ordinance. I fear, my dear brother, that the trials which you have already experienced, are not the last which may arise from these causes. But the Lord, who has been a wall of fire round about you, will be a glory in the midst, and a continual defense, as long as you are honored to be laborers. This, however, is the dark side of the subject. There are cheering views of it to be taken. None of your competitors work with your instruments. The Gospel which you preach, though it counts near twenty centuries, rejoices in eternal youth. It ever possesses Pentecostal strength and majesty. Having slain the enmity of many of the actual murderers of the Lord Jesus, it can now fill with love and joy the hearts of their descendants. There is a strong hope that the novelty of the views you advocate may serve, like the fiery meteor which crowned the apostles with a living glory, and called ancient Israel to the feet of Heaven's own teachers, effectually to introduce you to Judah and his brethren. May both Esau and Israel yet rejoice in your labors!

Our God is the hearer and answerer of prayer. You and your missionary family are the objects of the unceasing supplications of thousands in our wide spread country.

The reflex influence of all this work of Christian missions upon the churches at home is of the highest utility. It excites benevolence in giving, and benevolence of feeling, opening the heart to a lively appreciation of the wants and miseries of the dying world. The expectation of news from the "far countries," to which the missionaries have gone, will incite the Church to keep its vigils, and serve for oil and trimming to our lamps. The Lord give you, amidst your privations, self-denial and comfort, and enable you to report to us abundant success in the field of your labors! Indeed your recent rich harvest is an encouraging first-fruits, which leads to the hope of an abundant return for the toils of seed-time and after cultivation.

I have never seen your family, but they have become endeared to me and mine, and are not forgotten in our approaches to that presence where all Christians are welcome and are at home. There is one Jerusalem where we all shall meet.

Be so kind as to present me most affectionately to brother Lazarus Murad, your future coadjutor. May the Lord give you comfort in his aid, and to you both great success! Your labors are arduous, but you are naturally cheerful without excitability, and you know in whom you have believed. But I must close this hasty letter.

Your brother in the kingdom and patience of the Lord Jesus Christ, D. S. BURNET.

LETTER TO DR. BARCLAY — NO. II.

My Dear Brother:—Jerusalem has become a point of much interest to the American, and doubtless to the English church, since your arrival there. From the circumstances, yourself and family have become most vitally associated with this interest. Everywhere Jerusalem and the Mission are talked of, and the latest intelligence concerning them is sought for with avidity. It is a matter of importance, then, that this public expectation should be met, as far as possible. To answer these ends some system might be adopted.

And first, all the members of the missionary family, now amounting to six persons, should contribute to the public gratification by keeping, as likely they now do, a diary, inclusive of all the principal or most interesting events. As a matter of course, none of these should be given to the public, in any form without your consent, and your previous inspection. This exercise of daily writing would prove a most instructive exercise to all the parties engaged in it, especially if the daily memoranda should embrace a great variety of details. All can write such, and all love to read them, much more than mere generalizations. Very few places on earth furnish a richer field. There hangs a story on every stone of the old foundations, especially of Solomon's porch. The early architecture and other evidences of the age of the city, the progressive development of new systems of architecture, indicating the change of times and the change of races, from the era of Melchisedek, and his peaceful sway, to the time of Turkish misrule, and a complete view of the present architecture and manner of living, including manufactures, however scanty and rude, agriculture and horticulture, with a description of the palm, the fig, the sycamore, olive, cedar, cypress, oleander, hyssop, cactus, etc. It might be inquired whether the rose of Sharon, the lily of the valley, and balm of Gilead, are there yet, for though some have the works of travelers, the mass of our readers and the public at large, have very partial information concerning places and scenes that are sufficiently sacred, without the superstitions of Romanism, to make any item of information of peculiar interest. And it must be borne in mind that the world is at this time vastly indebted to the missionary for geographical and archeological knowledge. Has Jerusalem any commerce? How is it conducted? How do the box and the barrel get from Jaffa, the ancient Joppa, to the great city? Which is the most common, the mule, the horse, the camel, or dromedary? Do any caravans arrive now, and of what kind, and whence? Are pilgrimages made to the holy sepulchre by Romanists, Greeks, Armenians, Nestorians? etc. What are the ridiculous services of Easter and other supposed holy seasons, and what the cordial co-operation or desperate hate of the pilgrims and officials to each other? What can be said of the Jerusalem Jew, of his civil and religious disabilities, of his habits, and the habits of the other "dwellers at Jerusalem;" how and what do they eat and drink, what are their salutations, modes of marriage, burial? etc. As I intimated to you in a former letter, much matter useful for illustration of the sacred Scriptures, can be thus gathered, the freshness of which would add to its value. The Jew, the Mohammedan, the Arab, the Druses, the Nestorians, the Egyptians, their dress, manners, avocations, etc., all open a fountain of curious particulars. Your sons and daughter could select their topics, and out of all the materials thus brought before you, a most interesting monthly or semi-monthly report could be collated. I have not yet alluded to the real and most absorbing objects of your mission, the records of which would have such a thrilling effect upon us here; I mean the daily experience of each one of you in teaching, colportage, conversation, medical practice, and preaching. Can one of you describe the first celebration of the Lord's supper by yourself, and particularly the first celebration of it after the baptism of Dragoman Murad? A valued correspondent, in his letter received this evening, makes some very excellent suggestions on this subject, as will be seen by the following extract from the letter, which should have appeared entire had not his modesty forbade.

"Our publications, the Age especially, will be greatly increased in interest and usefulness, provided Brother Barclay writes out reports of his labors in a style adapted to the taste and capacity of general readers. In reading his letters I wish to ask him a hundred questions. Many brethren and friends are anxious to know how he employs his time: what sister Barclay is doing, how she enjoys a missionary life, how our young brethren, his sons, and our young sister, his daughter, employ their minds and hands in the 'Holy City?' We look upon them all as missionaries, and we feel as desirous of hearing from them as from their father.

"We are also inquisitive about the city. How great a population? How many Jews, Mahomedans? How many Romanists, Greek Church, Armenians, Protestants? What number of communicants in these various sects? How many schools, pupils, physicians, soldiers, merchants, mechanics? The health of the city and the surrounding country. The possibility, probability, etc., of ancient and modern accounts of the scarcity or quantity of water in and about the city.

"But above all things, Brother Barclay must make us intimately acquainted with all the converts. We are anxious to know the names, ages, employments, etc., of those immersed. Tell us how they became acquainted with Jesus, when they confessed him, in what language, etc. Who are the opponents. The grounds of their opposition, etc.

"Many of us have read a most interesting account of John Mushullam. We have anticipated much good to result to Brother Barclay from an acquaintance with him. A man of Mr. Mushullam's goodness of heart, and able to speak some *fifteen* languages ought to be of great benefit to such a missionary as Brother Barclay, and yet in his letters he has not once alluded to him, or the fruitful vale of 'Artos,' or Bethlehem."

My dear brother, these friendly remarks will serve to show you how deep an interest is felt in this glorious **work, and** how much the public thirsts for information.

The Board would feel stimulated to greater exertions, if we were in more constant communication with you But my paper is full. Once more I would commend you to God, and to the word of his grace.

Yours truly, D. S. BURNET.

August 1, 1851.

JERUSALEM, July 17, 1851.

MY DEAR BROTHER CRANE:—Having an opportunity of sending communications post-free as far as England, and perhaps all the way to America, I can not consent to let it pass altogether unimproved. But having written to you so recently, I shall not now trouble you with another letter, but merely send you, by way of a more extended report than I have heretofore made, the foregoing account of our voyage from New York to Beyroot, and our trip thence to the Holy City.

The time is not far distant, I hope, when the Board will send out to these regions more "witnesses unto the truth of Jesus," and if so, some useful hints may be found in the foregoing pages.

For the conveyance of this journal—at least as far as Liverpool—I am indebted to Mr. Sinyauki, a missionary of the "London Jews Society" to the Jews of the Holy Land, who visits the United States with a view of committing to the press a new version of the Old Testament, or at least his proposed emendations;

for which important undertaking, his intimate acquaintance with the original and the Talmud, the manners and customs of the Jews, and the physical history of this country, pre-eminently qualifiy him. His great kindness and valuable services have laid me under lasting obligations; and should he visit Cincinnati, his Christian courtesy will prompt him cheerfully to furnish the Board with much useful information. Will you, therefore, regard this brief notice as a kind of introductory note should he ever call upon you.

While I have pen in hand I may as well mention that I expect to baptize, in a few days hence, a very respectable physician and his wife, daughter and son-in-law, and also a Greek Catholic and his wife, who took refuge in this city a few weeks ago from the persecution raised against them by the Greek bishop of St. John d'Acre, for professing the broad principles of Protestantism. I have many more applications for medical aid than I can possibly attend to consistently with my duty to other departments of missionary labor, and have already been compelled to refurnish myself with the more important and leading medicines. We cannot but praise the Lord for the past and present, and implicitly trust him for the future.

Most cordial salutations to the Board and brethren generally, by whom, we trust, we are remembered at the Mercy Seat.

Indeed, believe me, dear brother, with affection sincere and warm, most truly, yours in the Lord,

J. T. BARCLAY.

TO THE BRETHREN OF THE EASTERN VIRGINIA CO-OPERATION.

JERUSALEM, August 5, 1851.

DEARLY BELOVED IN CHRIST:—On passing through Richmond this day twelve months ago, the sum of four hundred and sixty-nine dollars and four cents was placed in my hands by Brother Quarles, through your liberality, and it is right and meet that you should have an account of its disbursement and special application.

The one half of this amount you designed to be appropriated directly in support of this mission, and accordingly it has been thus applied—having been first transferred to this missionary committee at Cincinnati, and by them retransferred to me for the direct maintenance of the mission in conjunction with their own appropriation. The other half you wish devoted to the distribution of the Bible; and it is upon this indirect, though valuable, if not indispensable auxiliary support of the Mission that I propose making a few remarks; not, however, without first most sincerely thanking you, as well as blessing the Lord for such an indubitable proof (the more highly prized because unsolicited) of the interest you take, not only in behalf of the objects of this Mission, but I would fain hope, of the instruments (however unworthy such a testimony) of accomplishing the intention of the patrons of the Mission—" not because I desire a gift; but I desire that fruit may abound to your account"—to the good of man and the glory of God.

The American Christian Bible Society having also

made a donation for the purpose of disseminating the good seed of the word; their contribution ($300) forms with yours, a common fund for the distribution of the Scriptures. I made it my business while in London to have frequent interviews with the officers of the British and Foreign Bible Society, that great manufactory of Bibles in all languages, in order to procure such versions as I might want, on the most favorable terms, either from their own rooms in London, or from their more accessible depositories at Smyrna or Malta. And having made arrangements by which I could procure them on the same terms from either of these depositories as from London, I only purchased from their city depot, to the amount of one hundred and sixty-six dollars and seventy-five cents, lest in my ignorance of the most approved versions and the particular dialects spoken in Jerusalem and the surrounding region, or by the pilgrims resorting here, I might get such as would be ill adapted or altogether unsuitable for distribution—the propriety of which precaution has since been but too evident—for I learn that some versions are far superior to others in very important points. This supply having been considerably reduced, and some versions entirely exhausted, I lately purchased from the American Beyroot Mission a temporary supply to the amount of fifty dollars and thirty-five cents—awaiting a direct opportunity, in prospect a few weeks, to procure a full supply from Valetta.

These purchases are made from the joint fund; but deeming it expedient and indeed highly important to publish occasionally, according to the requirement of the times, separate portions of the Scriptures, such as the second chapter of Acts of Apostles, collections of the Messianic prophecies, small oracular tracts, etc., I shall take the liberty, in the continued absence of any intimation of your disapprobation, of charging to your contribution a small but very efficient hand Press and Types, which I purchased at the low price of seventy-five dollars. But should any of the brethren deem this a misapplication of the fund, the Press will at once be set down to the account of one who knows too well the importance of such instrumentality in scattering the laws of Divine Truth, which are for the healing of the nations, to regard a cost so low compared with the amount of good to be expected from its proper management in this benighted part of the earth. I have now in course of preparation, two small tracts, the object of the one printed in English being to correct misrepresentations in quarters otherwise inaccessible, so framed also as to give a synopsis of the distinctive characteristics of Primitive Christianity contrasted with paganized and judaized Christianity as exhibited here and elsewhere—a work very much needed and sometimes asked for by travelers, and even missionaries from the ends of the earth, who are frequently visiting this city. The object of the other lithographed in Arabic, is to call the attention of the people away from the traditions and inventions of men, to the Word of the Lord—a purpose, the great importance of which, you who are privileged to live in a land where every one can procure a Bible, and examine for himself, can form no adequate conception.

While you will be both grieved and surprised to learn that not a few persons are to be found in this land of Revelation—and they not Mussulmen either—who refuse to accept any portion of the Bible except the Old Testament, you will be pleased to learn that I occasionally find in quarters least promising, even among the Jewish Rabbis, a few who joyfully accept the entire word of the Lord—though *Nicodemus like*, for fear of the Jews. But what will surprise you still more, if indeed you can credit it, is that some who style themselves Christians of the "Holy Apostolic Order" utterly refuse to let the Word of the Lord remain in their houses, albeit, some of them say, they would like to read the Bible, if their priests would let them do so. It is gratifying, however, to know that though the Jews and nominal Christians so generally refuse the Living Oracles, many of the Gentiles gladly receive them. We had been here but a short time before an officer in the seraglio earnestly asked for an entire copy of the Bible in Turkish; but whether he is a sincere inquirer after truth, or whether he merely wished to satisfy himself, that the book which he heard I was circulating, contained nothing dangerous to the welfare of the empire, I am unable to say. I have lately been agreeably surprised to find, as my acquaintance increases among the Effendis, that though they are generally bigoted votaries of Islamism, yet many of them converse with much freedom and toleration on the subject of Christianity, and have embraced, even with eagerness, the opportunity of possessing our "*Koran.*" Now although this is but the mere shadow of a spark in the oriental horizon, yet so different is the spirit of liberality and tolerance manifested by the Mohammedans, from what I had expected, that I cannot but say—"it is the Lord's doings and is marvelous in our eyes." And could you but see the various manifestations of the kindness and consideration with which we are treated, not only by the Effendis of the city, but the sheiks of the neighboring villages, and even by some of the Bedouins of the desert, you might be tempted to say that it is altogether unaccountable upon any other hypothesis than the supposition, that the Lord is granting us this favor in the sight of the present possessors of the Lord, in order that Primeval Christianity might again be planted in its native soil.

Should you infer, from the small number of books already distributed by us, that there is not much demand for the Scriptures, you would be indulging a sad mistake—for I doubt whether there is a spot upon earth where more can be profitably done in the way of Bible distribution than in this city. But it must be remembered that it is at the close of the Easter and Christmas festivals, when so many thousands of pilgrims are taking their departure for distant countries, that the best opportunities for this book are presented. It is to be regretted that I was not prepared to avail myself properly of this advantage, during the only season of this kind which has occurred since my arrival here. It will, doubtless, be gratifying, however, to know that through your liberality the rays of Divine truth are now illumining some of the dark corners, not only of Asia and Africa, but some solitary spots of Europe scarcely less benighted. This immediate region has been so lavishly supplied with Bibles by the "Prusso-Anglico-Hibernio Hebrew Christian Mission" of this city, that it is necessary to exercise some discretion in their further distribution. It is a lamentable fact, which I have noticed myself in the forum of the "Church of the Holy Sepulchre," which is used as a house of merchandise during the "holy days," that the Word of the Lord was used for wrapping paper! On this account I am very cautious in giving away a large Bible to a citizen or merchant from any quarter, without a sufficient acquaintance or satisfactory reference. Such a discrimination is painful, but absolutely necessary to a judicious distribution of the Word of the Lord.

I have sometimes been offered payment for Bibles, but in the absence of all instruction on this score, I have deemed it best to give away the Bread of Life without money and without price. Should the Lord continue to prosper you in basket and in store as well as in all spiritual privileges, (as I most earnestly pray that he may) so that you shall feel privileged to give vent to your liberality through the same channel again, will you please accompany your donation with suitable instructions?

Our hearts overflowed with gratitude, as did our eyes with tears, on learning that we had been made the special objects of your prayers. We thought and felt as much before we heard it; for what else but the special favor of the Lord, bestowed in answer to your intercessions, could have sustained us so well, on several trying occasions! Allow us, dear brethren, to invoke a continued interest in your supplications. And may the blessedness of them that water others be many fold yours.

October 7, 1851.

The above was written (or at least much of it) more than a month ago, but since that time I have been compelled to suspend business of every kind except such as was indispensable, on account of very protracted cases of fever in my family, from which we are now, by the kind Providence of the Lord, nearly exempt; though two of my children are still confined to bed.

That grace, mercy, peace, and every blessing, temporal as well as spiritual, may be abundantly vouchsafed to you, dear brethren, most fervently prays your brother in Christ,

J. T. BARCLAY.

JERUSALEM, October 7, 1851.

MY WELL-BELOVED BROTHER:—Although I have blundered amid the distracting cares of the sick chamber, and have accidentally written two communications on the same paper, yet as I am desirous that the report of the Virginia Co-operation should be received before its fall meeting, and as an opportunity has unexpectedly offered of sending it by private conveyance to Beyroot, so as to ensure its committal to the steamer, I take the liberty of sending it just as it is—without copying it. We found, when, alas! it was too late to correct our error, that we ought either to have followed the example of the English and other foreigners, in spending the summer in camp near the city, or else in some more salubrious spot, for Sarah and John have been sick nigh unto death. But the Lord had mercy upon them, and not only upon them, but upon us also. Indeed, my dear Brother, the Lord was with us in this seventh trouble in a most gracious manner. The next summer we expect to spend in Safet, just above the shores of Lake Galilee. Beside slighter attacks, this is the fourth week with Sarah and the third with John. Oh! my beloved brother, could you but just see them! Having only a few minutes at command, I cannot now particularize, but hope to write in detail by next steamer—perhaps, indeed, by this. All missionary operations have of course been suspended. I have baptized two Greeks since I last wrote to you: and two other persons are at the portals of the kingdom. Limited as is my space, all insist upon sending their love. Messages, of course, excluded. Dear brother, continue to pray for us; pray without fainting, even though you receive not any evident answer to your petitions. Love to all. Do write soon and often. May every blessing be yours,

J. T. BARCLAY.

TO THE CHRISTIAN MISSIONARY SOCIETY.

JERUSALEM, October 13, 1851.

BROTHER CRANE—DEAR SIR:—Your very kind and welcome favor of July 21st was received more than a month ago, but owing to the distressing care of the sick room, it has remained thus long unanswered. We have all suffered, more or less, for the last three months, under repeated attacks of intermittent, remittent and continued fevers; but the most serious cases are those of my daughter's, (now in the fifth week of her attack, but, thanks to a gracious Providence, now considerably convalescent) and of my youngest son, who was confined to his bed two or three days later, now also improving; though neither of them is able to sit up more than a few minutes at a time. We were strongly urged by many of our friends not to spend our first few summers in the city; but all of us possessing good health and fine constitutions, somewhat inured, as we thought, to malarious exhalations, we concluded that our chance of escape was as good in our elevated and airy premises, into which the north-wind blows freshly every evening over the neighboring wall, as it would be in tents near the city—where the English, Germans and others are encamped. But had we then known as much of the insalubrity of the city during this season of the year, as we now do, to have continued in our house would savor more of *tempting* than trusting the Lord. Should we be spared another year, we propose spending the latter part of the summer and the early part of the fall at Saphet, just above the shores of Lake Galilee, which is a promising field for missionary labor, and quite a place of resort on account of its salubrious situation. Certain it is that it will be highly improper to spend this particular season in the city, until we shall have been somewhat acclimated. The present season is, however, unusually sickly—*three-fourths* of the inhabitants having been swept off in several of the native villages. The former attacks that we have had yielded very readily to the ordinary medical treatment; but the two present cases were so very anomalous in their character that I deemed it expedient, at a very early stage of the complaint, to request a consultation with the medical faculty here—two of whom, Drs. McGowan and Faukel, were kind enough to continue their attentions for ten or twelve days—my wife and self also having slight attacks in the meanwhile. You will be gratified to learn that we were sustained in a most remarkable manner during this trying time; and when it appeared as if the Lord would certainly take away one, if not both of my children, we became perfectly willing to give them up—unnatural as it may seem. But how would it be otherwise when they were so willing themselves, and beside, we could but fear that they might never be so well prepared for an exchange of worlds. It is sweet, indeed, thus to kiss the rod that smites us, and be enabled to feel that it is good to be afflicted. We have to regret, however, that for more than a month our missionary operations have been greatly interrupted, our studies altogether suspended, and medical practice almost entirely discontinued, although three or four dozen patients were daily applying for aid—this, however, must necessarily soon have been the case from want of appropriate medicines. Our public Wednesday night meetings have for a still longer time been discontinued on account of sickness in the families of our usual auditors; and one meeting on Lord's day is as much as we have been able to maintain during all this while.

There has been no rain for more than six months; but the "early rain" is expected now in a week or two, and then we may hope to see health restored to the city again. Had I written to you a few weeks ago, I might have given you an account of a very intelligent and pious German lady who, upon hearing one or two expositions of the truth, exhibited a certificate of her baptism by an American missionary, and joyfully cast in her lot among us: but alas! she has already fallen a victim to the prevailing fever—greatly rejoicing in the truth. Brother Murad has had a long though not very dangerous spell; but is now nearly reinstated in his usual health.

The Board having decided not to send a physician

to our aid, my sons, who have for some time been engaged in laying a good foundation for a course of medical studies, have determined to prepare, with all practical dispatch, to assist me in this department of my labors; and I hope one of them will soon be enabled to substitute me entirely in all ordinary cases, so that I can give myself constantly to the ministry of the word—until which time, however, I must, so far modify present arrangements as to spend one or two hours each day, or perhaps every other day, in dispensing medicines, giving medical advice, etc.

Yours in Christ,

JAS. T. BARCLAY.

DR. BARCLAY'S REPORT

TO THE BOARD OF MANAGERS OF THE AMERICAN CHRISTIAN BIBLE SOCIETY—CHRISTIAN SALUTATION.

JERUSALEM, October 13, 1851.

DEAR BRETHREN:—Although I have nothing of special interest to communicate in relation to the subject upon which I am about to address you—the distribution of the Scriptures purchased by the appropriation you were kind enough to make to this Mission; yet, as it is doubtless expected, and is altogether proper, if indeed not requisite, that you should be furnished with an account of the manner in which the commission confided to my charge has been executed, I embrace the present opportunity of communicating with the United States, to write you a fraternal epistle, by way of Report, upon the subject.

The brethren of the Eastern Virginia Co-operation having kindly placed in my hands the sum of two hundred and thirty-four dollars and fifty-two cents, for the purpose of circulating the Scriptures abroad, this amount has been united with your grant of three hundred dollars for the purpose of forming a common fund for the purchase of Bibles. Of this sum only three hundred and forty-four dollars and ten cents have been as yet vested in the sacred stock and material; but owing to high rates of exchange, and attendant expenses, only one hundred and ten dollars and thirty-one cents now remain on hand; the net amount realized being only four hundred and seventy-six dollars and six cents, and the purchases, costs, and discount amounting to three hundred and sixty-five dollars and seventy-five cents. But in order that you may have a more specific explanation, the following detailed statement is subjoined.

From the foregoing statement you perceive that in order to make your donation of money available in London, where the Scriptures in foreign languages are generally purchased, it must needs be subjected to discounting operations amounting to about one-eleventh of its amount, and this loss is still farther increased by a discount of five or six per cent. here—at least fifteen per cent. in all! Now should you find it in your hearts to make another grant, as I sincerely trust you will, I am glad to inform you that this heavy loss **need** not be incurred. Mr. J. Hosford Smith, our excellent consul at Beyroot, informs me that for every dollar deposited with E. O. Hamilton, Esq., No. 31 Bond street, New York, he will pay me ninety-six cents, or their equivalent in Turkish currency. But might it not be still better to purchase Spanish pillared dollars in New York, and ship them directly to Beyroot or Jaffa, for each of which places there are now regular conveyances several times a year from New York? We would then deal exclusively with the depository at Valetta. I doubt not that Brother Parmly of Bond street, New York, could furnish you with very exact information in relation to this whole matter.*

The version of Scripture principally distributed is, of course, the Arabic, that being the language universally spoken, and most generally read, throughout all these regions. But beside the Arabic translation, I have also distributed a goodly number of the Coptic, Syriac, Syro-Chaldaic, Judeo-Arabic, Turkish, Hebrew, modern and ancient Greek, Spanish, Judeo-Spanish, Italian, German, Armenian, and our own vernacular, here, as well as on the route hither. Bibles to a much larger extent might easily be distributed here in a short time; but Palestine has been so well supplied, that I deem it best to direct my main effort to the supply of pilgrims from a distance, of whom there are vast numbers here at the festivals, who come—the Greeks from Russia and Greece, the Armenians, from Constantinople and Armenia, the Copts,

---

* There is no such house now in existence.—BURNET.

and Abyssinians from the banks and sources of the Nile, the Mohammedans from far beyond the "Great River," the river Euphrates on the one hand, and from the Southern Pillar of Hercules on the other, the Romanists from the opposite Pillar of Gadez to the remotest of the many waters upon which the meretricious Scarlet Lady sitteth, and the poor outcast Israelite, "from every nation under heaven." For, strange to say, Jerusalem is as much the focus of religious feeling as it ever was. Hither the Tribes (not alone) of Israel, but of all the kindreds of the earth still come up.

From what you know of the Papal Apostasy, even in your own favored Valley, you are prepared to hear that very few members of the Roman Catholic, Greek, or Greek-Catholic Churches will accept a copy of the Word of the *Lord*, however implicitly they receive and obey the word of *man*. The Armenians, Copts, Abyssinians, and Syrians, are far more accessible, and frequently receive the Scriptures with readiness in the absence of their priests. The "common people," among the Jews, will generally receive at our hands the Hebrew Old Testament and frequently the New; and even among the Rabbins I have found some few, who will receive the New Testament, and promise to examine its claims upon their credence. But most of them obstinately reject it, even though they confess that they have never read it! The dogged obstinacy of some of these cabalistic devotees of the Talmud may be inferred from the following conversation (verbatim, as translated), which I held one evening with one of the most intelligent Scribes among them, in whose family I was administering medicine:

"I wish to talk with you about the Messiah;" said I to him, at what I thought might be an opportune season.

"But what's the use?" said he.

"Why this is the use; I believe that Jesus of Nazareth was the promised Messiah; and I accordingly worship and serve him. Now this is very wrong if he be not the Christ. But if, indeed, Jesus of Nazareth is the Messiah, it is very wrong in you not to acknowledge and obey him. Now I declare to you, if you can prove that the Messiah has not come, I will become a Jew this very evening; for if Christianity is not true, Judaism undoubtedly is. That's the use of talking about it. And if I prove Jesus of Nazareth to be your Messiah, will you not forthwith embrace him?"

"Oh! I can never believe that Jesus of Nazareth is *our* Messiah!"

"But don't you believe that Isaiah and Daniel were inspired prophets?"

"Oh, yes."

"How long, then, since the decree of Darius went forth to restore and rebuild Jerusalem?"

"I don't know exactly—(hemming)—I don't care about that."

"But has it not been more than seventy weeks, and was not Messiah the Prince to come in seventy weeks, or four hundred and ninety years from the going forth of that command?"

"I——, I —— (balked, silent, and confused), I——."

"Don't you really think that Shiloh has come?"

"No. I can never believe it."

"Well; has not the scepter departed from Judah, and the lawgiver from between his feet?"

"In some sense; but not as you Christians seem to think."

I went on to specify some of the Messianic prophecies of Isaiah, Micah, etc.; but he told me rather petulantly, that I need not tell him about any of these things; "for you certainly misunderstand them," said he, "for when the Messiah comes, there will never be another war, nor even a sword or *pistol* upon earth," quoting Isaiah ii.

"You take that passage literally, then?"

"Yes: certainly."

"Do you understand all the Scriptures in the same way, whether they be prose or poetry, narrative or prophecy?"

"Most certainly I do."

"Then you think that the wolf and the lamb shall be on good terms, and the lion, feeding no longer on flesh, shall literally eat grass like an ox, etc., when the Messiah comes?"

"Oh, yes; all Scripture must be construed literally, none of your figures!"

"Then you think that the three *branches* of which Pharaoh's butler dreamt are three *days really* and not figuratively?"

"Yes."

"And the three baskets three days too?"

"Yes."

Well, thought I, if it be a true axiom that things which are equal to the same are equal to one another, then a grape-vine and a basket are identical! So finding the rabbinical logic of this poor deluded son of Abraham so egregiously at fault, I was constrained to let him alone, knowing that

> "He that's convinced against his will,
> Is of the same opinion still."

He derives his support from the foreign Jewish contribution! and that is the secret of his ignorance and obstinacy. Of what a large class of these teachers may it be truly said, "they be blind leaders of the blind."

But it is gratifying to know that though the Jews and Christians so generally reject the Word of the Lord, some of the most influential devotees of Islamism not only willingly accept, but occasionlly earnestly ask for it. The truth is, Moslem intolerance and fanaticism are wonderfully on the wane. Never have I been more agreeably disappointed than by our reception at the hands of the Mohammedans! Instead of surly looks and even open insult and meditated injury, with which I expected to be treated, they have demeaned themselves with the utmost civility, respect, and kindness; particularly the upper classes—the effendis of the city, and the various officers who have been sent here from time to time from Constantinople. Some of the most influential among them have even gone so far as to wish me success! It is not, however, to be supposed for a moment that they have visited me in quest of the truth. Their curiosity may be the only motive; or they may be actuated by a desire to ascertain whether I have come to spy out the land; or, what is more probable, respect to the United States alone has dictated this respectful consideration for us. For at this time there is no power on earth so high in favor with the (*de*) crescent "moon and star," as the stars and stripes that "wave o'er the land of the free and the home of the" *blest*.

Although I have omitted much that I wished to say, yet my near approach to the end of the sheet compels me to come to a conclusion; and when I mention that this desultory communication has been written, amid unceasing interruptions, at the bedside of my children during their convalescence, I trust it will be regarded with that indulgence, to which the circumstances entitle it. And now, brethren, I commend you to God and the word of his grace. May your efforts to disseminate that Word, by which you are built up in the most holy faith, be crowned with the richest success; and may the beauty of the Lord our God be upon us, and the work of our hands, may *He* establish it!

With highest Christian regards, yours in the Lord,

J. T. BARCLAY.

DR. BARCLAY IN ACCOUNT WITH AMERICAN CHRISTIAN BIBLE SOCIETY.

Amount appropriated by American Christian Bible Society	$300 00	
Amount appropriated by Eastern Virginia Co-operation	234 52	
Total amount contributed in United States' funds		534 52
From this amount deduct 10⅓ per cent. discount on Bill of Exchange on Baring, Brothers & Co., at sixty days	56 07	
Further discount for cashing bill in London	2 39	
		58 46
Amount realized in London		476 06
Deduct bill with British and Foreign Bible Society	166 75	
Bill with Society for Propagating Christianity among the Jews,	32 50	
Other purchases for S. School, etc	12 00	
Bill with Depository at Valetta,	7 50	
		218 75
		257 31
Draft for this sum discounted in Jerusalem at 5⅓ per cent		14 15
		243 16
Freight, storage, commissions, etc		7 50
Balance on hand March 1, 1851		235 66
Bill with Beyroot Mission, for Arabic Testaments, etc., (July 29)		50 35
		185 31
Printing Press (purchased on account of Virginia contribution)		75 00
Leaving balance on hand, October 1, 1851		$110 31

DR. BARCLAY AND THE POLANDERS.

JERUSALEM, January 30, 1852.

MY DEAR BROTHER BURNET:—Providence permitting, this will either be handed to you in person by Captain Tabaczynski and son, or else mailed for you in New York. In the former event it will serve the purpose of an introductory note; and in the latter, you must regard it as a mere familiar epistle. Should they conclude to stop at Cincinnati on their way to Iowa, you will find them accomplished gentlemen, of polished manners, and, what will interest you far more—Christians of the primitive stamp.

The Captain and his son were brought to serious reflection by the unfortunate issue of the Hungarian struggle; and they came to the resolution, during their long detention in Turkey, to visit Jerusalem as soon as liberated, in the hope of finding a religion that would afford them rather more solace than that of "The Beast." But vain were all their *Diogenes-like* investigations, for a length of time. Instead of finding that pure, soul-cheering religion which they expected could but be flowering around the tomb of our Saviour, the mummery and superstition which they found so rife in every chapel of the "Church of the Holy Sepulcher," led them to the conclusion of those who visited the Sepulcher eighteen hundred years ago— " they have taken away the Lord, and we know not where they have laid him." At length, however, they accidentally (or I should rather say *providentially*), found one of our proselytes engaged in reading the Bible; and on learning that no man had a right to *forbid Scripture*, that they should not be privileged to read and judge for themselves, gladly accepted a copy of the Bible, and eagerly read it—particularly such portions as they were told would teach them the nature of true Christianity. When I inform you that these earnest inquirers twice attended our public services, and also received instruction informally some half a dozen times, according to the form of sound words, you may safely guess the result. They were so impressed by the simplicity of our services, contrasted with anything they had ever witnessed before, in the way of devotion and instruction, that they were literally ready to "fall down on their faces, and confess that God was in us of a truth." It would greatly rejoice your heart to witness their joy in the possession of the *Truth*, and the earnestness with which they study the Bible. Brother Julius says his highest ambition is to become prepared to preach the Gospel. Those brethren, not content with enjoying this great salvation themselves—like one of old, who, when he had found the Messiah, made it his first business to tell others that he had found Him of whom Moses (in the law) and the Prophets did speak—embrace every opportunity of

> " Telling to sinners all around
> What a dear Saviour they have found."

Accordingly they explain the nature of the Kingdom to a Polander, with whom they met, who, like themselves had come on a pilgrimage to Jerusalem from religious considerations; and so much of the truth had he already learned from them and another convert, that I felt fully assured, from his earnest countenance and suffused eyes, that the instruction thus conveyed was by no means in vain; and after only two interviews with him I was fully persuaded, that he was altogether a fit subject for baptism; and accordingly (after spending much of the intermediate time in giving him further instruction), I baptized him the next morning. After spending a few days with us he will have to return to his business in Smyrna—a fact that I can but regret—though he is doing a good business there, and I have every confidence in his steadfastness.

The abjuration of Romanism by these three gentlemen has excited "no little stir" in the Latin Quarter, as I am informed. The Romanists of this city are exulting not a little over a proselyte they have made from the Lutherans—a fact which I deeply regret; for, notwithstanding the mere *tweedledum-tweedledee* difference of *con* and *trans*, in a very important matter, yet Lutheranism, in its very worst state, is infinitely preferable to Romanism in its best dress—even as seen in the United States. And beside, the gentleman referred to is a man of some standing in the medical world, and quite a friend of mine. Strong and peculiar influences, however, have been brought to bear upon him, and there is "still hope in Israel concerning this matter." Considerable interest was excited a short time ago, by a rumor that the Roman Catholics of Bethlehem were about to become Protestants *en masse*, and join the Prussio-Anglican church of this city; and, from all that I could learn, they would have done so but for the interference of the French Consul. The matter, it seems, was in this wise: The Pacha wanted money, and the Catholics of Bethlehem being *natives*, were assessed in common with other subjects of the Sultan throughout his Pachalic: but believing that should they turn *British* Protestants, and place themselves under the protection of the Lion and the Unicorn, they would be beyond the reach of such exactions, they began to think that auricular confession, saint-worship, indulgence, *et id omne genus*, were not such good things after all, and had well nigh come to the conclusion, that to read the Word of God was not so *sinful* as their "*padres*" had represented it! But in the meantime, their levy was paid off by the French Consul, (it is said, but most probably by the Latins of this city), and lo! reading the Bible again becomes a sin, and indulgences, purgatory, etc., are as orthodox as ever.

Only two of the four individuals, who, I think, I informed you some time ago, had determined to be baptized, have put on Christ—owing to an unfortunate family disagreement, but with the conduct of these two, I am much pleased.

I addressed you, some time ago, a report in relation to the Bible Fund, intrusted to me, and I believe, one or two others, communicated since, all of which, I hope, reached you safely. I also addressed a communication to our well-beloved Brother Crane, which I hope was received in due time.

No one knows better than yourself, the important bearing of Christian intercourse upon practical Christianity. I trust, therefore, my dear brother, that should the Captain and his son tarry a few days in Cincinnati, you will (if convenient) introduce him to some of the brethren, who will be kind enough to favor them with their fraternal intercourse and Christian instruction. It is no easy matter, as may be well conceived, to discard all errors and adopt truths, utterly subversive of all they have ever learned on the subject of religion.

Will sister B. and yourself please accept assurances of the highest Christian esteem and affection from all my family as well as myself. All my time, not necessarily appropriated otherwise, being almost entirely occupied in teaching these new converts, I know you will readily excuse these crude thoughts thus hastily thrown out. As there is still room for a line or two, I will just add, that the Jews are now more accessible than they have heretofore been; but what will be the effect of the chief Rabbi's tyranny, in withholding the *portion* of the *common fund* from a Rabbi with whom I have lately had several very interesting conversations, is yet to be seen. Pray to the God of Abraham, Isaac and Israel, that this poor wanderer, and many others with him, may be brought into the fold of the Redeemer.

As ever, Yours most sincerely,

J. T. BARCLAY.

The Brother Tabaczinsky, mentioned by Brother Barclay, brought the above letter to this city during the summer of 1852. His history possesses much of interest. As a Polander, he was involved in the struggle which issued in the downfall of his country. Before that event he was imprisoned for several years. His patriotic feelings implicated him in the defection of Hungary from Austria. He was a captain of Polish lancers under General Bem, who makes honorable mention of him in papers which I have seen. When he visited Jerusalem, he was but just released from prison at Aleppo. Then he thought himself a rich man. He went from Jerusalem to Egypt; thence by ship to London, where, instead of meeting his wife and the proceeds of his estate, he was informed by letter, that he was a widower without a farthing. He is familiar with the French, German and Italian languages, but speaks the English yet imperfectly.

ANNUAL REPORT OF THE JERUSALEM MISSION.

JERUSALEM, February 9, 1852.

WELL-BELOVED BRETHREN:—Had I the opportunity of meeting with the saints in the church gathered together, it would afford me great pleasure to "rehearse all that God hath done with us," and for us, since we entered upon the work whereunto we have been called; but as the nature of existing circumstances necessarily precludes the enjoyment of such a privilege, I must be content merely to make, to those by whom I have been more specially " commended to the grace of God," a brief written statement of such matters only as may seem more particularly to claim attention—a duty which the expiration of the first year's existence of the mission naturally suggests, by way of Report; for it was on yesterday twelve months ago that we unfurled the banner of primeval Christianity within the precincts of the "Holy City."

The initiatory operations of a mission in a foreign field are necessarily attended with peculiar difficulties; hinderances of a temporal as well as a spiritual nature. Beside the difficulty and delay attendant upon the establishment of a household in a land so deficient in the most ordinary comforts of civilized life, the missionary has to become acquainted with the peculiar views and habits of the people, as well as their language, before he can reasonably expect to become useful. And these difficulties, necessarily incident (more or less) to all foreign missions, are greatly aggravated, where, as in the present case, there are rival religions, some of which are maintained by the purse, and others defended by the sword. And when, in addition to these great obstacles, he finds that the cause he would present has been so perverted and degraded among them, that the very name he wears is a standing term of reproach; and that, while he is unable to *preach* Christianity to the people as he would wish, owing to his ignorance of their intricate language, he is also greatly hindered from commending its excellence to their contemplation as a living reality, owing to the very serious disabilities arising from his subjection to an unhealthy climate, it is evident that no little time must elapse before these formidable obstacles can be surmounted; and hence our inexpressible gratitude to the Author and Giver of all good—temporal and spiritual—that notwithstanding these disadvantages, we are still in the enjoyment of such abounding mercies; and that during the short space of our sojourn here, twelve persons have already practically embraced the "truth as it is in Jesus," and seem determined, with full "purpose of heart, to cleave unto the Lord." It pains me, however, to add, (as I must in faithfulness do), that one lately numbered with our little flock, taken from among the lost sheep of the house of Israel, who ran so well at first, and of whom we entertained such fair hopes—influenced by considerations of a carnal and pecuniary nature—placed before him for the express purpose of drawing him away, so frequently absented himself from the ordinances of the Lord's house, that we were constrained to exclude him from the congregation. I ought to add, however, that owing to the shameful laxity of discipline that prevails here, even among some styling themselves Protestants, he was induced to believe that his remissness and obliquities of conduct would be tolerated. And although he deems himself rather harshly dealt with, I understand he has expressed himself willing to return, provided no explanation or apology be required of him; but the spirit he still manifests renders a profession of repentance and amendment of life an indispensable prerequisite to his restoration. Owing to our protracted illness, and the indisposition and absence of Brother Murad, the two Greek members of our congregation have doubtless suffered for instruction, and hence they evince rather too much partiality for some of the superstitious notions of the Greek Catholic Church, in the faith of which they have been raised. But so great was their ignorance, and so inveterate their prepossessions in favor of certain tenets which have grown with their growth, and strengthened with their strength, that they have not only needed line upon line and precept upon precept, but no little forbearance with their waywardness. With these exceptions (and possibly another), our little flock may be said—if not in *all* things to adorn the doctrine of Christ—at least to be very orderly, and observant of the means of grace. Exclusive of the individual above alluded to, and two immersed persons regularly worshiping with us, and usually reckoned with us, (one of whom has fallen asleep in Christ, and the other not being a permanent resident here), the names on our church list amount to seventeen. One, however, resides in Smyrna, and two are about to set sail for the remote west of your own favored land; so that the number now worshiping here, and constituting our church, is only fourteen.

Had it been my intention merely to establish a church of numerical strength, the number might have been considerably increased. But I have been constrained by a sense of duty, either to reject some applicants outright, upon their own statement, or on detection of an improper motive; or else to urge upon

JERUSALEM MISSION. 221

them the necessity of a closer examination of the Bible and their own hearts, in such terms as have generally prevented a renewal of their application. This, of course, has been a most painful duty, and deeply do I feel the responsibility thus incurred. But that I have acted properly, (at least in most of these cases), I am happy in knowing that I have the entire approbation of my own conscience. And that I may enjoy the approval of your valued judgment also, I will briefly state such of the cases as will enable you to form a just estimate of the whole.

A, brings testimonials highly commending him as a teacher, etc. He is already in the service of a mission, but tells me, in plain terms, that if I will give him a little more than his present allowance, he will join our church. The proposal of this Herodian is, of course, rejected without hesitation.

B, a gentleman of very high literary and scientific attainments, and possessing undoubted piety, wishes to know whether our society would employ him, were he to unite with us. Now, while I have great respect for the individual, I could but speak to him in language so discouraging as to deter him at least from the repetition of any such proposition.

C, who has long been a sub-officer in a Protestant church, asks the appointment of an hour for a special interview; and comes in very respectable company to make a formal proposition to unite with us himself, and also bring along a number of others with him. These persons, he alleges, are compelled from conscientious considerations to withdraw from their church; and they propose to form an "independent church," upon principles of "toleration and union," under my direction. Now this seemed quite laudable in some respects; but upon explaining to him the nature of the Christian Institution, he is found to be not only ignorant of its very first principles, but in direct opposition to some of them. Upon further conversation, it is discovered that they propose sending agents abroad to solicit funds for their maintenance in the Holy City, after the manner of Jews, Christians, and heathens here. And so the proposition being clearly ascribable to carnal motives rather than principle, it is entirely discountenanced: the divinely-appointed plan of contributing toward the support of the saints when unavoidably poor, is explained; the sin of supporting a church in willful idleness is exposed, and the good old way of Christian union, according to sound words and sound principles, is urged upon their consideration.

D, a youth of some promise, whose history may be found in the Jewish Intelligence, Vol. 15, No. 174, as detailed at an annual meeting of the London Jews' Society, states that he has heard that we discard all human forms and ceremonies, and have a plain religion, which he thinks must be the religion of the Bible; and beseeches me to receive him into our congregation. But it is discovered on conversing with him, during this and subsequent interviews, that he is entirely ignorant of the difference between us and the church of which he is a member: and it plainly appears from all the circumstances of the case, that he is influenced more by a desire to obtain *personal* protection, than by love for the truth. But although it is evident that his proposed change is too much the dictate of wordly policy, the "good old way" is plainly set before him; he is exhorted to search the Scriptures, to see whether the things I tell him are so, and to scrutinize his motives more closely.

E, a member of a popular Christian community, who, though at first much opposed to us, yet, on attending our meetings, and hearing the Christian system explained, was convinced of the truth; but on avowing his dissatisfaction with his creed, was forced, strange as it may seem, to make choice between a removal to a distant station, and a continuance here (should he remain in his church), under restrictions most galling to a sensitive conscience; or in the event of dissolving his ecclesiastical connection, and becoming obedient to the faith once delivered to the saints— severe persecution. After long halting between two opinions, he adopted the alternative of a removal to a distant post. Notwithstanding his distrust of Providence, and his dread of persecution, he seemed, in the main, to be under the influence of proper principles; and I could but lament that one so nigh the kingdom, should feel himself constrained to go away so sorrowful. He compounded matters with his conscience, by resolving to return and obey the Lord fully, after he shall have secured the means of living here independently of others.

F, was acquainted with Messrs. Whiting, Lenneau, etc.—likes them very much, and wishes to become an

American Christian! But upon familiarly conversing with him, and dwelling upon the evil of being actuated by sinister motives in professing religion, so much ignorance of the Scriptures, and such superstition and carnality of motive are developed, that I am compelled to content myself with advising him to probe his heart, and imitate the example of the noble Bereans. But after a few more visits, during which I instruct him how to become a *Bible* Christian and to continue one—and dwell upon the necessity of rigid discipline, I see him no more.

G, and wife, Jews, lately from Egypt, seem to be sincere inquirers after truth. They are poor—scarcely able even now to maintain themselves, and know full well that they will not only be deprived of their portion of the general fund for the support of the Jews residing here, but will be dreadfully persecuted as soon as it becomes known that they profess faith in Jesus of Nazareth. In this predicament, they inquire whether we can afford them any shelter and assistance if they are baptized. Now, although this circumstance is apparently much against them, yet, after making due allowance for their ignorance, there seems, upon further inquiry, to be no sufficient ground to challenge the sincerity of their motive, however much we may pity their indecision and distrust.

I might mention the case of a Copt, and several other persons, professing faith and repentance, and yet unfit subjects for baptism, in my estimation, for various reasons; but to multiply cases would only be consuming time uselessly. The state of society in the

"Holy" City (the city of three *Sabbath* days per week), is deplorable in the extreme; and it would seem that there are few places on all the earth where the propagation of Christianity (even when somewhat accommodated to the taste of the age, by a liberal admixture of philosophy, Judaism and Paganism) is attended with greater difficulties than at this same Jerusalem, where it succeeded so triumphantly at first. In proof of this, I need only refer to the vast expenditure of treasure and effort here on the part of several powerful missionary societies. The American Board of Commissioners for Foreign Missions sent two missionaries here as long ago as 1821; and their mission was well sustained (with occasional interruptions) by a strong band of most excellent, devoted and talented men, till about four or five years ago, during all which time three converts were all the fruits of this great outlay. The persevering efforts of the Lutherans have been still more barren of good results. The London Jews' Society have had missionaries here, more or less constantly, for more than a quarter of a century; and in 1834 they established a regular mission on a very extensive scale, which has been lavishly supplied with chaplains, missionaries, colporteurs, helps, governments, etc., under its learned "Lord Bishops." A splendid church edifice has been erected, at a total cost, as I am informed by the architect, of £70,000; an extensive and well-conducted Hospital established; well-endowed literary and manual-labor institutions founded, and money funded for the purpose of "aiding inquiring Jews," "assisting to establish converts in business," etc. Beside the money already so extensively invested in real estate by the society, thirty or forty thousand dollars are annually expended in support of the missions, which is not only under the auspices of that powerful and wealthy society, (one of whose patrons alone has recently given it $300,000), but is under the special care and patronage of two of the most enlightened and potent monarchs in Europe, (Victoria and Frederick William), both of whom maintain able consuls in the city, for the special protection of its members. And yet, during the thirty years' labors of its various well-sustained and energetic agents, the number of converts made in this city, even with all the worldly inducements set before them, amounts to only a score or two, more than three-fourths of whom are retained in the service of the society at salaries far more than adequate to their support.

Not a single convert from Mohammedism has been made by either of these denominations, nor by the combined efforts of the dozen different Christian sects of Jerusalem; but on the contrary, several Christians have actually gone over to the Moslems and Jews!

And yet, notwithstanding all these great discouragements, I can but regard Jerusalem as one of the most important missionary stations on earth; and cannot help believing that "the faith once delivered to the saints" would soon number its converts here by hundreds, but for one main difficulty, which, although we have not the power to remove entirely, can yet be counteracted to a considerable extent. The site originally selected by Divine Providence as the grand radiating point of the light of salvation, possesses all the advantages now that it ever did, for enlightening the greatest possible number of the benighted sons and daughters of Adam; for hither, as to no other place on earth, the tribes, not only of Jews but of Gentiles of every nation still resort for religious purposes. With Africa, the dwelling-place of the children of Ham, on one side, and Asia, the hive-like abode of Shem's descendants, on the other, and in front the Mediterranean (that great highway to the everywhere-dwelling sons of Japhet) dividing, yet uniting, the lands of Shem and Ham, and the Isles of the Gentiles, what spot could be more admirably situated for the wide and speedy diffusion of truth! Be it, then, that "the city is walled up to heaven," and the children of Anak dwell here—drawing our resources alone from the armory of Heaven, are we not able to fully rescue "the city of the Great King" from its Canaanitish oppressors, by whom it is trodden under foot—whether open enemies or pretended friends? The great obstacle to which I alluded as so formidably opposed to the revival of pure religion in this city, and upon which I wish to say a few words, is confessedly one of some delicacy; but the importance of the subject, I trust, will sufficiently plead my apology for using so much plainness of speech only as will enable me to make myself understood by you. I allude to the practice of *supporting converts*, which prevails here, to a greater or less extent, among all professions of religion—Christians, Jewish and Mohammedan? But as this assertion may sound rather strangely and uncharitably if unsustained by evidence, I beg leave to adduce the testimony of several persons (at least so far as Christian converts are concerned), whose character and position constitute them unimpeachable witnesses. Mr. Spencer, an Episcopal minister who spent some time here in 1849, remarks, (page 275—" Sketches of Travel in Palestine," etc.), when speaking of the Luthero-Episcopal mission here, that "the mission to the Jews has not only got to convince them of their guilt and perversity in rejecting the Messiah, but, on their professing Christianity, is obliged to undertake their temporal support also, as a necessary consequence."

Mr. Williams, chaplain to this same Prussio-Anglican mission, observes (page 570, vol. 2, of his "Holy City,") when speaking of the proselytes made by the missionaries of the American Board of Commissioners for Foreign Missions, that "there were three of these men—I believe not more. The Missionaries have taken charge of their families, as they were bound to do." Dr. Zischendorf, in his "Travels in the East," page 159, goes so far as to say that "conversions in Jerusalem are framed to an accommodation with the most modern Judaism, and six thousand piasters (about £50), with other advantages, are offered to the converts as a premium." Now, while I cannot believe that the gravest item of this charge is literally true, yet I lament to say, there is far too much of truth in it; for it is undeniably true that worldly inducements of a very tempting character are held forth, the effect of which (not to say design), is both to make proselytes and to retain them in ecclesiastical connection, upon principles not countenanced by the Word of God. It is a matter deeply to be regretted, that gentlemen so worthy as I know some of the members of this Mission to be, should have fallen into a practice so unfavorable to the interests of pure religion. The existence of a custom so fraught with evil tendencies, renders great circumspection necessary on the part of the evangelist, who would have his converts influenced alone by moral principle, apart from all worldly motives. And in this time-serving latitude, nothing seems better calculated to render his efforts abortive, than the necessity (imposed upon him by such a state of things), of frequently and solemnly protesting against a practice so congenial to the vitiated taste of a crooked and perverse generation; and especially when, as in the present instance, his meaning is perverted, and undue advantage of his protestation is taken, to create the impression that the opposite course argues not only a want of interest in the temporal, but spiritual welfare of the convert!

But while this practice of placing before the *sinner* any worldly motive to embrace Christianity, or *retain* him in the church, is so much to be deprecated, yet situated as matters are *here*, it may nevertheless be both proper and expedient, to provide a kind of asylum to which the poor persecuted convert might retreat, should it be necessary, and keep himself from violence and starvation, on becoming obedient to the faith, but by no means *before* he yields obedience. For surely it is not the dictate of sound philosophy, to be deterred from the proper *use* of a good principle, on account of its *abuse* by others; and that poor suffering saints should receive the sympathy and aid of their brethren is a truth, that none professing a regard for the Bible will deny. I venture, therefore, to suggest the propriety of having such an asylum, for reasons which will fully appear, when we consider the consequences attendant upon a change of religion in the East generally, but especially in this city.

When a Jew or Mussulman becomes a Christian (and the same may be said of a member of any of the Oriental sects of Christians who turn Protestant), he is immediately regarded as an outcast; and if he is so fortunate as to escape stripes and imprisonment, he is at least anathematized and outlawed. His former brethren will neither buy from him nor sell to him, nor indeed have any dealings whatever, except to maltreat him. And in many instances, not only is his portion of the public fund withheld, but his wife and children are forcibly taken away from him; or, if he happens to have influence enough to retain them, they must share his persecution. Nor is the ill-treatment confined even to himself and family, but extends far beyond the sphere of his own immediate household. Let his avocation be what it may, he can no longer derive a support from it, if at all dependent upon the patronage of the community of which he was a member. And few indeed are the occupations in which he can compete successfully and honorably with the mendacious Arab, the circumventing Turk, the wily Jew, and the tricking *Christian!* or which he can pursue profitably enough to gain the most scanty livelihood—so general is overreaching among tradesmen, mechanics, and persons of all classes! Truly fortunate is it for our converts here, that such as are dependent, happen to derive their support from travelers and other Franks.

Under existing circumstances, the conviction has forced itself upon my mind, that if we had a small piece of land, near the city, with a few cheaply-constructed houses, or an establishment within the city, with a few rooms for workshops, tools, etc., where persecuted converts could retire in case of necessity, and escape starvation by cultivating the earth, or laboring at some trade, such an asylum, presenting, as it would, no worldly motive to embrace religion, and yet affording to such as might need it, a safe temporary retreat from persecution, would be a great desideratum; for while it would accomplish all that would be desirable in the way of assistance, it would be entirely exempt from the objections that apply with so much force to those arrangements by which carnal considerations are placed before the sinner, which, whether designed or not, cannot fail to operate as inducements to embrace Christianity from mere secular considerations. Nor would it be any slight proof of his sincerity, if the convert is willing to embrace Christianity in Jerusalem with the understanding that, beyond this temporary shelter, he is to expect no temporal relief whatever, except what all helpless saints are entitled to from the weekly contribution, should he become unavoidably poor and disabled.

It may be said, however, that if a person is not willing to bear the brunt of persecution and even endure the pangs of starvation, he is unworthy of admission into the kingdom, and that we ought therefore to rejoice in having his faith subjected to such a test; and this is readily conceded, provided his opportunities and means of information are such as to enable him to discriminate properly on these subjects. But to suppose the ability of doing this, at least between the Christianity of the Bible, and Protestantism, as taught in some of the less exceptionable creeds, would be conceding far too much to the great majority of persons in this anti-Bible-reading part of the world. So superior to all the religions of the East, is Protestantism, in its very worst garb, that a person, in forsaking any of these corrupt communities, may be expected readily to embrace the views of any of the Protestant sects, with their "loaves and fishes," in preference to primitive Christianity, with disfranchisements and persecutions. Some little allowance must undoubtedly be made for the defective optics of those from whose eyes the scales of rabbinical cabalism have not yet entirely fallen, or, who, being as yet on the outskirts of Babylon, still view the matter through a misty medium. There are now in the city, a Jew and a Greek priest, who, from all I can discover, are proper subjects for baptism; but they are both rather poor, and would no doubt be dreadfully persecuted—particularly the latter. The Jew, having an independent trade, could easily make a living, were he sheltered awhile; but the priest being unaccustomed to do anything but swing a censer, hear confessions, etc., could do but little, till he could be instructed in some handicraft, which he earnestly desires. Such facilities, with ample protection, are afforded by all the denominations here; and it is highly probable that they will, therefore, become members of the "Hebrew Christian Church," which has, in addition to these facilities, so many lay benefices at its disposal.

What is to be done? Should such an asylum as that suggested, be provided or not? But the question is submitted entirely to the decision of your better judgment, assured as I am, that you can best determine whether the time has arrived, that the Disciples should grant the proposed relief to the brethren who dwell in Judea, and should again " send their liberality to Jerusalem."

Notwithstanding the almost total suspension of my usual medical practice, for several months, on account of my own illness, and that of my family, I have had the pleasure of relieving about two thousand cases of sickness, during the past year. And the conclusion to which my experience brings me, is, that the practice of medicine is a most important auxiliary to missionary operations, and should by no means be discontinued. I know of no means whatever, by which access can be had to so many, and so cheaply and favorably, too, as by the gratuitous administration of medicine to the poor of the city and its dependencies.

We had hoped to enjoy entire exemption from fever

during the winter, and become well fortified for the next sickly season; but we are still subject to frequent slight attacks, of a few days' continuance, notwithstanding all our precautionary measures as to exercise, diet, etc. Had we such a place, however, as that proposed, where we might occasionally retire and recuperate, beyond the reach of the miasm of the city, I think we would soon and safely become acclimated.

So greatly have our studies of language been interrupted by sickness, the absence of our Dragoman, and other unavoidable circumstances, that our progress has not corresponded with our desires or expectations. That the Arabic, however, is very difficult of acquisition, even on the part of one who devotes the most of his time to it, you will readily infer, from the fact related to me a few days ago, by a missionary from Gafit, that a missionary from Lebanon, who had been assiduously studying it for six years, was requested by some Arabs, at the conclusion of his *Arabic discourse*, not to speak to them any more in the *Turkish* language, but in the *Arabic*, so that they might understand him!

Another consequence of our sickness has been the dismission of the few scholars we had, till recently, when we gave notice of our readiness to resume our little operations in the way of teaching; but as yet, we have only one regular and two irregular scholars. As there is no express apostolic precept or precedent in relation to schools, and it is by no means proposed to plead the example of others, as a rule of practice for us, yet, I may be allowed to mention, that the

English and Germans have large and flourishing schools in various parts of this city, and in some of the neighboring towns, upon which they mainly base their hopes of ultimate success.

A Jewish Rabbi, with whom I have lately had several interesting conversations, wished me, some time ago, to teach two of his children, and says that other Jews would send their children, if I would open a school on Mount Zion; but it was impracticable to attend to it at the time, and his children are now in one of the Episcopal schools. I entertain some hope that the fulminations of the synagogue and the withholding of his stipend, consequent upon this resistance to the authority of the chief Rabbi, may so open his eyes that he will heartily confess and gladly obey the Messiah, which, I am persuaded, he would already have done but "for fear of the Jews."

Invoking a continuance of your highly valued counsel, prayers and co-operation, I remain, dear brethren, most sincerely and affectionately,

Yours in the Lord,

J. T. BARCLAY.

The portraiture of Eastern duplicity and incorrigibleness, given in the above report, presents no very encouraging aspect of missionary success. But this picture is not as dark as one delineated by the *Historical Sketch of the Presbyterian Mission in Damascus*, drawn up by order of the Association of the

Mission, and presented at its meeting held in Bludan, on Wednesday, July 15, 1851.

It was resolved, in July, 1841, by the General Assembly of the Presbyterian Church, in Ireland, "to establish a mission to the seed of Abraham." They commenced the mission in Damascus, in 1843, with strong force.

Previous to that time Damascus had been sometimes visited, but never permanently occupied by Protestant missionaries. In 1824, it was included in a missionary tour by Messrs. King, Fish and Cook. Ten years afterward it was visited by the Rev. Eli Smith and Dr. Dodge. In 1837, Mr. Holmes, now of Constantinople, who came to Syria to devote a year to the study of Arabic, spent a few months in the city. During his stay he had a few boys under his instruction, and he is still gratefully mentioned by some of the natives. Damascus was again visited in May, 1841, by the Rev. Mr. Wolcott. All these persons were agents of the American Board of Commissioners for Foreign Missions. Several persons from the London Jewish Society, and perhaps also from other societies, have made passing visits; but no permanent occupation was attempted by any of them, nor were any abiding results produced.

The Report embraces a period of eight years, and in different parts of it we have such statements as these:

"Soon after Doeb's affair, Yusef Shatela, a member of the Greek Church, applied to be received as a Protestant. Applications of a like nature have indeed often been made, but generally by ignorant persons, sometimes by immoral persons, and always for some worldly object, which they scarcely ever attempted to conceal."

To this add :—

"Sometimes Jews, and sometimes Christians, came seeking to join us; but they went away as soon as they learned that they could not gain the particular worldly object which they had in view."

All this demonstrates that Brother Barclay has not fallen upon the worst population of the East. His success has also been greater than usual among the sons of Shem. Not to mention the first six years of fruitless labor by Judson, with similar cases in the South Seas, and those alluded to by Brother Barclay himself, this Presbyterian report of the Damascus mission, thus discourses of the first success, after more than seven years' labor among the native Damascenes:—

"At the afternoon service on the 9th of January, 1851, held in the house of Meshakah, for the occasion, Mr. Robson baptized Ibrahim, son of Mikhail Meshakah, born on the 29th of November preceding. This was the first administration of a sacrament to a native."

There were but few other conversions of Greeks, etc. An infant of six weeks is the first fruits of Damascus, where there had been regular Hebrew and Arabic service for many years.

We have reason, then, to be much encouraged with the **first** year's effort to plant the standard of the Cross in the land where it was originally used to torture our Lord, and to crucify his cause. We should devoutly thank and praise the Author of our Holy Religion, for the blessings which he has conferred upon his cause. We should beseech our Father above to continue his benignant smiles upon Immanuel's land.

DR. BACON AND DR. BARCLAY.

JERUSALEM, February 15, 1852.

DEAR BROTHER BURNET:—Soon after my arrival here, a rumor was bruited from Dan to Beersheba, that a man who did not even believe in the divinity of Immanuel, had dared to come to teach Christianity even at the spot where our Lord was entombed; of the existence of which I was kindly informed by Dr. DeForrest, of Beyroot, who had it from the Vicar of "my lord Bishop," Gebat. I promptly denied the foul charge, and demanded through Dr. DeForrest an explanation from my traducers; and greatly to my surprise, Dr. Leonard Bacon was given as authority. But I can by no means believe that he could have been guilty of such an aspersion, after our repeated conversations on board the steamer, in one of which I remember distinctly to have taken occasion expressly to disclaim a tenet so derogatory to the character of the Divine Redeemer.

Now, my dear brother, I learn that Dr. Bacon is appointed to preach the introductory, at the meeting of the American Board of Commissioners for Foreign Missions in your city next fall; and deeming it right to allow the doctor the opportunity of denying the paternity of such a slander, I merely add this note, that if you deem it expedient, and it be altogether convenient and agreeable, you can apprise him of the blot that thus stains his escutcheon, and allow him the opportunity of wiping it off. You will not understand me as making a *request*, but simply submitting the matter to your superior discretion.

We get some hard cuffs in undergoing our probation, but such a thrust as this, (at such a time, and in such a place), is surely " the most unkindest cut of all. The good Lord give us grace " patiently to endure all things, that we may inherit the promises."

With affection and esteem most sincere,

Yours in Christ,

Jas. T. Barclay.

———

To wait till next autumn seems tardy justice to either of these gentlemen. If Dr. Bacon has been misrepresented by the Vicar of the Bishop of Jerusalem, the sooner his disclaimer is published, the better for his own justification, and for the comfort of the wrongfully accused missionary. If Dr. Bacon has done to his brother an injury in affirming of him what is incorrect, the case is still more urgent, and, therefore, the earliest opportunity should be afforded to the latter to make the amende honorable. Further, if Dr. Bacon has accused Dr. Barclay of serious error in Palestine, it is to be supposed that he would repeat his assertion in Europe and America, and, therefore, this public denial is demanded.

If any one will inform us of the present whereabouts of Dr. Bacon, this copy of the Age shall be forwarded to him, that our pages may contain his rejoinder.

The foregoing letter, and my appended remarks, I regularly mailed to Dr. Bacon on two occasions, but receiving no reply, I supposed that they never met his eye, or that he found it desirable to effect a retreat in silence.

MOUNT OLIVET, September 1, 1852.

BELOVED BROTHER:—My communications have been so numerous for the last few months, both by mail, and by private conveyance, that I could by no means reconcile it to my sense of propriety to tax you with another so soon, had you not specially requested a monthly communication—lest I should *terrify* you with letters. Some of my communications, however, must have been lost or greatly delayed on the way, as you mention in your letter of the 24th of June (which I had the pleasure of receiving a week or two ago), that you were "painfully anxious concerning" us on account of the length of time elapsed without intelligence from the Mission.

The eight hundred dollar draft which you mention

as *en route* for London, has safely arrived, as I learn by a letter received a few days since from Messrs. Baring & Co., and its avails will be applied to the purchase of a suitable piece of property for the purpose proposed, as soon as practicable. No little circumspection is necessary, I find, in order to guard against imposition, and secure a valid title; and I am, therefore, proceeding very cautiously.

The inclosed abstract of the pecuniary concerns of the mission, will, I hope, be considered sufficient as a reply to your request that I should "speak freely in relation to financial matters at large." Should you not have received a special account of the respective items constituting the aggregate of expenditures, please inform me, that I may forward them again. I should mention, however, that about fifteen dollars have been voluntarily contributed by travelers, and appropriated for the benefit of the sick, according to request (except brother Picket's subscription, which he wishes reserved toward building a house of worship). The medicines, books, etc., to which you allude, have not yet come to hand, nor ever been heard of; but still I hope they are not lost, but only delayed in transit, at the grand depot at Alexandria, as it is not unfrequently the case when the parcels are but few or small. Although I had but little occasion for medicine for some time after leaving the city, yet the non-arrival of medicinal supplies is now felt as a serious disadvantage, since our residence here has become generally known; for I now have very numerous applications, not only from the citizens of Jerusalem, but from the

Fellahin of the neighboring villages, the Bedawin of the desert, and pilgrims from the ends of the earth; many of whom I am compelled to decline treating altogether, or treat very imperfectly, for want of suitable medicines and materials.

The report of great numbers of skeletons, found jammed up in an erect posture, on digging out some old foundations at Jericho, is confirmed by two of my patients, to-day, from the Jordan.

The sickly season is now far advanced; yet, through a kind Providence, our health is unusually good. We have not had so much as a single chill during our sojourn on this airy mountain; but there is a good deal of sickness, of a very serious character, at the English and German encampment, on the other side of the city, particularly in the families of the missionaries lately arrived.

We have only one regular scholar at present, but were we suitably situated, we could easily have a large school.

Owing to the continued absence of the member alluded to in my last, I have not yet been able to ascertain the truth or falsity of the mortifying report about his alleged denial of his immersion, a second time. Another convert has given me some uneasiness, on account of his having partially yielded, for a few days, to an attempt on the part of a certain missionary, of a certain Protestant (?) church, to bribe him into the communion of that church. But he professes great sorrow for having suffered such tampering with his conscience, and I trust is rendered the more stable by it. With these exceptions, our little flock seems to be in a prospering condition; and I think will not suffer by comparison with any congregation of my acquaintance. Brother James Diness, the present dragoman of the mission, is much engaged in the good cause, and gives encouraging promise of usefulness.

The German and other Askenarim Jews in this city, are under able consular protection; but the Spanish and other Sephardim Jews are without any protection whatever; and in consequence, are subjected to many exactions, mortifications, and grievances from their Moslem masters. This oppression they are now attempting to remedy by an appeal to some of the great powers, but I fear to little purpose. I was told by Rabbi Cohen, yesterday, that they have already taken measures to represent their oppressed condition to Queen Victoria and the President of the United States. Great Britain manifests the deepest concern in whatever pertains to the holy land, and will doubtless attempt the alleviation of these grievances of her *proteges* through her ably conducted consulate here; but I fear Jerusalem presents too few commercial inducements to justify the establishment of a well sustained consulate here.

As to the "ownership of the Holy Land," about which you inquire, I give no credence to the rumor some time ago so generally current and credited, that it has passed into the hands of the Rothschilds; nor to the one now so rife, that England has just acquired a special interest in it. I am not informed as to the claims of which you speak, that "Great Britain has upon Palestine;" unless, indeed, her naboth-like cupidity may be constrained into a claim. Certain it is, however, that she is making all possible interest with all classes of Syrian population. And it is probable, in the highest degree, that when the great eastern Turkey comes to be carved up to gratify the august gastronomies of certain great state gourmands, England will have her peculiar penchant for the leg of the Turkey abundantly gratified.

I expected to have baptized two Romanists, who appeared to be sincere inquirers after truth, and expressly declared that they wanted no house-rent, nor anything else, except the truth; but after receiving instruction a few times, they have discontinued their visits — I know not why, but can ascribe it alone to priestly interference. I had, however, extreme satisfaction in baptizing, a few days ago, a former worshiper of the Beast, from Germany, whose history, had I space at command, I would like to narrate; but I have scarcely room to ask the acceptance of our cordial and affectionate salaams for sister B. and the Cincinnati brotherhood of my acquaintance, as well as yourself. But I must not conclude without entreating the continued intercession of the dear brethren in behalf of the mission. With love unfeigned,

Yours in the Lord,

J. T. BARCLAY.

ELDER BURNET, *Cor. Sec'y.*

THE JORDAN.

JERUSALEM, June, 26th, 1852.

MY DEAR BROTHER BURNET:—Day before yesterday, I returned from a brief excursion to the Jordan; and presuming a little upon your forbearance, will inform you of the occasion and circumstances of my journey there at such an unusual season.

A few weeks previous to this visit, Dr. Zimpel, a German gentleman of great intelligence, benevolence, and general moral worth, after listening most attentively to several public and private expositions of the Christian system, expressed his entire conviction of the truth as I taught it, according to the form of sound words, and earnestly desired baptism; expressing, at the same time, his preference — provided it was not asking too much, or did not savor of impropriety in my estimation — to be baptized in the river Jordan. Fully persuaded, from previous acquaintance, as well as from the conversation then held, that the desire arose from none of that superstitious veneration for " sacred localities," which is such a blotch upon the religious profession of the East, but rather from a laudable devotional feeling, I very readily acceded to his generous proposal to have myself and one of my sons avail ourselves of his escort, and accept the hospitalities of his tent. Preparations were accordingly made for the excursion.

Leaving the city about two o'clock, P. M., at St. Stephen's Gate, we descended into the valley of Jehosaphat, crossed the bed of the Kidron on the upper stone bridge, wound along the southern declivity of Mount Olivet, leaving the Virgin's Church and Gethsemane on the left, the tombs of Jehosaphat, Absalom, James, and Zachariah, and also the Mount of Offense, on the right, and took the most ancient and direct road "down to Jericho," passing through Bethany. Here were numbers of Fellahin, still engaged in treading out and winnowing their crop of wheat, oats, and barley, which for many weeks they had been depositing around their threshing-floors. They generally select for their threshing-floors such portions of the limestone rock, composing the mountain, as are flat or nearly so. The sheaves being placed upon this in a stratum of several feet thickness, animals are slowly driven over it until every head is hulled most effectually, and the straw is reduced to a fine chaff. In no one instance were the animals all of one kind; mules, donkeys, horses, oxen, and cows, were indiscriminately tied together by the neck, and urged with a goad all over the huge bed till the straw is sufficiently minced. Although this promiscuous intermingling of brutes is rather opposed to the law of Moses, which these Moslems profess to regard, yet I was pleased to see that they so far respected the anti-muzzling act of the great lawgiver, as to permit every animal to eat as much as he could without stopping. I saw none so silly as to "kick against the pricks," however much he might be goaded. While most of the grain seemed to be reaped with the hook, not a little of it was merely pulled up by the root. Wonder what these poor creatures would think of an American cradle and threshing-machine.

About one mile from Bethany, near a large ruined khan, a fine fountain of cool water cascades into a large marble trough, which conveys it into an adjoining stone reservoir, five or six yards square. These reservoirs are always found attached to fountains in this country; so that wherever you see a fountain — be it ever so small — there you are sure also to find a respectable *baptistery*. The sight of many busy bees, making honey, as we were entering the wilderness of Judea, forcibly reminded us of John Baptist. Fanned by a pleasant breeze, which is almost sure to spring up the latter part of every day, we found it delightfully pleasant, even when wending our way through deep narrow gorges of the mountains. No signs of culture were to be seen, a short distance below the fountain; but the tops and sides of many of the hills were all alive with sheep, goats, and camels. Soon afterward, however, all verdure disappeared, and scarcely a single article of the vegetable or animal kingdom was to be seen, and bleak, weary, wild, parched, and desolate, beyond conception, appeared the whole surface of the earth. We had entered the wilderness of Judea! What awful convulsions and throes this land must once have undergone, to produce such dizzy cliffs and terrific chasms. After two or three hours' dreary travel and indulgence in the solemn reflections and emotions suggested by the occasion, we were reminded, by the appearance of a few stunted trees and shrubs, that we had passed through the wilderness of Judea. We here overtook quite a cavalcade of Russians (or Muscoobs, as they are here termed). Some of the men were riding sidewise; not so the ladies, however. Well; *de gustibus non disputandum est*, thought we, and so (though somewhat disgusted by this singular fancy), the two parties merged into one, for we soon ascertained that they were on a pilgrimage to the Jordan; and in this land of banditti, bad indeed must be discarded company.

Just before we left the hill country and entered upon the plain of Jordan, we noticed several aqueducts, plainly indicating the attention formerly paid to agriculture on these now sterile hills, portions of which are in fine state of preservation. Noticed also a few remains of building just as we entered upon the plain, supposed to mark the site of the Jericho of Joshua. Crossing a beautiful stream of clear water several yards in width, upon the shaded banks of which the jackals were quietly roaming, we soon reached the canal and aqueduct from Elisha's fountain, which passed over a valley or two in sight, on handsome, well-constructed, Saracenic arches. It was conveying a rapidly-flowing stream, about eighteen inches deep, which, properly distributed, would render no small portion of this lovely plain once more "like the garden of the Lord," but which I believe is now all suffered to run to waste; another portion of the same water, however, is conducted by a shallow trench to Riha (the present Jericho), where it is applied to irrigation and other useful purposes. Just as the sun was gilding with his last mellow rays the neighboring mountains of Moab, we pitched our tent on a beautiful plat of green grass beside the bush-walled village of Riha. Men half dressed, and children in a perfect state of nudity, remind us of the doleful plight of David's condolers, when they were ordered " to tarry in Jericho till their beards be grown out." Such a poor mud and straw-hut village, and such a hard set of customers I have nowhere seen. An ill-shaped old castle where the Turkish government keeps a few soldiers to curb the incursions of the trans-Jordan Bedawin, is not a little venerated as the veritable house of Zaccheus, by many a devout pilgrim. The blind are seen groping their way along, but unlike the son of Timeus, they cry not for mercy to the Son of David, however much they need it; albeit, they cry vociferously enough for "buckshish." So complete is the desolation that reigns in and around the "accursed city," that not a single palm-tree can now be found in all the region of the "city of palm-trees." The tall, rawboned Abyssinians seemed to be the dignitaries of the town, and lorded it over the wretched, squalid Jericheans, as none but a son of Ham can do. In a very short time, fires were blazing all around, and white folks, black folks, and yellow folks, were all to be seen seated around the pool supplied by Elisha's fountain, engaged in various and culinary operations. The dispatch with which some of them would knead a parcel of pounded wheat into dough, and roll it out on their blanket, into cakes as thin as leather, and as broad as the head of a barrel, is really astonishing.

The column of atmosphere pressing upon our bodies at night, is four thousand feet higher than it was at noon, and one of the effects of this increased pressure—that of retarding evaporation, is quite obvious in our increased perspiration, even under diminished temperature. So many interesting events that have transpired hereabouts, are matter of sacred record, that our evening devotions, in which some of them come under review, are protracted to an unusual length — but not at the expense of their interest. With more fear of musquitoes *et id omne genus*, than of the Bedawin before our eyes, we retire to bed — but not to rest; for the constant yelling of jackals, on the one side, and the howling of dogs on the other, prevented some of us from sleeping a single wink the whole night. It was also the height of Ramadan, and the Mohammedans kept up the most dolorous music, revelry, and rejoicings, throughout the entire night, as is the universal custom of these singular fanatics during this month.

Having risen and breakfasted very early, we were off for the Jordan as soon as the faint outline of the dark blue mountains of Abarim was rendered visible by the first blushings of Aurora. What a lovely spectacle must have been presented by this beautiful plain, copiously irrigated and highly cultivated as it was when "Lot lifted up his eyes and beheld that it was well watered everywhere, even as the garden of the Lord," before the Lord destroyed Sodom and Gomorrah, and even as it was two thousand years later, when Josephus declares, "one would not have erred to call it divine." A donkey having been stolen from the Russian party during the night, the theft was of course charged to the nomadic sons of Ishmael, and hence, our sheik and his attendants made frequent detours, and scoured the plain in every direction, in search of their brother wild men. At the place where we approached the Jordan, its "second banks," (as the boundaries of the deep valley limiting the river's overflow, are called,) were very deep and precipitous, and washed into the most fantastic and picturesque shapes. The interval between this second bank and the river, was several hundred yards in width; and that on the Moab side appeared to be equally wide. What a mighty flood of water must have been rushing between these banks when Joshua arrested the impetuous tide — for the passage of the ark occurred "*at harvest, when the Jordan overfloweth all his banks.*"

We reached this ever memorable stream just as the sun was gilding its waters with his first golden beams. But despite the many pleasing reflections that crowded upon my mind, I could but feel disappointed when I saw such a narrow, rapid, and muddy stream — for I had fancied that it would at least be clear, and glide smoothly at this season of the year. Notwithstanding all that I had read about the river, my biblical romance received no small shock. I wondered not that the proud generalissimo of Syria thought that Abanna and Pharpar would be more efficacious in cleansing his leprosy, than this turbid water. The river here is scarcely twenty yards wide, but quite deep. It is, however, a beautiful spot for the administration of baptism; for the water, though so rapid and deep in the main channel, was almost eddy in some places, and possessed of every depth, from six feet to six inches. Having arrived a little in advance of our Russian fellow-travelers, we proposed anticipating their ablutions. But just as we were about to engage in religious exercises preparatory to the administration of the ordinance, they rushed up tumultuously; and our sense of delicacy was so shocked by an exhibition of their Russian modesty, that we gladly waited awhile, "that all things may be done decently and in order," without unnecessary distraction. We were no little astonished to see the naked old Magogian, attended by his equally naked serfs, leave a spot where they might have laved to their heart's content, almost concealed by the shrubbery crowning the curving bank of the river, and rush heedlessly and shamelessly into the water just where we were standing. This, however, we might have patiently endured; but when we saw the *ladies* also, in a perfect state of nudity, enter the river close beside us, we thought it was time to be off; and we accordingly retreated precipitately into the adjoining jungle — rather incurring the risk of encountering the lion in this famous place of his resort, than be a voluntary spectator of the sport of these ruthless Russian boors (bears)! Had these poor creatures all been serfs, such conduct would not have been so surprising; but one of them was a *priest*, and several others (specially of the ladies), were thought to belong to the upper circles of society. We could but remark the great gravity and devoutness with which a very gentlemanly looking young man entered the water, near the place of our seclusion, and carefully securing himself to the limb of an overhanging willow tree, thrice dip himself with various mutterings and crossings, beneath the deep-rolling flood. But this practice of trine self-immersion is by no means confined to the members of the Greek community. The Rev. Mr. S., of New York, publishes to the world in his "Sketches of Travel," that he three times bowed his head beneath the waters of the Jordan, pronouncing each time the name of the Father, the Son, and the Holy Ghost, and a very pious and benevolent pedobaptist of the same city informed us, that he thus endeavored to obtain the answer of a good conscience, and wash away his doubts about the validity of sprinkling, inquiring, simply enough, if it was n't probable that the Lord would accept his baptism? Being reminded of this circumstance, by witnessing the Greek baptism, I mentioned it to Dr. Zimpel, who confessed, that during a former visit to the Jordan, he had vainly tried to satisfy the qualms of his conscience by the same way; but he now rejoiced that he had been brought to see the difference between the assurance imparted by a "thus saith the word of the Lord," and the mere "mayhap," extorted from human vicarious inventions. He had traveled all over the world, he declared to a brother German, (whom in imitation of the brother of Simon, near this very spot, he was endeavoring to lead to the Lamb of God), in search of true religion, but never could be satisfied till he found it where it was first preached on the day of Pentecost. The Russian pilgrims continued their ablutions so long, that we were under the necessity of requesting them to retire and dress, in order that the baptism might take place. They accordingly retired; and this ordinance was then administered, as to manner and matter—(action, subject, and object)—in a way that the banks of the Jordan have not witnessed for, perhaps, more than seventeen long centuries. If ever I saw a happy person in all my life, the doctor was that individual, when he arose from the liquid grave to walk in newness of life. Such a cordial Christian salutation, in the shape of a holy kiss of charity, and a bruin-like embrace, while standing in the Jordan, it has never fallen to my lot to receive anywhere else. It was truly soul-cheering to see him thus start " on his way rejoicing!" And what heart could be so phlegmatic as not to be moved almost to transport on such an occasion?

We were "right against" Jericho, if we may credit the testimony of certain remains supposed to indicate its ancient site; and undoubtedly standing on ground which, though now covered with the flowing stream, was once laid bare and dry, when, at the command of Joshua, " the waters that came down toward the sea of the plain, even the salt sea, failed, and were cut off." Equally certain is it that we were near Bethabara, beyond Jordan, where John was baptizing in the river of Jordan, and where the great Redeemer fulfilled righteousness, by submitting to the very ordinance which had just been administered, " as it was delivered unto us." We lingered at this interesting spot, cherishing such reflections as long as we could; and would have remained ("in such a frame") much longer, but for the importunate entreaties of the sheik, enforced by the declaration that there was danger of the Bedawin. One of the Russian ladies came up and expressed most significantly her preference of immersion over sprinkling.

Instead of returning, as we had proposed, by way of Neba Musa, and "seeing what is not to be seen," (for be it known that though the Lord buried Moses in Moab, over the other side of the Jordan, "in a place which no man knoweth," the Mohammedans have got him buried, for the convenience of Moslem pilgrims, on *this* side Jordan), we went up the plain to visit Elisha's fountain. How often, while traversing this plain, did I look over to the mountain ranges of Moab, and endeavor to fix my vision upon some elevated peak, better entitled than all others, by its towering height, to lay claim to the distinction of being the identical Pisgah whence Moses "viewed the landscape o'er;" but vain was my search. Equally unsatisfactory was my effort to single out some "high mountain" on the opposite side, in the wilderness of Jordan, where I could bring myself to believe that Satan had taken the Messiah and "shown him all the kingdoms of this world, and the glory of them, in a moment of time;" but if the "exceeding high mountain" is to be taken in a strictly literal sense, and was situated in this wilderness, it may long since have been shorn of its height by the winds and rains of heaven; for many of the mountains of the Holy Land are still observed to be undergoing a rapid process of diminution by disintegration. Mount Quarantina, however, may still be called very high, compared with many of the neighboring mountains. And that this mountain has long enjoyed the distinction of being the scene of the Saviour's temptation, is obvious from the number of cells with which its lofty and precipitous sides are perforated for the residence of anchorite monks.

Arrived at Elisha's fount, we were glad enough to quench our thirst in its copious, cool, gushing waters. How different is this spot now from its condition previous to the miracle of the prophet, when "the water was naught and the ground barren!" This great caldron of "Adam's ale" appeared to be about thirty yards in circumference, and many fish were sporting in it. But it was time now to turn our faces toward Jerusalem.

What a melancholy contrast did we feel when we left the delightful plain of the Jordan, and ascended the rugged mountains of the wilderness, where "Jesus was led up of the Spirit to be tempted of the devil!" How important is it that we pray — "Lord, abandon us not to temptation!" — yet true it is, that "blessed is he that endureth temptation."

Some one in the rear of the caravan having fired again, our watchful sheik immediately started to the rescue, apprehending—or at least pretending to apprehend—that the Bedawin had attacked some stragglers, behind. We were thus reminded that we were on the very road, in all probability, (and near the very spot, as tradition saith), on which "a certain man went down from Jerusalem to Jericho, and fell among thieves;" and it was near this very place that, but a short time ago, two persons were "*stripped* of their clothes" by these lawless marauders, and though not seriously "wounded," were yet "left half dead" from sheer fright. Escaping all such dangers, however, and pursuing, doubtless, from the nature of the country, the identical route traveled by our Lord when he left the lowlands of Jericho, and made his triumphant entry into the Holy City, we passed over Olivet, where he ascended on high, and soon reached the city in safety, "the good hand of the Lord being upon us." May we ever follow in the footsteps of the "Lamb," during our travels over these low grounds of sin and sorrow; and passing through this wilderness world of temptation, may our spirits at last safely reach the New Jerusalem; and when Christ, who is our life, shall appear, may we also appear with him in glory.

With sincere regards, yours in Christ,

J. T. BARCLAY.

MOUNT OLIVET, November 1, 1852.

BROTHER BURNET:—Although the moon has many times waxed and waned since I last had the pleasure of hearing from you, yet in compliance with my engagement, I proceed, after a bare lunation since my last, to send you another monthly communication.

The rainy season having not yet set in, we are afraid to jeopardize our health by returning to the city, and hence we are still in summer quarters on this healthful and hallowed " mount, called the Mount of Olives ;" and I confess we like to linger about a place where our adorable Redeemer so often retired from the din and bustle of the city, and where we have been so richly blessed in body, soul, and spirit. But while *we* are in the enjoyment of such excellent health ourselves, I am sorry to say that our friends at Artos, and the Franks generally, are suffering very much from serious illness. I learned on visiting Bethlehem yesterday, that there were upward of three hundred persons in that village dangerously ill with the prevailing fever, and a very malignant species of ophthalmia, speedily terminating in total blindness. From several of the surrounding villages I have received the most urgent applications to visit them ; but the medicines having not yet arrived, and my present supply being exceedingly scanty, I have been under the painful necessity of confining my practice, as a general rule, to such as could come in person for medical aid. After having so long labored under the apprehension that the long expected medicines were all lost at sea, it was with no small pleasure that I received a letter from brother King, stating that they had recently been shipped from London; and we now hope to receive them in the course of a week or two. I discover, however, from the invoice, that many articles are exceedingly dear, and what is much to be regretted, that owing to the groundless fears of the captain, several very important articles are not sent—articles too, without which many of the other drugs would be altogether unavailing. But still I believe I shall be enabled, by mere accident, however, to procure most of the omitted articles, on terms that will be justifiable under the circumstances; and the supply will then suffice for several years.

In order to become the better and sooner acclimatized, I have deemed it important to take a great deal of exercise; and in accordance with my own convictions of duty, as well as in compliance with the suggestions of some eminent biblical scholars and antiquarians who have visited Jerusalem during the past year, (Drs. Robinson, Hacket, Bimoblodski, etc.,) I have been lately investigating some biblico-archæological questions of a topographical nature; and when a suitable private opportunity shall occur, I propose sending you the result of my investigations on some of these interesting topics. By-the-by, Dr. R. states, in a letter received from him to-day, that he has made many valuable discoveries during this tour, which he is now preparing for publication at Vienna, and was to have sailed from Bremen for the United States on the 7th ult. You will neither be surprised nor grieved to learn how mathematically demonstrable it is that Romish tradition is so egregiously at fault in her fanciful selection of "sacred localities," about the Holy City. Such of the questions as you may find too minutely or critically treated for the mass of your readers, may still repay *yourself* for their perusal, and perhaps afford an occasional excerpt for the Age.

That about the waters of Jerusalem and vicinity, was designed, in its inception, for the Harbinger; but the mass of facts already collected, however compactly they may be put together, will swell to a size inconveniently large for insertion in that inestimable monthly, (none the less valued though it has for more than two years entirely suspended that social intercourse which was formerly, every moon, an occasion of such delight and profit). This treatise on the adequacy of the waters of Jerusalem and its vicinity to the demands of Acts 2d, you will doubtless esteem rather prolix and uninteresting; but as a mistaken notion in relation to the water resources of Jerusalem contributes not a little to lead hundreds of persons annually to pervert an ordinance that so seriously concerns us to "keep as it is delivered unto us;" and this essay is designed to put an end to all controversy on this score—the sufficiency of water for the baptism of the three thousand. I hope you will bear with me in being thus tedious unto you.

You have concluded long before this, that I have entirely forgotten, or never received the queries you inclosed me in a letter several months ago; but if such is your conclusion you are entirely mistaken; they have only been "laid on the table" until correct information in relation to some few of them can be obtained To respond correctly and minutely to some of them, required a more intimate acquaintance with the natural history, resources, population, etc., of Palestine, than I have, until recently, possessed; but you shall now be furnished with minute information on all these topics by the first suitable opportunity. The many conflicting statements of travelers, even the most competent and impartial, afford ample proof that superficial observation is not to be trusted in most of these matters; and it is only the repeated and long continued in-door observations of the actual resident that can be relied upon with confidence. Had I replied to many of these queries immediately on their receipt, I should doubtless have misinformed you on some of these points, and been instrumental, however unwittingly, in propagating, instead of correcting, error.

A "big-bug" Basha from Stamboul (Constantinople) has lately arrived with a firman from the Sublime Porte, for the pacification of the long pending quarrel about the proprietorship of the church inclosing the reputed tomb of the Saviour. And how do you think the matter is settled? The Sultan gives it to neither of the claimants, the Latins nor the Greeks; but guarantees protection to all sects that choose to worship there, and reserves to himself the honor (and doubtless the *lucre*, too), of repairing its crumbling dome, together with the right of taking care of the premises hereafter. This decision, of course, gives satisfaction to none of the parties concerned; but it is to be hoped that such a curatorship will at least serve to bring them to their senses. The commissioner is said to be wonderfully toasted by all parties—the game of *buckshishing* having already commenced on a most liberal scale—and the church may now be considered as the property of the highest bidder.

Rumors are still current about the purchase of the

Holy Land by the Rothschilds, and have assumed a very definite form, detailing the exact cost, conditions, etc.; but Dr. Zimpel, from whom I received a letter a day or two ago, seems to be entirely ignorant of any such arrangement, though he is much interested in Jewish affairs, and has recently had several interviews with Baron Rothschild in Vienna. I am inclined to discredit the report altogether.

I am sorry I cannot cheer your heart by an account of any additions to our little flock during the past month; but though I am not privileged to report any actual additions, you must not infer that "the word of the Lord that goeth out of his mouth has returned to him altogether void"—"as though the word of God hath taken *none* effect." There is a gentleman of considerable learning, and great sincerity of heart, now sojourning here, who, from one attendance on the public ministration of the word, and a few private expositions, has become greatly enamored with most of the truth as it has been presented to his consideration, which he exultingly denominates real apostolical Christianity. As yet, however, he is unable to discard several long cherished, darling errors, such as consubstantiation, and the obligation of the feast of tabernacles. But I trust the light of heaven will soon dispel these errors, as it has many others, from his candid but beclouded mind. I hazard nothing whatever when I assert that you can have no adequate conception of the digging and plowing to which a heart spoiled by oriental philosophy and tradition must needs be subjected, before it can reasonably be expected that the good seed of the word can fall upon it as on " an honest and good heart." A Mussulman with whom my sons have ventured to converse freely, seems to be fully convinced of the folly of Mohammedism, and is almost — I might say *quite — persuaded to become* a Christian; but the fear of losing not only his property, but his head too, renders him reluctant yet awhile to make a public profession of Christianity; and he is honest enough to admit that he would openly profess Christianity at once, but for the dread of such a sad catastrophe.

Finding it impossible to procure, in the immediate environs of the city, a suitable place for the proposed asylum, on account of the high price demanded, I have extended my researches a little further than heretofore, and have at last found a very eligible place about six miles from the city, which is "*merie*" — a term used to designate the public domain, or property of the Sultan—and I have accordingly written to our highly esteemed minister at Constantinople, to ascertain upon what terms it can be obtained. I have every reason to believe that the sum demanded will not exceed that to which I am limited by the Board; and as it is a very interesting spot, and is surrounded by places of stirring interest, I will give you a brief account of my visit there.

Crossing Mount Olivet near the Church of Ascension, and taking the road down Wady Ru Waby, fifty minutes' walk brought us to the ruins of Al Kuby Sufre; and turning then abruptly to the left, after crossing a few inconsiderable hills, we found ourselves, in half an hour, within a few hundred yards of Wady Farar, the object of our visit. But having heard of a wonderful fountain a mile or two below, at the junction of this wady with Wady Fuwar, we determined to visit this fountain before descending Wady Farar. Our Moslem guide informed us, that though it burst forth from the earth as copious as a river, yet he could stop at command the rushing flood, merely by chanting a certain formula of prayer, the chorus and burden of which was — "the colored man whipped the white man;" and what to our occidental ears was equally marvelous, "could call the spirits from the vasty deep," and again cause the pent-up torrent to rush off down the valley in double-quick time, by reversing his declaration, and making "the white man whip the colored man." Arrived at the spot, we found that though not realizing the American idea of a river, it might still come up to his notion of one, and was certainly a most copious "fountain and depth springing out of the valley," capable of driving several mills as it gushes forth from the earth; and although we were not at all anxious to see such a noble spring suppressed, yet he proceeded at once to redeem his promise, as if unwilling that his character as a thaumaturgist should be doubted a moment longer. Imagine, if you can, what astonishment filled our minds, when, despite our disbelief in the miraculous pretensions of this follower of the "great *prophet*," the water actually began to disappear, and in a few minutes not a single drop escaped from the yawning fissure. It had entirely subsided and retired within the earth.

In order that we might be the more fully convinced of his miraculous powers, he inquired after a minute or two, if we did not wish to see him cause the water to flow again? to which, of course, we responded in the affirmative, and forthwith this rival of Canute, Xerxes, and Moses, commenced his lugubrious incantation, and soon, exultingly calling attention to the gurgling sound below, had the satisfaction of seeing the water burst forth furiously from its apparent imprisonment. In order to remove from our minds the least shadow of doubt, he again subjected the obedient waters to his magic influence. And as we still lingered at the fountain, he was about to renew his conjurations; but I thought it was now time to show him that " Saul was also among the prophets;" and by way of making " my rod swallow up his rod," told him I would neither sing nor pray about the white and colored men fighting, nor wave a hand or wand over the water, but would even walk out of sight of it, and yet make it appear and disappear at my bidding; for I noticed that it flowed about six minutes, ebbed six, and was quiescent about three; and the idea occurred to me at once, that the water from the fountains above, which he had told me disappeared after flowing about a mile, was received into a subterranean reservoir, which emptied itself every twelve or fifteen minutes by a kind of natural syphon. Anxious still to maintain his pretensions to familiar intercourse with infernal aquatic spirits, he defied me to do so at first, but seeing me pull out my watch and mark the moment of the water's subsidence, he discovered he could gull us no longer, and reluctantly confessed the trick he had been attempting to palm on us.

Returning by a circuitous route to the place whence we had started from Wady Farar, we descended with some difficulty into that " Valley of Delight"—for such is the literal signification of its name—and truly I have seen nothing so delightful in the way of natural scenery, resources, etc., in all Palestine. Ascending its bold stream from this point, we passed some half-dozen expansions of the stream, constituting the most beautiful baptisteries I have ever seen, the water rivaling the atmosphere itself in transparency, of depths varying from a fathom to a foot, shaded on one or both sides by the umbrageous fig-trees, and sometimes contained in naturally excavated basins of variegated marble, the common limestone of the country. These pools are supplied by some half-dozen springs, of the purest and coldest water, bursting from rocky crevices, at various intervals. Verily, thought I, we have stumbled upon Enon! " Many fountains," I believe, is what Dr. Robinson, the great biblical geographer and lexicographer, renders the "*polla hudata*" of Enon; and here are not only many fountains, but literally " much water." Portions of aqueducts, both of pottery and stone—and in a tolerable state of preservation too, in many places—are still found remaining on each side of the valley, indicating the extent to which the valley was at one time irrigated; and richer land I have never seen than is much of this valley. Several herds of cattle were voraciously feeding on the rich herbage near the stream, and thousands of sheep and goats were seen approaching the stream, or "resting at noonday," near the "shadow of the great rock" composing the cliff, here and there. Many birds of many kinds, from the chirping little sparrow to the immense condor-looking vulture, were sweetly caroling or swiftly flitting across the valley, or perched upon its cliffs, and the most delicious perfume pervaded many spots in this beautiful little Eden. Rank grasses, tall weeds, and shrubbery and trees of various kinds, entirely conceal the stream from view in many places, forming around its pebbly little pools, just such shady and picturesque little alcoves and bowers as Latin, Greek, and English poets picture out for their naiads, sylphs, and fairies. But instead of nymphs and sylphs, a very wizard-like old Arab was wading about, gathering crabs and snails for the dignitaries of the Greek convent. By-the-by, whence came the fishes that were sporting about in these pellucid little lakes? Have they made their escape from the muddy waters of the Jordan, and wended their way through subterranean channels to this great height? or are they the remains of an old piscatory colony planted here by the old Canaanitish, Jewish, Roman, Persian, or crusading residents of this valley? Certainly not by Turks or Arabs. Higher up, the valley becomes very narrow, and the rocky precipices tower to a sublime height. In these perpendicular cyclopean walls are found many caves of great extent; and what we at first took for sepulchral excavations, we found, on further examination, to have served as habitations for the living, furnished with reservoirs, and admirably devised for defense. A short distance below the upper fountain were very evident remains of a sugar or oil-mill, and scattered about were also tessera, fragments of pillows, and other indications of an ancient town. But what impressed me more than anything else that I saw, was a somewhat regular, though altogether natural hemispherical excavation in the cliff, with its overhanging dome of towering height, being an inverted cave, of depth, or rather *height*, unfathomable by the sight. Oh, what a devotion-inspiring cathedral for the worship of that exalted Being that "dwelleth not in temples made with hands," and who has made this gigantic temple out-and-out himself. Ascending a neighboring hill, we had a most commanding view of the land of Moab, the Dead Sea, Jordan, Mickmash, Rimmon, Geba, Ramah, Gibeah, and some other villages; and then, after having spent a most delightful day, we reluctantly left this sweet retreat, and reached our quarters in an hour and a-half, passing through Anathoth, near to which lay the field of Jeremiah; and recrossing Mount Olivet at Nob, where the haughty Assyrian king halted before he laid siege to Jerusalem (Isaiah 10.) But want of space precludes the opportunity of making any remarks in connection with these interesting places.

Having had no tidings of you either by pen or type for so great a length of time, you may conceive our anxiety to hear from you. But I trust you are not forgetful of us at a throne of grace. Earnestly indeed do we desire, and much do we need the intercession of the saints. With highest regards of myself and family, most cordially and affectionately yours in the Lord.

JAS. T. BARCLAY.

ARRIVAL OF SUPPLIES.

JERUSALEM, December 5, 1853.

DEAR BROTHER BURNET:—We have returned to the city, as you perceive; and though so " unworthy of the least of the mercy and truth that the Lord has shown his servants," we are still the recipients of the richest blessings of a kind Providence. The winter campaign having commenced in earnest, I am excessively engaged; and having nothing specially interesting to communicate, I shall only occupy half a sheet, my wife having already delivered a whole one to sister Burnet, to be sent in the same envelope with this.

I have lately had much religious conversation and disputation, in declaring both the elementary principles of Christianity, and the whole counsel of God; and while much of the good seed of the word has fallen upon sterile soil, some, I trust, has taken root in good and honest hearts. It is evident, however, that my well known disapproval of all "*buckshishing*" missionary operations, has served to diminish the number of professed inquirers. The late movement, too, on the part of the Jews in London, and other parts of Europe, having for its object the colonization of the land about Jerusalem with Jews, has greatly favored the restrictive policy of the rabbi of the city; so that the Jews are not now as accessible as they were a short time ago.

Our long expected articles have at length arrived; but, alas! in such sad plight! It would grieve you to see what sad havoc sea-water has made among the medicines; nor would you be less grieved to see the injury done to the books and other articles; though knowing their comparative value, I lament the injury sustained by the latter less than that of the former. Although the medicines were packed very securely in small boxes, canisters, etc., yet nearly every article not contained in bottles, is more or less injured; and such as were soluble in water, entirely dissolved and washed away. The damage may be fairly rated at one-half the cost of the articles. Brother King took the precaution of having them insured in London, and I intended to have written to him on the subject, and inclosed the necessary certificates, but I am told that inasmuch as the boxes were not opened in Jaffa, the claim for damages cannot be sustained. Under these perplexing circumstances, I have taken the responsibility of supplying the deficiency out of the fund intended for the purchase of land; though not without much hesitancy, notwithstanding the great importance attached to the proper maintenance of the medical department of the mission. To effect this, in this high drug market, has cost the sum of seventy-eight dollars and fifty cents (inclusive of some purchased before their arrival), which, together with nineteen dollars and fifty-two cents, the cost of freight, commission, storage, carriage, etc., has been charged to the appropriation above referred to. But should the brethren place the same estimate on the healing art that I do, as a pioneer and adjuvant to the more direct object of the Mission, they will not disapprove, however much they may regret, the necessity of such a step. The books could have been somewhat restored, notwithstanding their discoloration, had not the vessel been laden with sugar; but this being all dissolved, and penetrating the books along with the solution of drugs, so effectually stained and glued them together, that a complete perusal of them is impossible. You will be pleased to learn, however, that owing to its excellent binding, and the compact manner in which it was put up, the elegant Bible, so kindly presented by the American Christian Bible Society, suffered much less than the other books. The seeds, cuttings, etc., were, of course, entirely destroyed; but the half-eagle, so adroitly put in by the right hand, apparently without the knowledge of the left, came safely to hand, and will be devoted to supplying seats for our meeting-room. Many thanks for this and other things so kindly presented by your family and other endeared brethren.

I was informed this morning, by one of the leading priests of the Latin church, that the dispute about the possession of the "Church of the Holy Sepulcher," is as far from settlement now as it was before the arrival of the envoy from Constantinople. He spoke with great bitterness of the envoy's proposed compromise " to give the Latins entire possession of the 'keys' at Bethlehem, upon condition of permitting the Greeks to have precedence (merely) in the solemnities in the city;" for he says " that is all these cheating fellows want ; for they would then entirely exclude the Latins, by protracting their services through the whole period of the sacred occasion." Surely, as Jew loved Samaritan, so do these Eastern and Western branches of the " holy apostolic church " love each other. The Latins now console themselves with the avowed hope that when the " Prince President" shall have become grand emperor, he will use an irresistible argument with the Sublime Porte, in virtue of his office as " keeper of the Holy Sepulcher," and forthwith put the Latins in full and sole possession of all the disputed property. But I guess the great ce-*zar*-ean autocrat is also pretty expert in the use of this same nitro-sulphurous logic, and he will doubtless make it convenient to be on the Dardanelles about the time of arguing such a case. *Nous verrons.*

So great a length of time has elapsed since we have received a single line from your pen or press, that we can but fear that our long expected bundle of papers and letters is either entirely lost, or has gone on, by mistake, to India. But though we get no communications from you, I trust you send many to *Heaven about* us. Fully assured that without the blessing of the Lord we can accomplish nothing, I earnestly invoke the continued intercession of the brethren in behalf of the Mission. Most sincerely, yours in Christ,

J. T. BARCLAY.

JERUSALEM, December 5, 1852.

MY DEAR SISTER BURNET:—I have several times thought of pleading the rights of the sisterhood in justification of the liberty of writing you a social epistle without the usual prerequsite of a personal acquaintance, but have heretofore refrained from so doing, lest I should offend against the laws of epistolary etiquette. You may therefore imagine how glad I am that your kind note has removed the embargo thus imposed on my pen. The substantial proof evidenced on the part of yourself, daughter, and mother, by the highly prized presents lately received, of interest felt, not only in the objects of the Mission, but in the persons of the missionary family, is highly gratifying and demands our most cordial acknowledgments; and while the almost total ruin of the articles sent is a matter of no little regret as a personal loss, it detracts not in the least from the warmth of our gratitude to the contributors. It was grievous indeed to find that not only the color, but the fabric of almost every article of clothing was destroyed by the joint agency of seawater and solution of drugs. What pleasure it would have afforded me to wear the dress sent by our aged " mother in Israel," Mrs. Gano! Will you be kind enough (if convenient), to convey to her and the others to whom we are indebted, our sincere thanks for these unmistakable tokens of their interest in our welfare. What an ornament to the table of our conversation room, would the handsome book you sent us have been, had it arrived in safety; but it is unfortunately so gummed, dyed, and otherwise injured, as scarcely to be legible. Happy indeed are we that the elegant copy of the Bible, for which we are so much indebted to the American Christian Bible Society, though illegible in a few places, and much discolored, is yet in a much better state of preservation. Even the pins and needles are so corroded as to be entirely worthless, except as mementos of your kindness. Were you to construe my expressions of thankfulness for these tokens of regard into a hint for other similar contributions, you would wrong me not a little; for we have sent to the United States for the few necessary articles which are not to be had here, and hope, through a propitious Providence, to receive them in the course of a month or two. 'Tis true, that were it not for the evil consequences which observation abundantly shows to result from the distribution of such things among the poor Jews, and especially those who manifest a spirit of inquiry or even tolerance, we we would like very much to be the almoners of the brethren to the poor of Jerusalem; but we are afraid even to make them such presents, lest it should operate as a motive to enter into our ranks unregenerate. "Loaves and fishes" are powerful motives and arguments in Jerusalem.

After numerous abortive attempts, we at last succeeded in deciphering the greater part of the contents of your very kind and affectionate note; but were less fortunate in regard to the other.

In taking the recreation necessary for the restoration of her health, Sarah endeavored to combine pleasure with duty, and has taken a great many sketches, illustrative of Bible history, oriental scenery, manners, customs, etc., some of which she wishes to send to your daughter by the first available means.

Dr. Barclay has had so much else to write about, that I believe he has written little or nothing about the poor, degraded females of this land; and I shall therefore devote the remainder of my sheet to some notice of this unfortunate class of the daughters of Eve, in the hope that I may stimulate your pen to write something in their behalf in the Age. You know it is the general opinion that the Moslem women are unfit for religion, inasmuch as they have no souls. Nor is the Jewish estimate of womens' souls much higher. But my observation abundantly convinces me that they are not a whit less *religious* than their domineering *lords*. We had nearly two dozen of these Moslem ladies in our conversation room on one occasion, and just as soon as the muezzin announced the hour of prayer, they all spread their shawls, sheets or mattings on the floor, and most devoutly engaged in their imposing worship; for although it looked too much like mere " bodily exercise," it was nevertheless rather engaging. Where is the party of ladies in the United States that are as punctual in attending to their religious duties? I am sure, from what I have heard of you, that had you been with us this eveniug at the "Jews' wailing place," you would have been affected unto tears, as I was; and could have come to no other conclusion than that the matrons, maids, and damsels of Israel are possessed of the deepest religious feeling. As they stood or sat clinging to the wall of the temple, with heaving bosoms and streaming eyes, how forcibly was I reminded of their mothers in Babylonish captivity, when "by the rivers of Babylon there they sat down, yea, they wept." Poor depressed creatures! their harps are now hung upon the palm-trees of their own down-trodden Zion, while they that "wasted them require of them," not "songs," but sighs. It was pleasing, however, to see that (unlike the Moslem women), they can nearly all read.

When the better classes of the Moslem females visit us, they generally ask permission to "furrage"—that is to say, take a peep at everything on the premises; and much as they wonder at many things, so different from their own household contrivances, nothing astonishes them so much as to see my daughter or myself reading. They seem to esteem it not only a useless accomplishment, but an outrageous infringement on the rights of man. Upon asking an Effendi, the other day, why one of his wives, with whom we are very well acquainted, had not accompanied him, he replied that it would be *wicked* for a Mohammedan to be seen walking with his wife. And yet this family are considerably imbued with Frank principles, as a little civilization is here called.

But I ought to mention here, that while walking out the other day, Dr. Barclay met one of the highest Effendis of the city walking before seven or eight of his wives. And a lady of another wealthy Effendi is so far under sway of Frank influence, that she actually unvails her face in the presence of Dr. Barclay and my sons, though she begs us not to tell the Mohammedans. So you must know that the march of refinement and improvement is not confined to you Occidentals altogether. But while Frank influence is somewhat felt in the amelioration of the upper circles of Mohammedan society—and we are there treated with lavish kindness and hospitality whenever we vist them—the lower ranks are still exceedingly bigoted and prejudiced. These poor, debased creatures frequently curse us all; and several times they have spit upon Sarah and myself, and hurt our persons as well as injured our bonnets by throwing stones upon us as we passed under their latticed windows. All this, however, and infinitely more, we expected to undergo, before we came here, and of course repine not, except on their account. But as yet we can do little more than pray for them, and operate upon them by example; for the Arabic is such a very difficult language, that years are required before a stranger can communicate with them intelligibly, and especially on religious subjects, where their vocabulary of words is so scant. Our removal to Mount Olivet deprived me of the only scholar that I had; nor have we but one now among us all. But Jerusalem is so well supplied with schools by the English, Germans, and French, that but little is needed in the way of mere elementary literary instruction; though a good school, in which the Bible shall be taught instead of the various conflicting catechisms, is very much needed. But keeping only one servant, and plying the needle for five, my various avocations entirely preclude the possibility of my giving a regular school personal attention; and in this country young persons would not be tolerated as teachers. There is a lady lately settled at Artos, in connection with Mr. Mushullam and the Americans, in their laudable enterprise, who is fully competent, and entirely willing (I might say anxious) to take charge of such a school. The lady to whom I refer is sister Mary Williams, formerly of Cincinnati, to whose accomplishments and zeal, I doubt not, you can testify, as I have frequently heard her speak of you. *Cannot some of our wealthy sisterhood support such a school on Mount Zion for the benefit of the daughters of Israel?* I need not assure you how delighted I would be to receive an occasional epistle from yourself or Miss Cornelia. We all feel so well acquainted with dear Brother Burnet through his pen, that I take the liberty of sending assurances of sincerest affection to him, as well as to yourself and daughter. Dr. B. and the children wish also to unite with me in such expressions.

Believe me, dear sister B., yours most cordially and affectionately,

JULIA A. BARCLAY.

After consultation with some of the female members of the churches here, Mrs. Burnet has determined, with their co-operation, to make a special effort among the sisterhood, in favor of the Christian School in connection with the Mission; any lady, therefore, who desires to forward this good work, can send funds for that object to Mrs. Mary G. Burnet, and they will be properly acknowledged and appropriated. A few sisters will present copies of this letter to their sister professors of the holy faith, for their contributions. We wish success to the enterprise, and feel assured that it cannot be in any better hands than when Christian ladies take hold of it.

D. S. BURNET, *Cor. Secretary.*

PERSECUTION.

JERUSALEM, December, 29th, 1852.

MY DEAR BROTHER:—Being less engaged to-day than I expect to be for some time, I conclude to write you a few pages, although only a short time has elapsed since I wrote my last monthly communication, and I have not been favored with a single line either from your pen or press for many a long month.

With the exception of a slight attack of sickness, from which I have just recovered, our health has suffered but little by returning to the city. Until to-day but little rain has fallen; and the present copious rain is no doubt regarded as an answer to the prayers of the dervishes, who yesterday paraded the streets, and commanded all the "faithful" to repair to the mosque and pray for rain, on penalty of five hundred stripes! The weather is still quite pleasant during the most of the day; but woe to the shepherds that would "abide in the field, keeping watch over their flocks by *night*," at this season of the year, for the nights are very cold.

Having never witnessed the "grand ceremonies of Christi Missa," we visited Bethlehem on last Friday evening, for the purpose of attending them. About 8 o'clock at night we repaired to the Church of the Nativity, and in half an hour afterward, as we were all seated in perfect order and silence, the Latin patriarch of Jerusalem came up to me very menacingly, and inquired through a priest, who spoke imperfect English, whether I was a Catholic. "Yes," I replied, "I am a Bible Christian, and of course a Catholic." "And do you believe in the real presence?" continued the heretic detector. "I believe that the Divine Redeemer is everywhere present," was the reply which I made, not being aware that the question was asked in special reference to the mock-devotions upon which they had just then entered. "But," said he, with real inquisitorial ken, "you do not believe in the real presence," pointing to the chalice, "and therefore cannot stay here; and you certainly are not a Roman Catholic!"

"No, thank God, I am not a *Roman* Catholic," said I, rising to my feet, "but a *Bible* Catholic Christian."

'Well, sir, it is not a possibility that you stay here."

" This is a public place for all Christians, and I *shall* stay, sir!"

"I tell you, sir, that it is not permitted that you stay here any longer."

" Yes ; but I tell you, sir, that I don't intend to be driven away."

" Jeeb kawass!" the patriarch furiously vociferated; which being interpreted means, " lictors, bind him!" and forthwith several subalterns hastened off to bring the janizaries."

" Have I misbehaved since I have been here ?"

" No, not at all."

" Then why do you wish me to leave ?"

" I tell you," said the officiating dragoman, " his grace says you must immediately go."

" *His grace! Whose* grace ?"

" *His* grace !" he indignantly exclaimed, placing his hand near the patriarch's person.

" Whew!" was my half whistled, half uttered exclamation, in retort to which he frowned indignation, and again resumed his twaddle about the real presence.

" But I give you to understand, sir, that I do not recognize any right you have to be thus catechizing me, unless I can ask you a few questions in return. Do you allow your people to read the Scriptures ?"

" No, we do not," he spasmodically replied, almost choked with rage. " But you must go, sir! His grace says this chapel belongs to the Roman Catholics, and no Protestant whatever is permitted to stay here during worship."

" Very well; if that is the case I will go. But I beg leave to inform you that I will be glad to see you all in Jerusalem, where I preach the gospel;" and off we leisurely walked, just in time to escape the talons of the ruthless janizaries; for as we were leaving the room, several of these worthies, who had been dispatched from the chambers of the inner temple for our apprehension by the French and Austrian consuls, made their appearance. After passing one or two rooms, entirely out of sight and hearing, we halted at the end of a long corridor, and soon received a message from "his grace," that we were still on Latin premises, and must *immediately* leave. Anxious to avoid a row, we retreated in good order into the portion of St. Helena's church owned by the Armenians, where we were heartily welcomed and assured of protection by various sympathizing friends, who had witnessed our shameful expulsion. The door leading into the Latin apartment was forthwith guarded by the French and Austrian janizaries, to keep out the American heretics, or "devils," as "his grace" calls us. But while *we* were so carefully excluded, other Protestants, as well as Greeks, Armenians, and Moslems were permitted free ingress and egress. One of the priests now came and apologized for himself, alleging that he was compelled to obey the orders of his superiors. But a surly bishop was dispatched from the inner fane, to keep us under espionage, and report our movements to the patriarch; and faithfully did he discharge the duties of his post, brushing by us most contemptuously every few minutes, and then retiring to a distant door, keeping us all the time under the strictest surveillance.

Some of our party having not yet visited the reputed sites of Jerome's cave, Joseph's *house*, and the manger, we concluded, on being assured that these were not the property of Rome, to spend a few minutes in visiting these traditional spots. But on descending into the latter—the grotto of the Nativity—we soon received a message, very loudly and audaciously delivered, that "his grace" wished to visit the star and manger, and that we must depart! Being fully assured, however, that here, at least, I had the right of staying as long as the church was open, I determined to resist the mandate of "his grace," and accordingly remained some minutes after receiving the summons. But, refusing to bow the knee to the uplifted wafer during some exercises preliminary to the entrance of "his grace," the officiating priest ordered me, in a very authoritative tone, to kneel; and finding his orders set at naught, commanded an officer to expel me; but this little dignitary satisfying himself with coming up and making divers frightful, pugnacious demonstrations, the priest raised the cry of "Protestant," Protestant!" and forthwith the vaulted archways rung with the odious epithet—" Protestant!" "Protestant!" "Protestant!" and "being upon the stairs, so it was, that I was borne" of the zealots for the violence of the priests—having scarcely had time to call upon the people to bear witness that I had done nothing amiss. More than half-a-dozen other persons beside our party were standing there all the time, and yet I alone was singled out as an object of insult and vengeance.

Foolish and abominable as are the orgies and mysteries practiced in these convents, and galling as it must be to have them witnessed and exposed by protestant spectators, it can yet scarcely be credited that either their hate or shame would be so great as to drive the Romish priesthood to the adoption of such harsh measures; and hence it may be supposed that I had given them some special cause of offense. But I am not at all conscious of having given the slightest offense, or any just cause of provocation whatever, unless, indeed, healing the sick and instructing the ignorant of Bethlehem may be so construed. The following facts, however, very materially assist in forming a correct judgment of the whole affair.

About two weeks ago I received a message from some of the leading Bethlehemites, principally of the Latin rite, that about six hundred of them wished to become Protestants, and get me to "stand up for them, and read prayers, and bury their dead," as they expressed it. I soon had an interview with them, (though of course I could not think of seriously entertaining their proposition), and found them apparently very sincere and earnest. But being aware that some of the Bethlehemites had formerly made overtures to the English of rather questionable propriety, I could but call in question the purity of their motive, and I accordingly told them of a similar movement among the Latins of Jerusalem—that about a dozen of them had come to me as the representatives of forty or fifty others, and requested to be baptized, but that I had declined receiving them, because I had discovered, after much conversation with them, that they wanted a *buckshish* to pay their house-rent. They immediately declared that such a thing was very wrong, and that *they* wanted no money, nor anything else but to be taught "the way and the truth;" expressing, however, a strong desire that I would undertake the instruction of their children, if any of their rooms should be found suitable for conducting a school; and declared that if I " doubted their faces," twelve of their chief men would give me a paper that should they ever draw back, all their property should become mine. I told them, in reply, that I would have their children educated, provided I could do so conveniently, and would take great pleasure in showing them " the way and the truth," without money and without price, and that if any of them would receive and obey it in sincerity, I would be very happy, but that it would be wrong to receive them as they proposed, in a *body*, and without a knowledge of what I taught. The idea that we had no litany, and that we derived our religion entirely from the Bible, though so entirely new and astonishing, yet soon secured their approbation. They expressed great satisfaction, on further explanation, and wished me immediately to receive them under my superior guidance. But the occurrences of a few hours served to abate the ardor of some of them not a little; for the patriarch, hearing of their determination, summoned them, under awful threats, to return to the bosom of mother church, " dealing damnation all around." These *spiritual* anathemas, however, most of them would have disregarded; but the cunning priests induced them to believe that all the ringleaders would be thrown into prison by order of the pasha, and that I would be unable to procure their release; and hearing that one of them was already imprisoned, I determined, without loss of time, to call upon the pasha, and explain the matter to his excellency. I accordingly went to the seraglio, in company with Mr. Murad, the American consular agent, and informed him that some of the Latins of Bethlehem, having requested me to give instruction to them and their children, had been threatened with imprisonment; but that confiding in his excellency's impartial execution of the Sultan's firman of toleration to Protestants, I intended forthwith to comply with their request. We were very politely received by the pasha (an influential effendi being present, who entertained him with an account of the wonderful effect of my electric machine upon his palsied arm), were treated to coffee and pipes, and assured that I had an undoubted right to grant their request, and that no one should be imprisoned on that account. But scarcely had I left the city to return to Bethlehem, when he sent in haste for the agent, telling him to notify me immediately, that on reconsideration he had come to the conclusion that I had no right to comply with the request of the Latins of Bethlehem, without a special firman from the Sultan, and, consequently, that I must desist. I sent him word for answer, that it was contrary to my principles to violate the laws of the land; and that if he could show me a counter firman, of later date than that I had shown him, I would desist; otherwise I should certainly proceed. The secret of the pasha's sudden change of mind was soon explained by the fact that some priests had just been in audience with him, and had doubtless presented an argument that uniformly secures the Q. E. D. in oriental halls of justice. The priests soon returned to Bethlehem, and triumphantly reported that the pasha had empowered them to have the recusant ringleaders imprisoned. Many, of course, became disheartened and drew back; but still a good many persevered amid all opposition, and I accordingly hired a room — deeming it best to pay a moderate rent, in order the better to secure possession — and commenced a school with sixty-one scholars. The patriarch fulminated furiously, and forthwith anathematized the owners of the house; but finding his curses unavailing, changed his tone, and promised to give them a higher rent than I was giving, and would then make them a *present* of it, and also establish a good school. But his promises and his threats were alike unavailing; for the three brothers who owned the room seemed determined no longer to submit to such tyrannical domination as that which had been exercised over them by " his grace." The patriarch then sent them word that the house should be pulled down; but though trembling for consequences, they are still firm in their resistance.

Last Wednesday was a trying time for the poor

trembling Bethlehemites, on account of a great demonstration made by the Latin authorities. About midday a large number of armed horsemen, headed by the pasha and by the French consul (the avowed patron of the Roman Catholic church), suddenly made their appearance in town; but it was soon ascertained that the object of the pasha's visit was, apparently, merely to *assist* in the ceremony of replacing the silver star, which the Latins accuse the Greeks of having stolen some time ago in a scuffle for " holy places !" What the Latins paid for the lavish waste of gunpowder, and the pasha's apparent countenance of their fraternity, " his grace," I trow, would not like to tell. A still more imposing procession was gotten up on Christmas eve. Indeed, this month has been signalized by religious demonstrations, Papal, Protestant, and Moslem; that, however, made on occasion of the arrival of two pilgrims from Mecca, if not the most *magnifical*, was, at least, by far the most enthusiastic. How ridiculously absurd and inconsistent with the spiritual nature of the christian religion are these pompous pageants, no one can form a correct idea without witnessing them. But what was the disgust I felt at the martial display attending the *entree* of " his grace," compared with my grief at finding the whole Lord's day, and especially the hour of " his grace's" departure from the convent, so abominably desecrated by scenes of tumultuous revelry and the incessant roar of firearms at the door of the church of the Prince of Peace. " His grace " tried very hard to intimidate or entangle me, by sending messenger after messenger to know what answer I would make to the decision of the pasha; but the only answer I made was, that if he wished to know, he must call on me in person, and I would inform him. He had declared his intention of extinguishing all the lights in the church, and causing the priests, robed in black crape, to go through the awful ceremony of anathematizing the recreant members and their *houses*. Nor was his threat entirely unavailing this time; for I had the opportunity of addressing but few on that day, either in the schoolroom or on the street, and some few even refused to receive the word of God as a present. There is also a diminished attendance of scholars, though I am pleased to find two or three grown females, not heretofore scholars, now receiving instruction. The uncertainty of being able to maintain the school under strong and long-continued opposition, induced me to open a dispensary in the town; and I doubt not that it will afford a very desirable means of access to many persons otherwise inaccessible. Two or three dozen persons thus receive medical aid almost every day, for Bethlehem is very sickly at present. My eldest son has gone to take charge of the dispensary, and is much pleased with the prospect of usefulness—dispensing to them, also, the word of life, as opportunity offers.

Miss Mary Williams, late of Artos, but at one time a resident of Cincinnati (with whom I believe you are acquainted), conducts the school (with a little occasional aid from my children and dragoman), charging nothing for her personal services, so that the expenses of the Bethlehem station are but trifling compared with the good that may reasonably be expected to result. And yet, knowing as I do so well what artful tricks a wily priesthood ("working with all deceivableness of unrighteousness,") will put in requisition when other means fail, I would not induce the expectation of realizing any great *immediate* good. But still, under the most discouraging aspect of the matter, the voice of Providence has been too loud and cheering to justify me in disregarding its demands, be the ultimate result what it may. The adhesion of some of the malcontents (of the Greek rite) is known already to have been purchased by a restoration of their lands, which the convent had seized and appropriated to itself some time ago. Others have been cajoled into a persuasion of the bliss of having their children, as well as themselves, remain in ignorance and idolatry. But should Sarphazeah, a celebrated sheik of the neighboring tribe of Ta'amirahs, send his children to the school, as he has expressed his intention of doing, it will inspire the people with new confidence and courage.

Owing to the absence of Mr. Marsh from Constantinople, I have not yet received a firman for Wady Farah; and Mr. Brown, the charge d'affaires, writes as if its procurement would be attended with a good deal of trouble and delay.

There is quite a civil war now waging between the Sephardim and Askenazim (the Spanish and Polish Jews), growing out of an order lately given by the pasha, depriving the Sephardim, who have heretofore monopolized the butchering business, of the liberty of any longer slaughtering sheep, goats, etc. The slaughtering of an animal for food is regarded by the Jew as a matter of such momentous importance, that the installation of a *butcher* is no small affair among them, and the slightest deviation from the prescribed form and ceremony of butchering *a la Talmud*, is regarded as a mortal offense. Among other matters deemed of vital importance, by the Sephardim, is the extraction of the wool from the spot at which the knife is thrust into the animal. But this the Mohammedans have lately decided is too cruel a practice to be tolerated any longer, and they have accordingly determined to suffer it to be done no more. So their dervishes created a great uproar, preaching a successful crusade against it, as contrary to the law of the "faithful," and besought the pasha to deprive the Jews of all right of butchering, as the only means of keeping a clean conscience about the matter. Poor Sephardim! unable to incur the expense of buying chickens, deprived of the right of butchering animals, and forbidden by their remorseless rabbis to eat anything killed by others, even by their Polish brethren, they are truly "in evil case." But the Askenazim (or, at least, the Polish portion of them) are blest with more elastic consciences than their Spanish brethren, and are willing to slaughter without first removing the wool aforesaid; hence, the deadly strife between them for compromitting the honor of Israel in a matter of such unspeakable importance!

Will you not pray that the "light" which has again

sprung up to them that sat in the region and shadow of death, may indeed shine into the hearts of these poor benighted Bethlehemites, and give them saving knowledge of the glory of God in the face of Jesus Christ?

In great haste, yours in faith, hope, and love,

J. T. BARCLAY.

ELDER BURNET.

JERUSALEM, January 10, 1853.

DEAR BROTHER BURNET:—With great pleasure do I avail myself of the kind invitation extended to any of the missionary circle, to communicate with you upon matters pertaining to the mission, or other subjects of interest in this land of patriarchs, prophets and apostles. Amid such a multiplicity of subjects it is difficult to select those which would be most interesting to the readers of your highly valued paper, and which have not heretofore appeared in your columns. Supposing, however, that answers to the interrogatories you propound in one of your letters to father would be acceptable, I cheerfully give you the experience resulting from two years' observation in the East. And first in relation to your query on architecture.

Though not one stone rests upon another, or even a vestige of Solomon's temple and porch remains, still will stimulate some of their neighbors to redoubled energy on behalf of this once so fertile soil; and even to the present day it will yield as much as any other land, if properly attended to.

For many years the Romanists held in their possession the key to the Church of the Nativity at Bethlehem, but owing to the influence of money, and through sophistry, the Greeks induced the Sultan to give it into their possession. The Latins tamely submitted to this until a few months since, when they proclaimed themselves protectors and owners of the holy places, and at the same time showing them the key; they also bribed the Sultan to permit them to replace the star, which the Greeks had stolen from them.

But, by-the-by, notwithstanding the great contrariety of opinion that has always existed respecting what day in the year should be fixed upon as Christmas, it is even more astonishing that three different days should be signalized and commemorated as the birthday of our Saviour; the Latins contending that the twenty-fifth of December is the veritable day, while the Greeks as strenuously contend and endeavor to prove that the fifth of January is the real day; and the Armenians just as plausibly assert that the seventeenth is the true date.

During their festivities the church was indeed a house of merchandise; for such banqueting, feasting, frolicking, etc., would not be exceeded by one of our gayest gala days. When the Greek patriarch approached Bethlehem, the priests went out with their lamps beautifully ornamented with flowers, also large candlesticks one or two yards long; and some of the pilgrims were so highly honored as to bear the painted screens in the procession of the priests who escorted him into the church.

While I am penning these lines I am interrupted by two very respectable Turks, on business; and during their conversation they refer to the late movement in Bethlehem among the Roman Catholics to emancipate themselves from the overbearing tyranny and misrule under which they are placed by their *Babas* (the priests). They informed me that there were some Jews who would become Americans, or Protestants; but that they must have a present for so doing. I told them in the plainest terms that our religion was free to every one who had pure intentions and was not actuated by sordid motives, but that we did not pay any one to become a Christian. One of them, however, gave me to understand that nothing could be accomplished here without money; as for himself he would not join our church for the room full of money, for he had several wives. He spoke in very disparaging terms about the Bible, denying its inspiration because it was written by men, *Hanna* (John), *Butros* (Peter), etc., but the Koran was from God. He contended that Mohammed was a prophet, and that David, Abraham, and all the prophets had foretold his mission, etc. I told him if he would show me any place within the lid of the Bible where Mohammed was spoken of he might cut off my head, and that Mohammed had never uttered a prophecy in his life, I thought it best not to tell him all the truth at once, and accordingly concluded by saying that Mohammed wrote the Koran in a cave, and the portions of it that were inspired he had transcribed from the Bible into their book. He then frankly confessed that he knew nothing but what his superiors told him, *i. e.*, the dervishes.

As father will write to you in a few days, and my disposable space is nearly exhausted, I shall say nothing about the mission further than that we are all well, and the prospect is at least as encouraging as it has ever been.

But for a fresh outbreak among the Bedouin about Hebron, which required the attention of the effendis, the purchase of Wady Farar, for sheltering persecuted converts, would have been consummated several days ago. But we hope it will be bought in a few days hence.

All the family wish to join me in the sincere love and esteem I have the pleasure of entertaining for my dear brother B.

J. JUDSON BARCLAY.

JERUSALEM, January 29, 1853.

MY DEAR BROTHER BURNET:—Since my last, I have had the pleasure of receiving your very kind and interesting letter of November 16th. The same mail brought me also a letter of notification from the

Barings, of London, apprising me of their receipt of the bill alluded to in your letter—£202 16s. 7d. But why are we deprived of the cheering visits of the Christian Age? The last number that reached us was dated about six months ago; and among various other postmarks, was stamped with those of Trieste and Vienna; a hazardous route, truly, for such an uncompromising advocate of civil and religious liberty to take. But I have reason to believe that many of my papers and letters safely reach the city without ever reaching me; for on making formal inquiry at the Seraglio, I learn from the officer who first examines the mail-bag, (and who can read English manuscript), that it nearly always contains something for me; but after the parcel leaves his hands, any Frank so disposed, can take every letter and paper in the mail not directed in Arabic characters, by the payment of a few piasters. Great complaints are made on all sides of foul play *somewhere*, and none the less since the late consular interference.

Some considerable time must elapse, I fear, before we shall be permitted to see much fruit of the Bethlehem movement, of which I gave you some account in my last. The rapid succession and alluring festivities of three Christmases in as many weeks, produced a state of things very unpropitious for religious reformation. In consequence of these " phantasies," and the promises, intrigues and threats of the Latin clergy, the number of those who seemed concerned about their souls has diminished from six hundred down to a mere tithe of that number; and the greater portion of these are so much intimidated that they are afraid to come to the meeting-room for instruction, but must be sought for on the streets or in their houses. Nor is this the worst of the matter. Upon the minds of some of these poor priest-ridden people, the truth of Heaven seems to make but little more impression than upon so many brutes. Such is the baleful influence of the system under which they have been trained, that they cannot conceive it to be either their duty or privilege to read and judge for themselves. And even when evidently concerned for their eternal salvation, they still cling with unaccountable pertinacity, to the embraces of their indulgent alma mater, that imposes such slight restrictions upon the gratification of their sinful propensities, and yet guarantees salvation so confidently upon mere application at the confessional. Hence such of them as have already been excommunicated, are exceedingly dejected, and hesitate not to declare that they would rather have lost every earthly possession than be thus cast off and disgraced in the eyes of the world. To increase their chagrin, the patriarch has caused to be posted up, in the most conspicuous places, admonitory notifications that they must not enter the convent under any pretext whatever.

A very respectable and influential priest, (the one represented in a tract I printed some time ago, entitled "A Conversation between a Priest and a Disciple of Christ,") fearing lest his silence might be construed into an indorsement of the patriarch's conduct, called upon me a few days since, in order to wash his hands of all participation in the patriarchal outrage. He left me after a long interview, with the intention of inducing the French consul to join him in his remonstrance, and shame the patriarch into an apology; but he has been suddenly dispatched to Malta, perhaps to get rid of him, and so the matter rests in *statu quo*. Public opinion is strongly against "his grace," since it has become generally known that Protestants were never excluded before, and that nothing was done or said to others (who really were misbehaving), while I, who, by their own confession, was chargeable with no offense, save that of being a Protestant, was treated with such indignity. Very grave charges have been tabled against the English and forwarded to headquarters, as I am informed by the dignitary who wrote the address to the Pope, on account of improper interference in the religious affairs of the East, contrary to the express stipulations of the fraternal letter of his grace the Archbishop of Canterbury.

The Greek priests are so much more independent and tolerant than the Latin padres, that they sometimes come to the dispensary and converse with great freedom about religion. Their patriarch, however, exerted his utmost to make the owner of the room in which the dispensary is kept, dispossess us of it. But our host effectually put his graceship to shame by asking him why he should turn out a young man who feels such an interest in them as to leave a pleasant home in the Holy City and come here to give them five hundred piasters' worth of medicine every day, while the Convent wouldn't even give them a sour orange without charging them full price? Although he greatly overrated the cost of the medicines daily dispensed, his logic was by no means lost, for he has not been molested since he drew this disparaging contrast.

The school was quite flourishing for a while; but the liberal distribution of handsomely ornamented silver crucifixes among the families of the owners of the school-house, soon induced me to fear that our tenure of the premises was becoming rather uncertain; and I had the mortification of hearing the owners declare that it was useless to hold out any longer— that the patriarch had not only excommunicated them, but had ordered them to close up their windows facing his palace—that they were really afraid of him, and that they would be ruined in the end. They frankly confessed too, that he had offered to give them a higher rent than *we* were giving, and not only allow them to retain possession of the house gratuitously, but purchase it from them at the end of the present year. Having no written contract for the premises, and having only paid one month's rent, I determined to lease a room elsewhere, and if possible, from a Mussulman; but just at this juncture an official of *the* Church Missionary Society gave the Bethlehemites notice that he would establish a much better school than we had—would assure them much better protection than Americans could possibly give, and would furnish the usual *buckshish*, (which I had positively refused to do). Of course there was a rapid declension in our school; and I felt constrained, under such adverse circumstances, however reluctantly, to yield the ground.

But although I have been so sadly disappointed in regard to the school, my expectations in regard to the dispensary have been more than realized. It is very highly prized by the people, and affords an excellent means of access to all classes. Seventy or eighty, and sometimes more than a hundred persons, from the town and neighboring country—Latins, Greeks, Armenians, and Mohammedans—daily receive medical treatment; and upon this effort to "heal all manner of disease and all manner of sickness," is based my main reliance, under Providence, for ultimate success in preaching the gospel of the kingdom. Some who are afraid to be seen at the meeting-rooms, freely resort to the dispensary, and *read*, as well as converse about the Scriptures.

Did I not feel such unwillingness to put your equanimity to so needless a trial, I might relate certain matters of recent occurrence in quarters whence so much better things might be expected, that would greatly excite your indignation; but for pity's sake I forbear.

The Jezebelian policy pursued by a certain politico-ecclesiastical institution, is about to prove successful ; and those pious, zealous and enterprising Americans will soon be dispossessed of the flourishing valley of Artos, after all their work of faith, patience of hope. and labor of love. The experiment, however, as regards the successful cultivation of maize, sweet potatoes, and other valuable exotic vegetables, grains and fruits, as well as the practicability of employing Jewish laborers, even in defiance of the precepts of the Talmud, the bulls of the Sanhedrim, or the still greater obstacles arising from their idle mode of living on eleemosynary contributions, is fully established. Did not the many disappointments to which I have been subjected admonish me not to be too sanguine, I might tell you (by way of offset to the discouraging circumstances herein mentioned) several encouraging circumstances, but I hold my pen in abeyance at present.

Observing one of the "bulls" of "his grace" lying before me, I conclude to inclose it, that you may see what manner of spirit is manifested by those who profess to be the special* guardians (jure divino) of the honored spot where first were announced the glorious tidings, "Peace on earth and good will toward men." But want of space compels me to conclude. Nothing very definite yet in relation to the purchase of land for the Industrial Asylum. Providence permitting, I may submit a few remarks to the Board at the conclusion of the current year of the Mission, (a week or two hence), and hope by that time to be enabled to congratulate you on the purchase of Wady Farar. With sincerest salaams and regards, as ever, dear brother, yours in faith, hope and love,

J. T. BARCLAY.

---

* "The Guardian of the Hill of Zion and the Keeper of the Holy Land"—one of the titles of his *lordship* the *patriarch*.

BULL OF THE PATRIARCH.

The Second Command.

"That it may be commanded by order of his Eminence, his Lordship the Patriarch, upon Antone Tweemey and his brother Elias: 1st. That news have been brought to the patriarchate, that the said individuals have still not yet withdrawn from letting their house to the Protestants, or Americans; and whereas this, in the present regulation, it is prohibited by the canons of the Holy Church, out of which will issue the foundation of heresy and the destruction of the souls. It is now necessary for the two persons to withdraw from such a practice, in order that not to bring upon their two selves the great anathema which will be hereafter announced against them both on condition if they do not dissuade themselves from the same; and this is the second order.

"Written in the house of the Patriarchate on the 4th of January, 1853."

The above is a literal translation, stamp and signature excepted. J. T. B.

JERUSALEM, March 1853.

DEAR BROTHER BURNET: — As if in compensation for past disappointments, we have been cheered by the receipt of two kind letters from your pen within the past week, to both of which I shall now reply, after first posting up current events to the present date.

With a view of occupying Wady Farah, and commencing operations preparatory to the settlement of several persons there, I visited the valley a few days ago, in company with my youngest son and an Arab servant. When within a short distance of the valley, our suspicions were aroused by the conduct of several Arabs near Irkan Ibrahim (Abraham's Cave), and on the tops of other neighboring hills, who were evidently on the scout; but we were not prepared for the events that transpired on reaching the valley. No sooner had we reached the brow of the hill overhanging the Wady, than the women began to yell and scream most prodigiously, which seems to have been a preconcerted signal for collecting the men together, for they forthwith began to creep out from the caves and to appear on the neighboring crags of rock. We were forthwith beset behind, before, and on each side, by several dozen men, women, and children, gesticulating most furiously, and threatening immediate death if we proceeded any higher up the Wady. But assuming as bold a carriage as possible, we pressed on, in hopes of intimidating them by so daring an act of temerity—for such it seemed to be to oppose this infuriated horde of savages, so well armed with clubs, swords, and fire-arms. Being thus surrounded and closely pressed, we were glad enough to come to a parley. They alleged, in justification of their attack, that they were the citizens of Hizmeh, a neighboring town, and had come to prevent our settlement upon their property.

We told them, in reply, that we had bought the place from the sheiks of Anata, the nearest village, and were not aware that they professed to have any claims upon it. They persisted in their claim, and told us that they had united with an encampment of Bedawin not far off, and intended to kill every Anata man they could find, and that they dare not make their appearance in the Wady. I thereupon informed them that I certainly would not take the land if it really belonged to them, and that I would immediately go and see the sheiks of Anata about it. They then told us that both we and our horses might drink—a piece of hospitality positively denied us at first—and I was proceeding to the water, when, all at once, they burst into violent exclamations, and turning my eyes in the direction they were looking, there stood a murderous-looking Arab, perched upon a lofty crag, with his gun still pointed at me, and doubtless he would have discharged it but for their declaration that a truce had been concluded between us. This was one of the men, to the lurking-places of whom the women had pointed on the cliffs of either side, when we were lower down in the valley, and admonished us not to get within their reach. But though they had professedly agreed to an armistice, they still prowled about, like so many howling hyenas, insulting, cursing, and menacing us, and badly misusing the poor Fellah that accompanied us. They followed us for some distance out of the Wady, but we had barely gotten out of reach of them and were congratulating ourselves on our fortunate escape, when, all at once, our ears were again saluted by the same hyena-like squalling that had greeted us on entering the Wady, and about twelve or fifteen men, accompanied by a goodly number of women, rushed from a cave, and rapidly approached a narrow pass, along which we must needs go. Our Arab companion was immediately seized, disarmed, beaten, and robbed of his gun and about one hundred piastres (the decorations of his daughter's head, which he happened to have in his bosom). The only reason alleged was that he had conducted us into the Wady. Though anxious to interpose a respectful distance between ourselves and these merciless marauders, yet we did not think it right to leave our faithful ally in their hands, and so I rode into the midst of them to intercede for him. But he seemed not much disposed to leave them, though in such sad plight (having everything to gain and nothing to lose, save a few tattered rags, and the little breath they had left in his lungs), and there he doggedly stood, as if appealing to their humanity, while they continued all the time kicking and cuffing him with their feet and fists, and dealing out liberal blows with sticks and gun-barrels. At last he agreed to leave them, on being promised that the matter should be properly presented to the pasha. But no sooner had they heard the word "basha," than several of them picked up rocks and began to throw at me. Not unmindful of Bishop Butler's definition of valor, I urged my horse vehemently until I was beyond the reach of such missiles, but, unfortunately, John was still very near them, and though he had neither said nor done anything at all offensive, they immediately commenced throwing at him. Urging his donkey to the top of his speed, he forthwith left them amidst a shower of stones, but just as he had nearly reached the spot where I had halted for him, and was beyond stone's throw, I discovered, on looking around, that a most ferocious-looking Arab had fallen upon one knee, and was deliberately resting his gun on the other to take aim at him. I immediately whirled around, and by way of diverting his attention from John, pointed at him a long gazelle gun that I had brought along, not only for the purpose of killing gazelles, large herds of which roam here, but certainly in some reference to personal protection—such a *vade mecum* being considered indispensable in all by-ways as security equally against the attacks of quadrupedal and bipedal hyenas, except when traveling in large parties. He was immediately intimidated, and desisted until reinforced by two or three of his comrades, when he fell upon his knee again to take aim, whereupon I wheeled around to resume flight (John now being at my side), and just as I did so, his well-directed ball came whizzing between us. A very few minutes sufficed to place us beyond gunshot range, on a commanding eminence, where we could watch their movement, and here we waited to see what would become of our hired servant. Knowing that according to Mohammedan law he could make them not only bring back his own gun, but deliver up theirs to the pasha, he several times endeavored to leave it in their hands, but they at last swore that if he did not immediately take back his gun they would cut his throat, and he then reluctantly took it back and came along, as best he could, halting and smarting from his wounds and bruises. Having ascertained the names of the ringleaders, from a friendly woman who happened to be among them, we repaired to Anata and reported the state of affairs to the sheiks, from whom I had bought the Wady, who declared their readiness to put me in possession of it next morning, but thought it best, in the meantime, to inform the pasha of the matter. Anxious to prevent a war between these two rival villages (Anata and Hizmeh), which was now openly declared, and concerned for the welfare of Frank travelers in these parts, as well as conscious of our own insecurity henceforth, I permitted this outrage to pass unrebuked. I lost no time in having the matter officially represented to the pasha through our consular agent, Mr. S. Murad. The pasha immediately took the matter in hand, and sent for me to appear before the Divan Effendi, and lodge the complaint in person. Having done so, his scribe immediately drew up a kind of writ addressed to the sheiks of Hizmeh, which he forthwith dispatched by the hands of six of his janizaries, for their apprehension, declaring that he would "show the regulations upon them—how to treat Franks hereafter." So far, so well. But here the Effendi—telling me, by way of preface, that he loved me very much—assured me that Wady Farah was "wakf," or church property, and belonged neither to Hizmeh nor to Anata, but to Neby Mousa (the reputed tomb of the "prophet Moses)," a few miles distant, and inasmuch as it was church property, it could not be sold! Great indeed was my disappointment. But what could be done? Deny the validity of their title upon the score of their misplacement of the great lawgiver's tomb? Of what avail would be the authority of Ezra against the testimony of "a prophet of their own?" Such an appeal would only have insured defeat. Right glad was I, therefore, to yield my claim, upon the positive assurance of the pasha that every para I had paid should be refunded. How much such an assurance is worth, however, remains to be seen, for as yet I have only received a little more than one-half, though I must do him the justice to say, he immediately imprisoned (of his own accord) all such persons as he heard had participated in its sale; but as I have taken security of the agent for the balance, I have some hopes of getting it back in the course of a few months. The mischief of the matter is, that though I was informed that it was purchased alone from the sheiks of Anata, the nearest village, nearly all the sheiks of the neighboring country have received a portion of the purchase money.

The loss of this delightful valley is deeply to be regretted, on many accounts, and I entertain no hopes of ever procuring such another spot; indeed, I shall make no further effort to purchase another place without first obtaining a firman from Constantinople. But the Divan Effendi was kind enough to say that so far from having any objection to my purchasing land, he would actually assist me in securing any place that could be disposed of, and would both countenance and protect the place with soldiers, if necessary. Although

I have used all practicable diligence and precaution from beginning to end, and have nothing to regret but misfortune, yet should the balance of the money not be forthcoming at the appointed time, the brethren must consider me as responsible for it. Set it down to my account—I will repay it.

The issue of the Bethlehem movement is another rather discouraging circumstance, of which I must inform you. The Greek patriarch had in vain offered the owner of the dispensary room twenty gazas (gold pieces of about one dollar each) to turn us out; and it was pretty much in vain that the Latin patriarch had brought a physician from the city; the patients still continued to come to the number of fifty, sixty, or seventy per day, until, by some cunningly devised trick, these " Reverendissimos," as they are blasphemously termed, leagued together, and so operated upon the fears, superstition, and cupidity of these poor oppressed people, that the number of applicants dwindled down to less than half a dozen per day, and not deeming this a sufficient number to justify the expense and trouble of maintaining the dispensary without a more encouraging prospect of benefiting their souls, it has been discontinued. What I surmised in a former letter, in relation to the sudden dismission of Padre Rush, by the Latin patriarch, is now an ascertained fact—*His* grace actually banished him to that stronghold of Romanism in Malta, merely for venturing to remonstrate with him on the impropriety or impolicy of his conduct toward me.

It is rather discouraging, but nevertheless true. I

fear that the large majority of the Bethlehemites who at one time seemed to be so much concerned, now either refuse instruction altogether—turn a deaf ear to it, or receive it only Nicodemus-like, while there is only one who is ready at all hazards, to unlearn his errors and learn the truth. But I must confess that had I been aware of the *intimate* nature of the *relationship* existing between this corps of " sacerdotals" and this progeny of Ishmael and the " Scarlet Lady," I could have anticipated no better result.

The weather is very hot, and the season is so far advanced, that the most serious apprehensions are entertained that there will be no " latter rain." The Mohammedans and Jews have been fasting and praying for rain, somewhat in concert, for the last three days ; but all in vain. To hear the doleful lamentations of the latter, as they mournfully pour forth their plaintive wailings, just opposite these premises at their " wailing place," could but draw tears from your eyes. So great is the scarcity of water in consequence of this unusual drought, that the supply now brought from the neighboring springs and tanks is greater than it was at any time during the summer. The water in both the cisterns attached to this house was found to have contracted so much impurity from the former occupants of the premises, that we had the largest one entirely emptied, and have been compelled to buy nearly all the water we have used for the past year, both in town and country, except the supply derived from the little rain that has fallen this winter, which will soon be exhausted. In consequence of the present drought and the threatened scarcity, every article of food has already materially advanced in price, and the population of the city will doubtless be considerably thinned.

March 6.— Your communication of October 14th, requiring more space for its reply than now remains, you will find fully answered in the inclosed sheet. That of November 29th, I find on reperusal, is virtually already answered by the contents of this, with the exception of your query about the precise locality of the pool of Bethesda, whose waters, you are aware, have been so much muddied of late, by the stirring of the three rival theorists, that I could not now reply satisfactorily without incurring double postage. Wherefore this subject is deferred till my next.

I am sure you will know how to excuse me for this abrupt conclusion, when I inform you that I can now be entertained by three such spirits as brethren Campbell, Burnet and Coleman, for the postman has just brought in one dozen Harbingers, one Christian Age, and one Christian Intelligencer. What a feast!

I am greatly comforted and encouraged in the assurance that the saints are supplicating a throne of grace in behalf of the mission.

With sincerest Christian affection and personal esteem, truly yours,

J. T. Barclay.

JERUSALEM, April 1, 1853.

DEAR BROTHER BURNET:—By the good providence of our Heavenly Father, I am again permitted to address you under circumstances of great mercy.

APRIL 2. — Just as I was concluding the foregoing paragraph, the post-man brought me a large budget of papers and letters, among which I was delighted to find one superscribed in the well known (albeit rather hieroglyphic) autograph of the much endeared brother whom I am now addressing. My pen was of course laid aside, and—taxing my tantalizing self-denial to the utmost—I now resume it at the earliest moment that my urgent engagements will allow.

The main points of the important matters you submit for consideration, you have doubtless found already sufficiently answered in my last two or three communications. In relation to some of the remainder, more time and investigation will be required to reply fully, than can now be bestowed upon them before the departure of the mail; but I will answer them (P. p.) *seriatum*, in the course of a week or two, by which time I hope to hear definitely about a matter of much interest to the mission, in reply to a communication addressed to the American Legation at Constantinople. The matter to which I allude is a proposition made by a very influential and respectable ex-pasha of this city, for the occupation of the fertile but uncultivated plain of the Jordan of Jericho, which can be had on very advantageous terms, provided the sanction of the authorities at Constantinople can be had. But I need not now enter into particulars. So indispensable is it to the extensive introduction of Christianity into the Holy Land, under existing circumstances, to have some suitable place where the poor outcast and persecuted proselyte can be employed, so as to eke out a living for a while, that I am not disposed to leave any proper means untried, to secure such a temporary shelter. After much trouble I have at last succeeded in getting a lien on a piece of land near the city as security for all the re-payment of the Ready Farrah purchase money, (not yet returned), except about fifty dollars, which I still hope to get; but the various expenses necessarily incurred in negotiating, transferring etc., as well as in the measures taken for the recovery of the purchase money, which must of course be a clear loss, will amount to about the same sum, I fear, before the matter is finally settled.

I am peculiarly indebted to the Pasha and Divan Effendi, for their prompt, liberal, and energetic action in this whole affair. Two of the Hizmeh men whom the Pasha had caused to be apprehended as accomplices in the assault made upon us, he considered on examination, to be implicated in so slight a degree, that he was disposed to liberate them upon condition of begging my pardon. Deeming the thirty-two days of imprisonment which they had already undergone, ample punishment for their offense, I readily assented to their liberation, and he accordingly sent one of them to me yesterday, and glad indeed was this humbled son of Ishmael to beg our pardon, as he did in the presence of Dr. Hamilton and other Americans. He even wished to kiss my feet, in token both of his deep regret and unfeigned gratitude, but to such degradation I would by no means suffer him to stoop. This is a mode of evincing gratitude which I have often had occasion to resist on the part of patients whom I had relieved. The Pasha has also caused the money of which our Arab escort was robbed, to be promptly returned to him. His Excellency assured me that although he had not succeeded in catching the ringleader, yet he had not at all relaxed his efforts, but had been scouring the country with horsemen, and having at last heard of his place of concealment, expected to get him in about five days. In reply to my remark, that there was nothing vindictive in my wish to have him brought to justice, and that I mainly desired it on account of Frank travelers, he said that I ought not to intercede for him; that he knew better than I did, "how to educate Arabs." So the probability is, that this daring Arab will have occasion sorely to regret his unprovoked attack upon us. This prompt interposition of the Pasha in favor of Frank interests, is more remarkable when contrasted with his singular indifference about the murderous warfare now raging between various villages near the city. Four men were killed the other day in the various skirmishes between the villagers of Surbahit and Siloam, almost under the very walls of the city; and it was but day before yesterday that a truce of forty days was concluded between the two contending parties of the Greek Christians of Beit Jala, after considerable havoc in slain and wounded, without the slightest interference on the part of the "powers that be," or any effort from any quarter, to suppress these shameful, petty, civil wars.

It would greatly delight you to witness the rejoicings of an Israelite whom I baptized two or three weeks ago. Having been among Romanists when he became convinced that Jesus is the Messiah, (six or seven years ago), he united with their communion, but discovering afterward that Romanism is but a poor counterfeit of Christianity, he became greatly dissatisfied; and hearing of those who profess to have revived the Christianity of the Bible, he came to inquire for "the good old way," and after twice attending public services, and several times receiving private instruction, he was found to be a suitable subject for baptism. "Now," said he, emerging from the pool, and going on his way rejoicing, " now I *know* I am baptized!" and away he went, glowing with zeal, Bible in hand, in search of the Latin patriarch and others, with whom he had been disputing, to reason with them about "the truth" that had now made him free indeed. With "eager pains" he still continues his search after all truth—" Following on to know the Lord," and seems to grow exceedingly in the faith. Well is it that he finds protection under the dome of a Gallio-like *pseudo* Protestant, now sojourning here! I think I will inclose, as a matter of curiosity, his Latin certificate of baptism. I also send you (inasmuch as you have requested something from his pen), brother Dennis's letter to the clergyman, now in London, who brought him into the Episcopal Church, and who lately deputed a lady now visiting the city, to induce him to return to the Anglican fold. It was written without the least expectation of ever being seen, either by you or myself, and although various inaccuracies may be detected in it, yet it shows great advancement in his knowledge of English since his baptism. His improvement in other respects has been much greater, and I trust he will become very useful.

I have been under the painful necessity of refusing baptism to two members of the English mission, the past week, because it was sought without such profession of reformation as the case evidently required; but I expect to administer the ordinance, a day or two hence, to a very interesting young man who seems to be a true and earnest inquirer after truth. When I inform you that several persons, who, I think would have made good disciples, have failed to unite with us on account of our failure to get a place of temporary retreat, you will probably rejoice that they were thus kept out; but I think you would not do so were you made fully acquainted with the state of things in this country. Six Greeks to whom I gave Bibles some time ago, expressed no little regret, the other day, that they could not be baptized, because I am unable to protect them. In vain are they told that "it is better to trust in the Lord, than to put confidence in princes." They seem incapable of comprehending an idea so contrary to the generally received opinion. The zealous Church-of-Englander who supplanted us in part, at Bethlehem, makes but poor progress there, even with the aid of liberal buckshishing operations. The country between this and Tayebeh, has been so insecure of late that I have not yet made them a visit.

Rain has at last fallen, and great is the strife among the various religious communities of the city, for the honor of bringing it! each ascribing it to the prevalence of its own prayers, penances, fastings, etc.

We have now in press an Italian tract, designed for the benefit of the Latins, which I wish to commence distributing in this city and Bethlehem, a few days hence, and send to distant points by the returning pilgrims. But want of space compels me to conclude. Are we not still remembered by yourself and others, who offer fervent, effectual prayers? As ever, dear brother, yours in hope.

J. T. BARCLAY.

AMERICA AND THE HOLY LAND

An Arno Press Collection

Adler, Cyrus and Aaron M. Margalith. **With Firmness in the Right:** American Diplomatic Action Affecting Jews, 1840-1945. 1946

Babcock, Maltbie Davenport. **Letters From Egypt and Palestine.** 1902

Badt-Strauss, Bertha. **White Fire:** The Life and Works of Jessie Sampter. 1956

Barclay, J[ames] T[urner]. **The City of the Great King.** 1858

Baron, Salo W. and Jeanette M. Baron. **Palestinian Messengers in America,** 1849-79. 1943

Bartlett, S[amuel] C[olcord]. **From Egypt to Palestine.** 1879

Bliss, Frederick Jones. **The Development of Palestine Exploration.** 1907

Bond, Alvan. **Memoir of the Rev. Pliny Fisk, A. M.:** Late Missionary to Palestine. 1828

Browne, J[ohn] Ross. **Yusef:** Or the Journey of the Frangi. 1853

Burnet, D[avid] S[taats], compiler. **The Jerusalem Mission:** Under the Direction of the American Christian Missionary Society. 1853

Call to America to Build Zion. 1977

Christian Protagonists for Jewish Restoration. 1977

Cox, Samuel S. **Orient Sunbeams:** Or, From the Porte to the Pyramids, By Way of Palestine. 1882

Cresson, Warder. **The Key of David.** 1852

Crossman, Richard. **Palestine Mission: A Personal Record.** 1947

Davis, Moshe, editor. **Israel:** Its Role in Civilization. 1956

De Hass, Frank S. **Buried Cities Recovered:** Or, Explorations in Bible Lands. 1883

[Even, Charles]. **The Lost Tribes of Israel:** Or, The First of the Red Men. 1861

Field, Frank McCoy. **Where Jesus Walked:** Through the Holy Land with the Master. 1951

Fink, Reuben, editor. **America and Palestine:** The Attitude of Official America and of the American People. 1944

Fosdick, Harry Emerson. **A Pilgrimage to Palestine.** 1927

Fulton, John. **The Beautiful Land:** Palestine, Historical, Geographical and Pictorial.   1891

Gilmore, Albert Field. **East and West of Jordan.**   1929

Gordon, Benjamin L[ee]. **New Judea:** Jewish Life in Modern Palestine and Egypt.   1919

Holmes, John Haynes. **Palestine To-Day and To-Morrow:** A Gentile's Survey of Zionism.   1929

Holy Land Missions and Missionaries.   1977

[Hoofien, Sigfried]. **Report of Mr. S. Hoofien to the Joint Distribution Committee of the American Funds for Jewish War Sufferers.**   1918

Intercollegiate Zionist Association of America. **Kadimah.**   1918

Isaacs, Samuel Hillel. **The True Boundaries of the Holy Land.**   1917

Israel, J[ohn] and H[enry] Lundt. **Journal of a Cruize in the U. S. Ship Delaware 74 in the Mediterranean in the Years 1833 & 34.**   1835

Johnson, Sarah Barclay. **Hadji in Syria:** Or, Three Years in Jerusalem.   1858

Kallen, Horace M[eyer]. **Frontiers of Hope.**   1929

Krimsky, Jos[eph]. **Pilgrimage & Service.**   1918-1919

Kyle, Melvin Grove. **Excavating Kirjath-Sepher's Ten Cities.**   1934

Kyle, Melvin Grove. **Explorations at Sodom:** The Story of Ancient Sodom in the Light of Modern Research.   1928

Lipsky, Louis. **Thirty Years of American Zionism.**   1927

Lynch, W[illiam] F[rancis]. **Narrative of the United States' Expedition to the River Jordan and the Dead Sea.**   1849

Macalister, R[obert] A[lexander] S[tewart]. **A Century of Excavation in Palestine.**   [1925]

McCrackan, W[illiam] D[enison]. **The New Palestine.**   1922

Merrill, Selah. **Ancient Jerusalem.**   1908

Meyer, Isidore S., editor. **Early History of Zionism in America.**   1958

Miller, Ellen Clare. **Eastern Sketches:** Notes of Scenery, Schools, and Tent Life in Syria and Palestine.   1871

[Minor, Clorinda]. **Meshullam!** Or, Tidings From Jerusalem.   1851

Morris, Robert. **Freemasonry in the Holy Land.**   1872

Morton, Daniel O[liver]. **Memoir of Rev. Levi Parsons, Late Missionary to Palestine.** 1824

Odenheimer, W[illiam] H. **Jerusalem and its Vicinity.** 1855

Olin, Stephen. **Travels in Egypt, Arabia Petraea, and the Holy Land.** 1843. Two Vols. in One

Palmer, E[dward] H[enry]. **The Desert of the Exodus.** 1871. Two Vols. in One

Paton, Lewis Bayles. **Jerusalem in Bible Times.** 1908

Pioneer Settlement in the Twenties. 1977

Prime, William C[ooper]. **Tent Life in the Holy Land.** 1857

Rifkind, Simon H., et al. **The Basic Equities of the Palestine Problem.** 1947

Rix, Herbert. **Tent and Testament:** A Camping Tour in Palestine with Some Notes on Scriptural Sites. 1907

Robinson, Edward. **Biblical Researches in Palestine, Mount Sinai and Arabia Petraea.** 1841. Three Volumes

Robinson, Edward. **Later Biblical Researches in Palestine and in Adjacent Regions.** 1856

Schaff, Philip. **Through Bible Lands:** Notes on Travel in Egypt, the Desert, and Palestine. [1878]

Smith, Ethan. **View of the Hebrews.** 1823

Smith, George A[lbert], et al. **Correspondence of Palestine Tourists.** 1875

Smith, Henry B[oynton] and Roswell D. Hitchcock. **The Life, Writings and Character of Edward Robinson.** 1863

Sneersohn, H[aym] Z[vee]. **Palestine and Roumania.** 1872

Szold, Henrietta. **Recent Jewish Progress in Palestine.** 1915

Talmage, T[homas] de Witt. **Talmage on Palestine:** A Series of Sermons. 1890

Taylor, Bayard. **The Lands of the Saracen:** Or, Pictures of Palestine, Asia Minor, Sicily, and Spain. 1855

The American Republic and Ancient Israel. 1977

Thompson, George, et al. **A View of the Holy Land.** 1850

Van Dyke, Henry. **Out-of-Doors in the Holy Land:** Impressions of Travel in Body and Spirit. 1908

Vester, Bertha [Hedges] Spafford. **Our Jerusalem:** An American Family in the Holy City, 1881-1949. 1950

Wallace, Edwin Sherman. **Jerusalem the Holy.** 1898

[Ware, William]. **Julian:** Or Scenes in Judea. 1841. Two Vols. in One

Worsley, Israel. **A View of the American Indians:** Showing Them to Be the Descendants of the Ten Tribes of Israel. 1828

Yehoash [Bloomgarden, Solomon]. **The Feet of the Messenger.** 1923